With the advent of increased capital mobility in the last two decades, financial factors have become of key importance for the processes of stabilization and growth in developing, developed, and transforming economies. The size of international capital movements and the financial intermediation industry has become so large that these factors could become the dominant impulses for individual economies and the global economy in the 1990s and beyond.

This book collects essays by well-known analysts in international economics and finance who treat these issues from relatively new perspectives. They focus on (i) the role of credit in the propagation mechanism of monetary policy; (ii) effects of monetary policy on the likelihood that a given economy will become a banking center; (iii) the implications of increased capital mobility for migration flows; (iv) the role of exchange rate bands in the transition from high to low inflation; and (v) the interaction between financial innovations and inflation.

FINANCIAL FACTORS IN ECONOMIC STABILIZATION AND GROWTH

FINANCIAL FACTORS IN ECONOMIC STABILIZATION AND GROWTH

Edited by

MARIO I. BLEJER
International Monetary Fund

ZVI ECKSTEIN
Tel Aviv University and Boston University

ZVI HERCOWITZ
Tel Aviv University

LEONARDO LEIDERMAN
Tel Aviv University and CEPR

CAMBRIDGE
UNIVERSITY PRESS

Published by the Press Syndicate of the University of Cambridge
The Pitt Building, Trumpington Street, Cambridge CB2 1RP
40 West 20th Street, New York, NY 10011-4211, USA
10 Stamford Road, Oakleigh, Melbourne 3166, Australia

H   © Cambridge University Press 1996

First published 1996

Printed in the United States of America

Library of Congress Cataloging-in-Publication Data
Financial factors in economic stabilization and growth / edited by
Mario I. Blejer . . . [et al.].
p.   cm.
Includes bibliographical references and index.
ISBN 0–521–48050–7 (hc)
1. Finance – Developing countries.   2. Monetary policy – Developing
countries.   3. Economic stabilization – Developing countries.
I. Blejer, Mario I.
HG195.F535   1996
332'.09172'4–dc20   95–16467
                                                               CIP

A catalog record for this book is available from the British Library.

ISBN 0–521–48050–7 hardback

Contents

Contributors

S. Rao Aiyagari, *Federal Reserve Bank of Minneapolis*

Mario I. Blejer, *International Monetary Fund*

Guillermo A. Calvo, *University of Maryland*

Lawrence J. Christiano, *Northwestern University, NBER, Federal Reserve Banks of Chicago and Minneapolis*

Fabrizio Coricelli, *University of Siena*

Alex Cukierman, *Tel Aviv University*

Jonathan Eaton, *Boston University and NBER*

Zvi Eckstein, *Tel Aviv University and Boston University*

Martin Eichenbaum, *Northwestern University, NBER, Federal Reserve Bank of Chicago*

Charles L. Evans, *Federal Reserve Bank of Chicago*

Mark Gertler, *New York University*

Simon Gilchrist, *Boston University*

Zvi Hercowitz, *Tel Aviv University*

Nirit Kantor, *Research Department, Bank of Israel*

Miguel Kiguel, *Central Bank of Argentina*

Leonardo Leiderman, *Tel Aviv University and CEPR*

Rafi Melnick, *Research Department, Bank of Israel*

Leora Rubin Meridor, *Research Department, Bank of Israel*

Eran Yashiv, *Tel Aviv University*

Preface

Financial factors have become key impulses for individual economies and for the world economy in the 1990s. Economic theory and experience indicate that these factors play a central role in the processes of stabilization and growth. A conference, Financial Aspects of the Transition from Stabilization to Growth, was held in Tel Aviv, Israel, on June 6–7, 1993. The conference was jointly sponsored by the David Horowitz Institute for the Research of Developing Countries at Tel Aviv University, the Bank of Israel, and the World Bank. We also thank the Bundesbank, the Bank of Italy, and the Bank of International Settlements for their financial support for this conference. The views expressed in this volume do not necessarily represent those of the sponsoring institutions. This volume is based on revised versions of the papers presented at the conference.

We thank our editor, Scott V. Parris, for his comments and suggestions on an earlier draft and for his cooperation all along. We also thank our production editor, Katharita Lamoza, for her valuable input into the production of this book.

M. I. Blejer, Z. Eckstein, Z. Hercowitz, and L. Leiderman

Introduction

During the last two decades there has been a sharp rise in the relative importance of financial factors to the processes of stabilization and growth all over the world, including developing, developed, and transforming economies. The size of international capital movements and of the financial intermediation industry has become so large that these factors could become the dominant impulses for individual economies in the 1990s and onward. This book brings together a collection of essays dealing with these issues from relatively new perspectives.

That monetary and financial variables play an important role for stabilization is well known from the work on inflations and hyperinflations. However, the mainstream view stresses the impact of these variables on the aggregate demand side of the economy. Interesting research in recent years has shown that in addition to these aggregate demand effects, monetary and financial factors can directly affect, in the short run, supply conditions. Accordingly, periods of monetary and financial contraction could be associated with direct repercussions on the real sector, which in turn may strengthen the extent of output loss under these circumstances. Three essays dealing with this topic from various angles are included in Part I of the book.

The essays in Part II deal with three different international financial factors: first, the shift toward increased exchange rate flexibility in the aftermath of disinflation; second, the formation of world financial centers at individual countries; and third, the impact of capital mobility on migration flows. The latter is especially important in light of the increased mobility of labor to be expected in the coming years.

When discussing the role of financial factors, the experience of the last twenty years points to a key element that gave rise to substantial discrepancy between ex ante forecasts and ex post experience: the role of financial innovations. The famous "case of missing money" is a salient example, in the United States, of such an innovation. Theory and applied work indicate that these innovations can have a significant impact on policymakers' attempts to disinflate, but at the same time they can have permanent effects for the economy's rate of growth. This area is covered in Part III.

Turning now to more detail, the three chapters in Part I deal with various aspects of the transmission of credit and monetary policies. The work by Gertler and Gilchrist focuses on the recent debate on how credit market imperfections may play a role in the transmission of monetary policy. There are two main approaches in this debate. One is known generally as the "credit view." This approach maintains that monetary policy directly regulates the availability of bank credit and thus it influences the borrowing and spending of bank-dependent loan customers. The second approach emphasizes a financial propagation mechanism. Because of various credit market imperfections, there is a wedge between the cost of internal and external funds. This wedge is affected by borrowers' creditworthiness, which in turn depends on macroeconomic factors. Shifts in monetary policy can alter this wedge and can magnify the overall impact of the shock. Specifically, a contractionary monetary policy that results in a slowdown in economic activity could have an enhanced impact on the borrowing and spending decisions of those agents who are most subject to the imperfections of the credit market. The evidence discussed by Gertler and Gilchrist points to a striking difference in the response of credit flows to small borrowers versus large borrowers, potentially consistent with the second approach. In particular, using flow of funds data to disaggregate bank assets, the authors find that consumer and real estate loans contract after tight money but that commercial and industrial loans barely respond. And when they disaggregate business loans using data from the manufacturing sector, they find that in response to tight money, loans to small firms contract relative to loans to large firms.

Whereas the foregoing discussion assumes that monetary shocks have been identified in a proper manner, Christiano, Eichenbaum, and Evans take a close look at various ways of potentially identifying these shocks. In earlier work, the authors found that following a contractionary monetary policy action there is a rise in short-term interest rates, in the value of the dollar, in manufacturing inventories, and in the rate of unemployment. In addition, monetary aggregates, output, employment, profits, and retail sales fall, and the price level remains unchanged for about a year. Last, in the very short run contractionary monetary policy is associated with a rise in the net funds raised by the business sector in financial markets. In their research, Christiano, Eichenbaum, and Evans attempt to determine the extent to which these previous findings (which are also in line with Gertler and Gilchrist's) are robust to two main alternative methods of identifying monetary policy shocks. The first method makes enough a priori assumptions to allow the authors to estimate the feedback rule of the monetary authorities. The second method consists of a narrative approach, where episodes are isolated on the basis of deliberations about those monetary authorities' moves that appear to have been large and visible in their size and effects. The authors' main finding is that the regularities mentioned are robust to the different identification assumptions that they consider.

Recent casual evidence indicates that credit policy could have played a key role in the precipitous fall of output and the systemic decline in economic activity throughout former socialist economies in Eastern Europe and the former Soviet Union. Beyond credit policy, numerous factors have been stressed in this context, such as the possibility of a statistical overstatement of the decline, the trade shock, and the change in enterprise incentives and behavior. Yet, in a series of papers Calvo and Coricelli have focused on the mechanisms whereby a credit crunch could lead to a fall in output, and have emphasized the risks of an excessive contraction of liquidity in a system, such as that prevailing in most Eastern European economies, characterized by unsophisticated and very rudimentary financial markets. In their present chapter, the authors extend their work by centering on the dynamic adjustment following an initial monetary shock. The focus is on the interrelations among firms and the process of creating mutual debts as a substitute for the credit that becomes unavailable through the formal channels. The authors show that within the soft budget constraints environment that has continued to prevail in many postsocialist countries, the accumulation of interenterprise arrears could be a factor softening the initial impact of the credit crunch but contributing to locking the system in a sustainable, although undesirable, low-liquidity and low-output equilibrium.

In addition to highlighting the importance of considering financial factors even in systems where they appeared to be irrelevant, this research has important policy implications. It does not imply that permissive credit policies should be the rule in the stabilization efforts of postcommunist countries but rather that, in the design of these policies, the provision of appropriate finance to prevent a collapse in activity should not be neglected. Moreover, the implicit lesson from this study is that observed misperformance at the enterprise level could simply reflect the intricate network of interfirm financial connections rather than the true economic and financial feasibility of the individual firms. It becomes apparent that the restoration of normal financial relations is a prerequisite for the evaluation of true profitability. Across-the-board, and excessive, credit contraction could only result, in the authors' framework, in across-the-board production cuts without facilitating the restructuring process that is the core of economic reforms in Eastern Europe and the former Soviet Union.

Part II is devoted to the analysis of international financial factors. The three papers in this section address different aspects of the topic, although they have a common interest in the effects of policies on international flows of various types. Cukierman, Kiguel, and Leiderman concentrate on exchange rate policy, and the possible tension between its use as a monetary anchor and the goal of maintaining international competitiveness of domestic goods. Specifically, stopping inflation by fixing the exchange rate involves a cost of real exchange rate appreciation, which in turn can lead to increasing current account deficits. Eaton addresses the implications of domestic monetary policy and regulations for the international flows of banking services. Hercowitz, Kantor, and Meridor focus on the role of international agreements, as special loans from international organizations or foreign governments, on domestic economic activity and migration flows.

Cukierman, Kiguel, and Leiderman develop a framework for the analysis of the evolution of exchange rate policy in periods after the implementation of a heterodox stabilization program. Accumulated experience with this type of program (e.g., in Israel, Chile, and Mexico) indicates the following sequence: fix the exchange rate first, produce a major disinflation, and shift to a more flexible exchange rate policy only at a later phase. While the fixing of the exchange rate plays a key role in bringing about a reversal in inflationary trends at the start of stabilization, it was associated with increasing real exchange rate appreciation and with a slow-down in economic growth. To avoid the risks associated with these phenomena, a shift toward increased flexibility of exchange rate policy was considered at some point after major disinflation had occurred.

After presenting a basic set of stylized facts for Israel, Chile, and Mexico, the authors develop a model that characterized policymakers' choices between a fixed peg and an exchange rate band. The choice of the exchange rate regime is modeled as the outcome of an optimization problem by a dependable policymaker whose objective function weighs the level of the real exchange rate against the level and variability of the nominal exchange rate. According to the authors, this formulation captures an important real world aspect of exchange rate policy determination, namely a case where the authorities are concerned about the external competitiveness of domestic products and the current account position, but at the same time they care about the possible inflationary consequences of nominal exchange rate depreciation. The determination of exchange rate policy is shown to involve a trade-off between credibility and flexibility. Among the main analytical results in the paper are the following: (i) the gradual replacement of fixed pegs with more flexible systems can result from a rise in the transparency of flexible exchange rate arrangements – a rise that follows the success of a disinflation policy; and (ii) under some conditions, this tendency toward increased flexibility can be explained by a rise in the authorities' relative concern for maintaining a competitive real exchange rate.

Eaton develops a model of banking intermediation with the purpose of identifying the policies that may determine which countries become banking centers. He also presents international data to motivate the analysis. A country is more likely to become an exporter of banking services when its inflation rate is lower and it is less reliant on revenue from seigniorage. This effect follows directly from the fact that inflation works as a tax on financial intermediation – given liquid reserves that banks are required to hold, or willingly hold for precautionary purposes. At a deeper level of preferences of the policymaker, this requires giving a higher weight to the interests of creditors relative to debtors. From Eaton's analysis it follows that integration of capital markets may be undesirable for some countries, without the prior coordination of monetary policies.

Hercowitz, Kantor, and Meridor extend the small-open-economy framework to include immigration flows and imperfect capital mobility, where the latter takes the form of an upward-sloping supply of foreign funds. The small-open-economy nature of the model implies that increasing capital mobility causes larger migration of labor. The traditional two-country analysis, in contrast, predicts that higher capital mobility is a substitute for labor mobility. In the author's model, increasing the availability of foreign funds (or reducing their cost) triggers capital accumulation and higher paths of real wages and probabilities of employment in the future. Correspondingly, the motivation to immigrate increases. The model is calibrated to Israeli data and used for a quantitative analysis of immigration to Israel. The particular case addressed in this analysis is the granting of loan guarantees by the United States government in 1992, for a total of $10 billion, which was captured in the model as an exogenous rise in available foreign funds.

The two chapters in Part III deal with the interaction among inflation, financial innovation, and economic growth. High inflations and various stabilizations in Latin America and Israel have provided substantial evidence on the comovements of monetary aggregates and real macroeconomic variables. This evidence on broad monetary aggregates is broadly consistent with evidence during the high-inflation episodes in Europe during the 1920s. However, there is less agreement on the evidence concerning the real consequences of accelerating inflation and abrupt stabilization programs on aggregate employment, unemployment, and output. A particular debate and research followed Sargent's (1982) claim that the evidence from the European cases rejects the hypothesis of a Phillips curve trade-off between inflation and unemployment; see Bruno (1993) and Leiderman (1993) for the cases of Latin America and Israel.

There is less disagreement on the comovement of inflation and financial sector activity. Following the initial work on the European hyperinflations, various authors have provided substantial evidence that high inflation is commonly associated with a sharp expansion of the financial sector, and that the latter is close to a collapse following sharp disinflation. Moreover, there is evidence that the growth rate of the economy declines as inflation accelerates to high levels. This is precisely the type of evidence that motivated the research by Aiyagari and Eckstein, who interpret the facts as suggesting that high inflation tends to attract resources to the financial intermediation sector, thereby reducing physical capital accumulation and the rate of growth. The authors stress that, in an attempt to minimize the costs of holding money, inflation induces individuals and firms to shift toward the use of credit. They refer, for example, to the Israeli case, in which annual inflation reached a peak of about 500 percent prior to the sharp stabilization plan of 1985.

Aiyagari and Eckstein provide an analytical model that relates the size of the banking sector, the growth rate of output, and the rate of inflation. There are two goods in their model, which are perfect substitutes in consumption and investment, but differ in terms of their production process until final use. One good is purchased with cash, and the other good is purchased with credit – and therefore involves financial intermediation as part of its production. The mechanism at work can be described as follows. As the rate of inflation rises (say permanently) the demand shifts toward the credit good, which saves on holding money, increasing the relative price of credit goods. Assuming that the credit services sector is labor-intensive, the demand shift is accompanied by a higher real wage, a lower real interest rate, and less capital accumulation. The latter, in turn, reduces the growth rate of output, given a production technology where the productivity of labor depends on total capital accumulation.

In the last chapter, Melnick and Yashiv analyze the comovements of inflation and various monetary aggregates, in the light of changes in regulation and financial innovations during both the high-inflation period and the poststabilization episode in Israel. In particular, they document the impact of certain financial innovations, such as the introduction of foreign-exchange linked deposits (PATAM) at the beginning of the high-inflation era, the increased use of short-term deposits, and the introduction of bank-teller machines on various measures of monetary velocity and the rate of inflation.

Melnick and Yashiv show that during the inflationary process the banking sector and the Bank of Israel increased the liquidity and decreased the cost of providing certain bank deposits. As a result, the relative shares of conventional monetary aggregates changed substantially during high inflation. In addition, there were sharp changes in these aggregates following the stabilization program of 1985. The authors attributed part of these changes to the substantial financial innovations in Israel during the relevant period. In their model, they developed a general equilibrium dynamic framework of money demand that allows for financial innovation to affect the rate of inflation. Money demand is modeled via a transaction cost function that depends on consumption, cash balances, and deposits. The authors show that increasing the liquidity of bank deposits leads to a reduction in the lending rate and to a rise in the steady-state levels of the capital stock and private consumption. Similar steady-state results are obtained from a substantial rise in the use of PATAM accounts, which is interpreted as a financial innovation in the transaction technology.

Earlier versions of the essays in this book were presented at the conference Financial Aspects of the Transition from Stabilization to Growth, organized by the Horowitz Institute, the Bank of Israel, and the World Bank, at Tel Aviv University, June 6–7, 1993.

REFERENCES

Bruno, Michael (1993), *Crisis, Stabilisation, and Economic Reform: Therapy by Consensus*, Oxford: Claremont Press.

Leiderman, Leonardo (1993), *Inflation and Disinflation: The Israeli Experiment*, Chicago: University of Chicago Press.

Sargent, Thomas J. (1982), The Ends of Four Big Inflations, in Robert E. Hall, ed., *Inflation Causes and Effects*, Chicago: Chicago University Press.

PART I

Transmission of Credit Policy

CHAPTER 1

The Role of Credit Market Imperfections in the Monetary Transmission Mechanism: Arguments and Evidence

Mark Gertler and Simon Gilchrist

> Further, with the rise of interest, the value of certain collateral securities, such as bonds, on the basis of which loans are made, begins to fall. Such securities, being worth the discounted value of fixed sums, fall as interest rises, and therefore cannot be used as collateral for loans as large as before.
>
> Irving Fisher, *The Purchasing Power of Money*

1. INTRODUCTION

How does monetary policy influence borrowing and spending? Is the traditional Keynesian–monetarist "liquidity effect" a sufficient characterization? Or do credit market imperfections provide other important dimensions? A series of recent empirical papers has given this long-standing issue a fresh perspective. Broadly speaking, this new work examines the response of various financial and real variables to shifts in monetary policy, and then interprets the significance for the nature of the monetary transmission mechanism. Our goal here is to review the arguments and evidence and to provide some new evidence as well.

We begin in Section 2 by summarizing the relevant theory. There are two distinct though complementary approaches. One is known generally as the "credit view." The credit view maintains that as a result of reserve requirements on deposits, monetary policy directly regulates the availability of bank credit. In this way, it directly influences the borrowing and spending of bank-dependent loan customers. Though the credit view has attracted considerable attention recently, it does not provide a complete characterization of the issues. Relatedly, the pure version of the credit view is tied to the question of whether reserve requirements in fact enable monetary

11

policy to constrain bank lending directly. As we discuss, whether this premise is reasonable in the current regulatory/institutional environment is the subject of current controversy.

The second approach emphasizes a financial propagation mechanism. It begins with the idea that credit market frictions may drive a wedge between the costs of internal and uncollateralized external funds. The size of this wedge depends on a borrower's creditworthiness, which in turn depends partly on macroeconomic conditions. Aggregate disturbances, including shifts in monetary policy, potentially alter the size of this wedge, and typically in a way that magnifies the overall impact of the shock. Examples date back to Irving Fisher (1911), who described how the effect on collateral values can magnify the impact of rising interest rates on borrowing. The financial propagation mechanism is also relevant (possibly more relevant) to the second round effect of monetary policy. The theory suggests that an initial decline in aggregate economic activity engineered by tight money should have an enhanced impact on the borrowing and spending decisions of those most likely facing credit market frictions, largely households and small firms.

Section 3 examines the evidence. We begin by reviewing existing work. The strategy in much of this literature is to identify the effects of credit market frictions by examining the cross-sectional response to tight money of different categories of loans and different categories of borrowers. We summarize this evidence and also present some new results on the disaggregated response of lending to tight money. As we discuss, the credit view suggests disaggregating the loan data into bank and nonbank sources, whereas the excess sensitivity hypothesis suggests disaggregating the data by borrower type. We perform both types of experiments and find that, although it is too early to draw firm conclusions, the data we analyze are more supportive of the latter approach than the former. Concluding remarks are in Section 4.

2. THEORY

We begin with a summary of the credit view. This approach is best understood in the context of the "money versus credit" debate.[1] We

---

[1] A detailed survey of both the traditional and contemporary literature on the topic is contained in Gertler (1988). Bernanke and Blinder (1988), Romer and Romer (1990), and Kashyap, Stein, and Wilcox (1992) offer recent formalization.

next turn to the "excess sensitivity hypothesis," which characterizes how credit market frictions may help propagate disturbances, including shifts in monetary policy.

2.1. The Money Versus Credit Debate

The money view embraces the traditional Keynesian–monetarist description of the monetary transmission mechanism. Supply and demand for money determine the short-term interest rate, which in turn affects investment and output. Any effect of a change in the money supply on the short-term rate washes out over time as prices adjust. Nonetheless, real effects are possible in the short run.

The response of the short-term rate to a change in the money supply diminishes as closer money substitutes become available. Offsetting movements of money substitutes, such as money market mutual funds, help reequilibrate money supply and demand, thereby dampening the required response of the interest rate.[2] The money view therefore rests on the idea that financial innovation has not yet generated perfect substitutes for money. Given that the money supply consists for the most part of bank liabilities, the money view tends to emphasize the special nature of the liability side of bank balance sheets.

Though it is not necessarily in conflict with the money view, the credit view tends to emphasize the special nature of the other side of bank balance sheets, the asset side. The key idea is that for a large class of borrowers, particularly households and small firms, close substitutes for bank credit are unavailable. As a result of informational frictions and the like, it is prohibitively expensive for these borrowers to issue securities directly on the open market. They must rely primarily on banks for external finance. An important implication is that any kind of disruption in the flow of bank credit potentially has important real effects.[3]

According to the credit view, monetary policy works at least in part by altering the flow of bank credit. An important step in the argument is the contention that legal reserve requirements on deposits provide the Federal Reserve with considerable direct leverage

---

[2] Brainard and Tobin (1963) originally formalized how the availability of money substitutes dampens the impact of monetary policy.

[3] Disruption in the flow of bank credit is a key aspect of Bernanke's (1983) theory of the severity of the Great Depression.

over the quantity of funds that banks may obtain. Assuming prices are temporarily sticky, an open market sale reduces the real quantity of bank reserves and therefore reduces the real quantity of deposits banks can issue. This in turn induces banks to contract lending, which ultimately constrains the spending of borrowers who rely primarily on bank credit.

Despite popular conception, nothing in the story hinges on credit rationing. The bank loan market may clear by price. The reduced quantity of available bank credit due to the open market sale may raise the bank loan rate relative to the open market lending rate. The gap in the rates may persist, because of the segmentation of the markets.

It is important to reiterate that two distinct hypotheses underlie the credit view: first, that bank credit is special; second, that monetary policy directly constrains bank lending. Recent criticism of the credit view is centered on the validity of the second hypothesis. Romer and Romer (1990) argue that because banks can fund loans at the margin using managed liabilities, the direct impact of open market operations on bank lending is minimal. The idea is that banks can mitigate the effects of tight money on lending by issuing large certificates of deposit (CDs) and other kinds of managed liabilities to offset any drop in deposits.[4] The Romers base their argument on the observation that, historically, the legal reserve requirement for demand deposits has been considerably higher than the corresponding rate for managed liabilities. They are careful to add that their criticism applies only to the issue of whether open market operations directly restrict bank credit, and not to the more fundamental issue of whether bank credit is special.

The Romers' argument deserves to be taken seriously, particularly in the current regulatory environment where there no longer exist reserve requirements on managed liabilities. There are several possible mitigating considerations, however. First, in periods of tight money, the Fed has often raised the legal reserve requirement on managed liabilities. This occurred in the periods of tight money that preceded each of the three recessions (74–75, 80, and 81–82).[5]

---

[4] Commercial banks obtain nearly as many funds from issuing managed liabilities as they do from issuing transactions accounts (546 billion versus 618 billion in May 1991). They obtain the majority of funds from savings deposits and small time deposits (1677 billion), but these kinds of accounts are not subject to reserve requirements. (Source: *Federal Reserve Bulletin*, June 1991).

[5] The Federal Reserve raised the reserve requirement on large CDs several times during both the 1973–74 and the 1979–81 periods of monetary tightening.

Thus, even though the Fed recently eliminated reserve requirements on managed liabilities, it is quite conceivable, at least infer-
ring from past experience, that they would not hesitate to reinstate
them if they felt the need to contract the growth of bank credit
seriously.[6]

A second factor involves whether banks can in fact elastically
issue large CDs at the margin. Large CDs raise the risk of the
bank's portfolio. They are not federally insured. As well, because of
informational asymmetries, there is potentially an incentive problem between a bank and its large depositors. It is conceivable that
these considerations make the supply schedule for large CDs
upward-sloping, rather than perfectly elastic. This scenario seems
particularly relevant to small banks, because they have relatively
less access to the CD market than do large banks.[7]

Weighing on the other side, in favor of Romer and Romer's proposition, is the consideration that a certain component of bank assets
are in fact liquid. These assets include government securities, as
well as private loans that may be securitized and sold on secondary
markets, such as mortgages. By holding sufficient buffers of these
kinds of assets, banks may be able to shield less liquid assets, such
as commercial and industrial loans, from the impact of tight money.
That is, they may be able to meet the contraction in deposits largely
by selling off their liquid assets, as opposed to reducing loans to
customers for whom bank credit is special. Indeed, as Bernanke
and Blinder (1992) note, following tight money, banks tend to sell
off securities. Only after security holdings have dwindled do loans
begin to contract substantially. (We present some evidence on this
phenomenon in Section 4.)

2.2. Excess Sensitivity and the Small Borrower Effect

The credit view is essentially a story about impulses to the economy
– the central bank perturbing the economy by directly altering the
quantity of bank lending. The excess sensitivity hypothesis, however, is about a propagation mechanism – a mechanism whereby

[6] A message from this discussion, though, is that empirical evaluation of the credit view
should take account of the institutional–regulatory environment, as well as any changes in
this environment that may have occurred over the sample period.

[7] On the other, small banks may be able to obtain funds from their (large) correspondent
banks, who in turn are able to issue CDs.

credit market frictions may serve to amplify the impact of disturbances on borrowers' spending decisions. Under the excess sensitivity hypothesis, credit market imperfections may play a role in
propagating the effects of monetary policy, even if the central bank
has no direct leverage over the flow of bank credit.

The theory underlying the financial propagation mechanism is
based on the voluminous literature that explores how informational
asymmetries introduce frictions in financial markets.[8] One enor-
mous difficulty with this literature is that the predictions are often
tied to a particular specification of the information structure, and
the associated incentive problem. Generalities are hard to obtain.
Several basic results nonetheless seem to survive across a wide
variety of frameworks.

First, informational asymmetries typically introduce a wedge between the price of uncollateralized external funds and the price of
internal funds. We refer to this wedge as the premium for external
funds. The informational advantage that borrowers have, for example, about the ex ante quality or the ex post returns opens up the
possibility that they may dishonestly appropriate value from
lenders. Roughly speaking, the premium for external funds com-
pensates lenders for the costs of mitigating this incentive problem.
As one example, this premium could reflect the expected costs of
evaluation and monitoring.[9] To the extent quality is unobservable,
another possibility is that the wedge could reflect a "lemons" premium.[10] In either case, the premium for external funds influences
the costs of borrowing at the margin, and thereby affects real economic decisions.

A second reasonably general result is that the premium for external funds depends inversely on the borrower's collateralizable net
worth relative to the obligation on the loan. Collateralizable net
worth includes net financial assets and also any tangible physical
assets or unencumbered prospective earnings that may be pledged
as collateral. The greater this value relative to the size of the loan,
the larger the borrower's percentage stake in the investment pro-
ject, and the smaller the potential net gain from cheating lenders.

Roughly speaking, the financial propagation mechanism is based

[8] Gertler surveys the literature that is directly relevant to macroeconomics.
[9] See, for example, Gale and Hellvig (1985), Williamson (1987), Bernanke and Gertler
(1989), and Furst (1991).
[10] See, for example, Myers and Majluf (1984), and Bernanke and Gertler (1990).

on the idea that economic disturbances influence borrowers' net worth, and hence the premium for external funds, in a way that likely enhances the overall impact of the shock. Examples of this kind of mechanism include Greenwald and Stiglitz (1988); Bernanke and Gertler (1989, 1990); Calomiris and Hubbard (1990); and Gertler (1992). In each of these frameworks, procyclical movements in borrowers' financial positions lead to countercyclical movements of the premium for external funds. The net effect is a "financial accelerator," which amplifies the cyclical fluctuations in borrowers' spending. This financial accelerator appears consistent with informal descriptions of how financial and real conditions have interacted both in prewar business cycles (Bernanke 1983; Mishkin 1991) and in postwar cycles (Eckstein and Sinai 1986). As well, numerous panel data studies have provided evidence that liquidity affects investment spending (e.g., Fazzari, Hubbard, and Peterson 1988; Gertler and Hubbard 1988; Oliner and Rudebusch 1992; Gilchrist 1990; Gilchrist and Himmelberg 1991; Kashyap and Hubbard 1992; Whited 1992).

This kind of mechanism may also propagate the effects of changes in the riskless interest rate. The rise in the interest rate reduces the discounted value of collateralizable net worth, thereby raising the premium for external finance. The response of the premium for external funds therefore serves to magnify the effect of changes in the riskless rate on the cost of capital. Gertler and Gilchrist (1991) and Gertler (1992) provide examples of this kind of phenomenon.

As with the "credit view," nothing in the story presented here hinges on credit rationing. Regardless of whether there is rationing, credit market imperfections distort the real investment decision, since the premium for external funds affects the overall price of funds that the borrower faces.[11] In the case of rationing, the nonprice terms of credit are likely to adjust in a way that amplifies the effects of shocks.

Ideally it is not controversial to suggest that the financial propagation mechanism is more applicable to "small" borrowers. It is

---

[11] Even in the case of rationing, changes in the riskless interest rate may affect investment. This result contrasts with the conventional wisdom, which seems to suggest that interest rates are unimportant when rationing is present. We think that argument usually ignores the impact of the riskless rate on the point at which the loan supply curve bends backward.

this group that most likely faces a consequential premium for external funds. There are a variety of reasons why this may be true. One possibility is that bankruptcy costs are proportionately greater for small borrowers, because of the existence of fixed costs in evaluation and monitoring.[12] Another possibility is that large borrowers have proportionately greater collateralizable net worth.[13] Finally, unobservable idiosyncratic risk, which is a central determinant of the severity of the incentive problem, is likely proportionately greater than for small borrowers, who are on average less well diversified.

The fact that loan rates for households and small firms are typically much higher than for large mature firms and the fact that this difference is probably much greater than simple default probabilities could account for is quite consistent with the proposition that small borrowers face a proportionately larger premium for external finance.[14] So too is the fact that small borrowers rely almost exclusively on internal funds and intermediated credit to finance their investments, while large firms obtain a considerable share of funding in direct markets (see Gertler and Hubbard 1988). Finally there is a volume of evidence from panel data studies suggesting that small firms are more likely liquidity constrained in their investment decisions than are large firms (e.g., Fazzari, Hubbard, and Peterson 1988; Gilchrist 1990).

At one level, the predictions of the excess sensitivity hypothesis regarding the impact of monetary policy are similar to those of the credit view. Both approaches would predict a larger impact on small borrowers.[15] A key prediction of the credit view, though, is that monetary policy can alter the flow of bank credit relative to other forms of credit. Empirical work analyzing the credit view therefore tends to emphasize the response of bank versus nonbank

---

[12] See Gertler and Gilchrist (1991) for an example of how scale economies in bankruptcy costs can introduce a "small firm" effect. See Morgan (1992) for references to the literature that suggest that bankruptcy costs are proportionately higher for small firms.

[13] In Gertler (1992), net worth is a function of the borrower's unencumbered discounted future earnings. To the extent that small firms have shorter expected horizons, their net worth is likely smaller in proportion to their current investments.

[14] Morgan (1992) presents evidence that small firms are less likely to have loan commitments. In future work it would be interesting to assess whether the small borrower effect we emphasized is closely tied to differential access to loan commitments.

[15] It should be noted that the idea that monetary policy might have a greater impact on small borrowers is not new. See, for example, Galbraith (1957) and Bach and Huizenga (1960).

credit to shifts in monetary policy. The excess sensitivity hypothesis, on the other hand, emphasizes the distinction between borrowers likely to face credit market frictions versus borrowers with costless access to the capital market. The corresponding empirical work therefore focuses on the differential behavior of these two groups.

3. EVIDENCE

In this section we present some evidence on the response of credit flows to tight money. To assess the credit view and the excess sensitivity hypothesis, we disaggregate credit by bank versus nonbank sources and by borrower type. Before reporting the results, we first review some of the existing evidence.

3.1. Existing Evidence

Using dummy variables obtained from a reading of the minutes of the Federal Open Market Committee to indicate periods of tight money, Romer and Romer (1990) find that M1 (the narrow monetary aggregate) tends to drop faster than bank credit in the wake of contractionary monetary policy. The growth rate of M1 falls precipitously within several months of a Romer episode, whereas the growth rate of bank credit does not drop until nearly six to nine months after the shock, roughly coincident with the time the growth rate of gross national product (GNP) takes to drop. Romer and Romer interpret these results as consistent with the money view. They argue that bank credit is more likely driven by demand factors than by monetary policy: first, because the decline in bank credit growth lags behind the decline in money growth; and, second, because of the nearly coincident movement of bank credit and GNP.

Bernanke and Blinder (1992) obtain similar results, using innovations in the Federal Funds rate to capture exogenous shifts in monetary policy. However, they interpret the evidence as consistent with the credit view. The fact that the drop in the growth of bank credit lags the drop in money growth is wholly consistent with the idea that bank credit is special. Following tight money, banks may not be able to reduce lending immediately because they may force many borrowers prematurely into bankruptcy. Indeed, credit demand may actually rise, because of the need to finance inventories.[16] Bernanke and Blinder present evidence that banks initially meet the decline in deposits in part by selling securities. If bank credit were not in some way special, there would be no reason for the ratio of securities to assets to fall quickly in response to tight money; borrowers could instead costlessly substitute from bank loans to open market loans.

The problem arising here, of course, is that the competing theories are capable of observationally equivalent predictions about the movement of money and credit. The fact that M1 growth contracts quickly in response to tight money is completely consistent with the credit view, which stresses the availability of close money substitutes. Conversely, a finding that bank credit growth declined sharply could be consistent with the money view, which stresses the availability of close substitutes for bank credit. Beyond this problem is the fact that it is difficult to distinguish between demand-induced versus supply-induced movements in money and credit. If movements in money growth are driven by money demand, then the fact that money leads output could be consistent with the pure credit view.[17] Conversely, if the Federal Reserve is targeting money growth, then the fact that money does not lead output is not evidence against the money view. Pitfalls also arise in interpreting the comovement of credit with GNP. That bank loan growth does not decline sharply in the wake of tight money is not necessarily evidence against the credit view, since credit demand for a substantial fraction of borrowers may actually be rising in order to smooth the impact of declining revenues. On the other hand, evidence that bank loans lead output does not provide support for the credit view, since credit demand could be driving the movement of this aggregate.

Kashyap, Stein, and Wilcox (1991) respond to the observational equivalence problem by examining the behavior of the mix of short-term business loans between bank credit and commercial paper. The idea is that the demand for bank credit and commercial paper

---

[16] If there is labor hoarding, inventories could include "inventories" of labor as well as of goods.

[17] The observation that money leading output is not proof that money causes output originated with Tobin (1970), of course.

should move coincidentally, since each is a source of short-term business finance. Therefore, if the two aggregates move together in rough proportion, demand factors are probably responsible for the overall movement. However, if the mix changes, it is likely the case that supply factors are at work. A decline in the ratio of bank loans to commercial paper likely reflects a contraction in the supply of bank lending, and vice versa for a rise in the mix.

The authors demonstrate that in fact the mix tends to decline sharply following periods of tight money; they interpret that tendency as evidence for the idea that monetary policy can regulate the flow of bank credit.[18] The behavior of the mix is not necessarily in contradiction with the money view, as we noted earlier (since the money view emphasizes the availability of substitutes for bank credit). On the other hand, the authors demonstrate that the mix contains considerable predictive power for real activity, particularly for the behavior of inventories.

Gertler and Gilchrist (1991) approach the issue by examining the cyclical behavior of small versus large manufacturing firms, and the differential response of the two classes of firms to various indicators of monetary policy. They exploit the idea that small firms are more likely sensitive to credit market frictions than are large, for the reasons emphasized in Section 2. The evidence suggests that monetary policy appears to have a larger impact on small firms. The result is robust to using either innovations in the funds rate to capture exogenous shifts in monetary policy, as in Bernanke and Blinder (1991), or to using the Romer dummies. Indeed, for more than ten quarters following a Romer episode of tight money, the sales growth for small manufacturing firms contracts at a much faster pace than that for large firms. The difference is statistically significant and averages more than 4 percent per annum.[19] Small firms also respond more than large to lagged movements in GNP, in keeping with the theory that predicts credit market frictions make small borrowers excessively sensitive to disturbances.

We also find a compositional effect on the behavior of bank lend-

---

[18] Kuttner (1992), however, finds that if nonborrowed bank reserves is used as the indicator of monetary policy, then factors other than monetary policy account for much of the variation in the mix.

[19] See also recent work by Oliner and Rudebusch (1992), who find a small firm effect in the investment data. They also study the link between investment and different types of credit mix variables, controlling for firm size.

ing, further suggestive of the idea that monetary policy has a more potent effect on small firms. Bank lending to small firms declines following tight money, whereas it actually rises for large firms. Relatedly, while the ratio of bank loans to sales following tight money is roughly constant for small firms, it tends to rise sharply for large firms. Large firms thus appear to borrow to smooth the impact of declining sales in the wake of tight money. Conversely, small firms do not. The excess sensitivity hypothesis suggests that credit market frictions impede the flow of liquidity to these firms.

An interesting aspect of the compositional effect on bank lending is that it is a prediction of the excess sensitivity hypothesis but not the credit view, which instead emphasizes the effect of monetary policy on bank versus nonbank credit. Further, since only large firms participate in the commercial paper market, these results raise the possibility that the behavior of the Kashyap, Stein, and Wilcox (KSW) mix (1991) may at least in part reflect compositional effects of small versus large firms, rather than substitution between bank and nonbank credit. We touch on this issue further in the next section.

3.2. Aggregate and Compositional Effects of Tight Monetary Policy on Credit Aggregates

In this section we present time series evidence on the response to tight money of various financial aggregates. Some of the results summarize existing evidence. However, we present some new evidence as well, including a disaggregation of the response of borrowing by firm size, by maturity, and by type.

We begin by estimating a set of vector autoregression (VAR) models. Each model includes four variables: the log of (detrended) real GNP, the inflation rate, the nominal Federal Funds rate, and the log of a (detrended) financial variable of interest.[20] Following Bernanke and Blinder (1992), we use innovations in the Federal Funds rate to capture exogenous shifts in the stance of monetary policy, on the basis of the idea that the Federal Reserve has direct leverage over this variable in the short term. Specifically, we consider the response of variables, particularly financial variables, to one standard deviation increases in the Federal Funds rate; and we

---

[20] We use quadratic time trend to detrend GNP and the financial aggregate.

interpret these experiments as analyzing responses to tight money. For all of the impulse response functions, the residuals are ordered: GNP, the price level, the financial variable, the funds rate. The funds rate is placed last in the ordering because it is thought to affect the other variables only with a one-period lag, whereas it may respond instantly (via open market operations) to contemporaneous movements in the other variables. Also, placing it last allows for the possibility that there exist some factors unrelated to the variables in the system that drive the movement in the funds rate, possibly shifts in the preferences of policymakers, for example.

The sample period is 1975:1 to 1991:4. We use this sample period and quarterly data because some of the financial series are only available in this form. The VARs are estimated using four lags of each variable. The figures report the cumulative response of the log level of a particular variable to a one standard deviation increase in the funds rate, along with one standard deviation error bands.

To help place the results in perspective, it is useful to recall Bernanke and Blinder's (1992) benchmark findings that a rise in the funds rate predicts a drop in GNP about two quarters later and a drop in bank deposits right away.

The top left-hand panel in Figure 1.1 reports that bank loans decline after a rise in the funds rate, though the pace is slower than the decline in deposits reported by Bernanke and Blinder (1992). The two lower panels illustrate how banks adjust their portfolios to offset the potential decline in deposits relative to loans. They sell securities, as the middle panel suggests, in keeping with Bernanke and Blinder's story. In addition, as the bottom panel shows, they issue money market liabilities such as large certificates of deposit, as Romer and Romer (1990) emphasize.

The right side of Figure 1.1 disaggregates bank credit into business, real estate, and consumer loans.[21] Interestingly, the overall response of business loans is not significantly different from zero, as the top panel illustrates. The overall decline in bank lending reported in Figure 1.5 is due to the drop in real estate and consumer loans. The bottom two panels report a steady decline in both types of loans that persists in each case for about eight quarters after the shock.[22]

The left column of Figure 1.2 illustrates the relative behavior of

---

[21] We obtained the various credit series from the Federal Reserve Board's data base.
[22] In future work we plan to ascertain how much of the drop in consumer and mortgage loans could reflect banks' selling off securitized assets as opposed to reducing new lend-

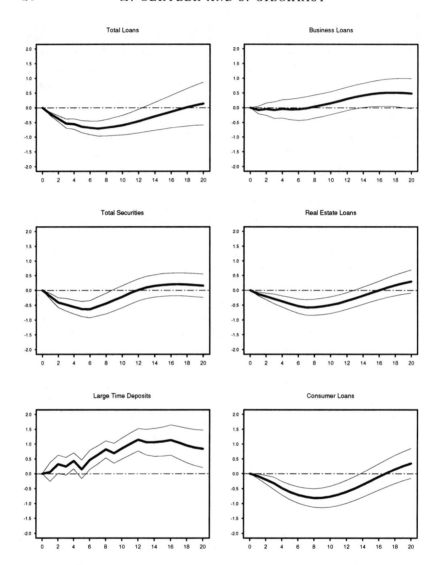

Figure 1.1. Impulse response to one standard deviation shock to funds rate. One standard deviation error bands included. Sample = 1975:Q1–91:Q4

business bank loans and commercial paper. As the middle panel illustrates, commercial paper expands rapidly following tight money. The result is a fall in the mix, as the bottom panel shows, in keeping with Kashyap, Stein, and Wilcox's (1991) observation. It is

ing. Since securitization is a relatively recent phenomenon, we doubt that it is responsible for the results.

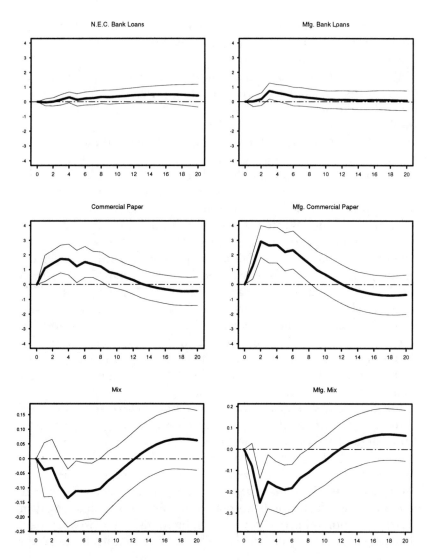

Figure 1.2. Impulse response to one standard deviation shock to funds rate. One standard deviation error bands included. Sample = 1975:Q1–91:Q4

worth emphasizing that the mix drops, not because business bank loans are falling, but only because commercial paper is rising.

We obtain further insight by disaggregating by firm size. Unfortunately, the broad business loan series do not contain the kind of breakdown we would like. A breakdown by size classification is available, however, for the manufacturing sector. The *Quarterly Fi-*

nancial Report (QFR), used by Gertler and Gilchrist (1991), reports a quarterly time series of real and financial variables for eight asset size classes of manufacturing firms.

We aggregate these size classes into categories: "small firms" and "large firms." By our construction, small firms account for 30 percent of manufacturing sales on average.[23] For several reasons, we think it is reasonable to view these firms as having more costly access to financial firms. First, about two thirds of these firms have less than $25 million in gross assets and the other third have gross assets under $250 million (in 1990 dollars). Relatedly, the capital stocks for these firms are about one third of gross assets, implying a rough upper bound of $75 million in physical capital for this group, with most having less than $10 million in capital. Thus, our small firm category squares reasonably with the microevidence on the size of firms that are likely to face liquidity constraints on investment (e.g., Fazzari, Hubbard, and Peterson 1988; Gertler, Hubbard, 1988; Gilchrist 1990; and Whited 1991).[24] In addition, the balance sheet data indicate that these firms are more bank-dependent than are the large firms. For example, small firms obtain about 80 percent of their short-term finance from commercial banks and, to first approximation, do not use the commercial paper market. Large firms, on the other hand, obtain about half their short-term funds from the paper market.

On the right side of Figure 1.2, we report the response of bank loans and commercial paper to a funds rate increase, using the QFR data. Interestingly, the QFR bank loans appear to rise, in contrast with the broader loan aggregates (portrayed in the panel directly to the left), which remain relatively flat. This "perverse" increase probably reflects the fact that, in the face of declining demand, manufacturing firms demand bank loans to finance inventories and other fixed short-term obligations. The broader bank loan aggregate does not rise significantly, probably because this

---

[23] For reasons of space we do not provide the details here. See the working paper version of this manuscript and our (1991) paper. One difficulty in using the QFR data is that the size categories are constructed in nominal terms. As a consequence, inflation causes firms to drift between categories. We control for the inflation drift here with a procedure that involves approximating the underlying distribution of firms. The procedure is more sophisticated than the simple approach in our (1991) paper and is ascribed in the working paper version. We have verified that the results in our (1991) paper are robust to the use of this new procedure. We are happy to make the algorithm available upon request.

[24] Our emphasis on firm size as an indicator of potential liquidity constraints is due to the fact that the QFR data are organized this way.

series includes loans to firms in noncyclical sectors and to firms that are smaller on average than manufacturing firms. Smaller firms may not borrow to smooth impact of declining sales, possibly because of credit market frictions. We next evaluate the "size effect" in the loan data.

Figure 1.3 presents the response of loans to tight money, disaggregated by size and by bank versus nonbank sources. The right side suggests a differential response of bank lending to small versus large firms, in keeping with Gertler and Gilchrist (1991). Although loans to large firms rise, as is consistent with the behavior of the total, bank loans to small firms eventually decline in the wake of tight money. Thus, bank credit does not appear to flow to small firms at the onset of recessions to the same extent that it flows to large firms.

Nonbank credit, which includes credit from other intermediaries and open market credit, is relatively unresponsive to tight money. This is probably true in part because the maturity of nonbank credit is typically much longer than that of bank credit, so that the former turns over at a much slower pace than does the latter. As well, bank credit is relatively more important for satisfying working capital needs, and nonbank credit (except for commercial paper) is relatively more important for financing physical capital. Typically, working capital stocks, including inventories, are more volatile in percentage terms than are physical capital stocks.

In Figure 1.4, we control for maturity by restricting attention to short-term debt, which we define as debt with maturity of a year or less. As the right side indicates, short-term bank lending to large firms surges after tight money, whereas it increases just slightly for small firms. The same pattern arises with nonbank short-term debt, portrayed on the left, which rises sharply for large firms but not for small firms.[25]

Figure 1.4 suggests that if we control for firm size and for debt maturity, then there is no striking evidence that firms substitute from bank to nonbank credit in periods of tight money, at least in terms of the data from the manufacturing sector. The one clear pattern is that liquidity flows to large firms but not to small firms. One possibility we have ignored thus far is that in periods of tight

[25] Short-term nonbank credit to large firms consists mainly of commercial paper. For small firms, short-term nonbank credit is relatively small and consists mainly of credit intermediated by nonbanks, such as finance companies.

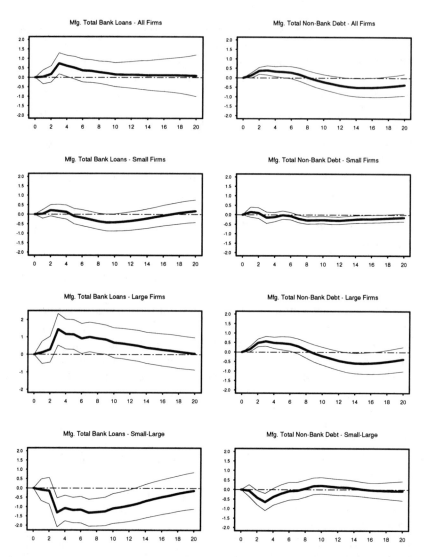

Figure 1.3. Impulse response to one standard deviation shock to funds rate. One standard deviation error bands included. Sample = 1975:Q1–91:Q4

money, small firms substitute from bank credit to trade credit supplied by large firms. Figure 1.5 indicates no support for the proposition, however. The left side reports the response of trade credit to tight money for large and small firms, whereas the right side re-

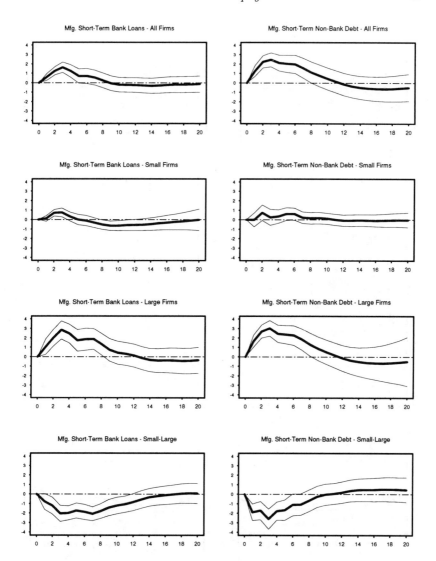

Figure 1.4. Impulse response to one standard deviation shock to funds rate. One standard deviation error bands included. Sample = 1975:Q1–91:Q4

ports the response of trade receivables. Trade credit to small firms actually drops after a rise in the funds rate. And the drop appears larger than the decline in short-term lending to small firms.

The evidence from the QFR is thus consistent with a differential

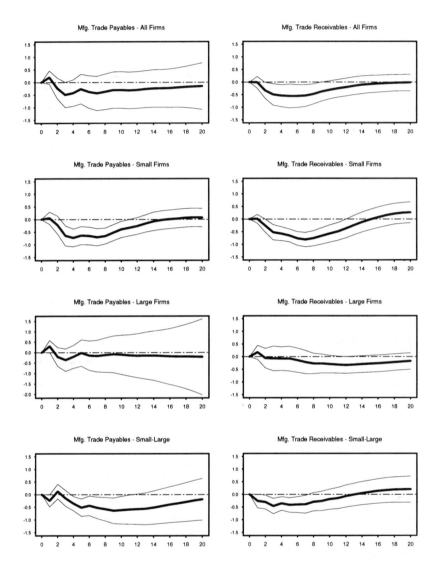

Figure 1.5. Impulse response to one standard deviation shock to funds rate. One standard deviation error bands included. Sample = 1975:Q1–91:Q4

effect of monetary policy on small firms. Credit market imperfections are relevant to the story, to the extent they may explain why small firms do not appear to smooth the impact of declining sales through borrowing at the same time large firms do. Could a nonfinancial theory explain why liquidity surges to large firms but not to small firms after tight money? One possibility is that small firms do not carry inventories. However, the evidence from the QFR suggests that the long-run average inventory–sales ratios for small and large firms are quite similar. A preliminary analysis of the data also suggests that large firms tend to raise the quantity of inventories they carry at the onset of recessions, whereas small firms reduce the quantity.[26] Credit market imperfections provide a natural explanation for this differential behavior. Milne (1991) and Kashyap, Lamont, and Stein (1992) provide some evidence from firm level data in support of this interpretation.

The results also raise the possibility that the behavior of the mix portrayed in Figure 1.2 could reflect differential behavior of small and large firms, and not necessarily firms substituting from bank loans to commercial paper. This conjecture stems from the observation that the surge in short-term bank lending to large firms after tight money closely resembles the behavior of commercial paper.[27] (Compare Figures 1.2 and 1.4.) Both small and large firms obtain bank loans. However, only large firms obtain commercial paper. For example, in 1986, firms that are small by our definition accounted for 55 percent of the short-term bank loans to manufacturers but only 1 percent of the commercial paper issued. If, in downturns, large firms are able to satisfy all or most of their short-term credit needs (through banks as well as the commercial paper market), but the same is not true for small firms, the mix will contract in periods of tight money.[28]

4. CONCLUDING REMARKS

There are two complementary ways in which credit market imperfections may be relevant to the monetary transmission mechanism.

---

[26] See Gertler and Gilchrist (1992b).

[27] In our working paper, we show that controlling for size eliminates the predictive power of the mix for real activity, at least on the basis of the evidence from QFR data. See also Oliner and Rudebusch (1992), who argue in favor of considering a broader mix variable.

[28] Note that under this scenario, factors other than monetary policy could generate movement in the mix. Any aggregate shock that leads to differential behavior of small and large borrowers could alter the mix. For example, a contractionary fiscal policy that reduces aggregate demand could lower the mix, as large firms borrow short term to smooth the impact of the decline in demand, but small firms do not (possibly because credit frictions constrain them).

First, credit market imperfections may force certain classes of borrowers to rely primarily on bank credit. Second, they may make this same class of borrowers, for the most part small firms and households, excessively sensitive to movements in riskless interest rates, as well as to demand disturbances. This second consideration is relevant even if monetary policy cannot directly control the flow of bank credit. It comes into play so long as open market operations influence the short-term real interest rate. Both approaches predict that the first-round effect of monetary policy should impact small borrowers more. The latter predicts that the same should hold for the second-round effect as well, everything else equal, because the overall decline in economic activity should force credit-constrained small borrowers to contract more sharply (i.e., they react more sharply to declining demand).

In analyzing the behavior of disaggregated forms of credit, we find that the sharpest distinctions arise between small and large borrowers, as opposed to between bank and nonbank credit. Following tight money, bank loans to households decline while bank loans to businesses actually rise slightly. Evidence from the manufacturing sector, further, suggests a strong compositional effect on small versus large firms. After tight money, lending to small firms declines relative to lending to large firms. Controlling maturity provides further insight. Short-term borrowing by large firms from both bank and nonbank sources rises substantially in the wake of tight money. This rise likely reflects an increased need for credit to smooth the impact of declining sales. But, interestingly, small firms do not appear to borrow similarly for smoothing purposes, even though they typically suffer a proportionately larger drop in sales.

The question on the table is why, after tight money, at the onset of recession, liquidity flows to large firms and not to small firms, and relatedly, why small firms seem to contract at a faster pace than large firms. Credit market frictions provide a natural explanation. However, although aggregate data provide a feel for the potential overall importance, fully resolving whether a financial propagation mechanism is at work in recessionary periods requires firm level data. As a step in this direction, Gertler and Hubbard (1988) present evidence from firm-level panel data indicating that for firms that are likely constrained a priori, liquidity effects on investment are stronger in recessions than in booms. Related evidence is in Whited (1991) and in Sharpe (1992), who studies employment.

Also using firm level data, Kashyap, Lamont, and Stein (1992) find that liquidity effects on inventory spending are particularly strong in periods of tight money. More work along these lines would be useful.

REFERENCES

Bach, G. L., and C. J. Huizenga (1960), Differential Effects of Tight Money, *American Economic Review* 53–80.

Bernanke, Ben (1983), Non-Monetary Effects in the Propagation of the Great Depression, *American Economic Review* 73: 257–6.

Bernanke, Ben, and Alan S. Blinder (1988), Is It Money or Credit, or Both, or Neither? *American Economic Review* (May): 435–39.

Bernanke, Ben, and Alan S. Blinder (1992), The Federal Funds Rate and the Transmission of Monetary Policy, *American Economic Review* 82: 901–21.

Bernanke, Ben, and Mark Gertler (1989), Agency Costs, New Worth and Business Fluctuations, *American Economic Review* 105 (March): 14–31.

Bernanke, Ben and Mark Gertler (1990), Financial Fragility and Economic Performance, *Quarterly Journal of Economics* 105: 87–114.

Brainard, William, and James Tobin (1963), Financial Intermediation and the Effectiveness of Monetary Controls, *American Economic Review* 53: 383–400.

Calomiris, Charles, and R. Glenn Hubbard (1990), Firm Heterogeneity, Internal Finance and Credit Rationing, *Economic Journal* 100 (March): 90–104.

Eckstein, Otto, and Alan Sinai (1986), The Mechanisms of the Business Cycle in the Postwar Era, in Robert Gordon, ed., *The American Business Cycle in the Postwar Era*, Chicago, National Bureau of Economic Research.

Fazzari, Steve R., Glenn Hubbard, and Bruce Peterson (1988), Financing Constraints and Corporate Investment, *Brookings Papers on Economic Activity* 1: 141–95.

Fisher, Irving (1911), *The Purchasing Power of Money*, New York: Macmillan.

Fuerst, Timothy (1991), The Availability Doctrine, mimeo, Northwestern University, November.

Galbraith, John Kenneth (1957), Market Structure and Stabilization Policy, *Review of Economics and Statistics* 39: 124–33.

Gale, Douglas, and Martin Hellwig (1985), Incentive-Compatible Debt Contracts I: The One Period Problem, *Review of Economic Studies* (October): 647–64.

Gertler, Mark (1988), Financial Structure and Aggregate Activity: An Overview, *Journal of Money, Credit and Banking* 20: 559–88.

Gertler, Mark (1992), Financial Capacity and Output Fluctuations in an

Economy with Multi-Period Financial Relationships, *Review of Economic Studies* (October): 647–64.

Gertler, Mark, and Simon Gilchrist (1991), Monetary Policy, Business Fluctuations, and the Behavior of Small Manufacturing Firms, mimeo, New York University.

Gertler, Mark, and Simon Gilchrist (1992a), The Role of Credit Market Imperfections in the Monetary Transmission Mechanism: Arguments and Evidence, mimeo, Federal Reserve Board, May.

Gertler, Mark, and Simon Gilchrist (1992b), The Cyclical Behavior of Short Term Business Lending: Implications for Financial Propagation Mechanisms, mimeo, New York University, August.

Gertler, Mark, and R. Glenn Hubbard (1988), Financial Factors in Business Fluctuations, in *Financial Market Volatility: Causes, Consequences and Policy Recommendations*, Federal Reserve Bank of Kansas City.

Gilchrist, Simon (1990), An Empirical Analysis of Corporate Investment and Financing Hierarchies, mimeo, Federal Reserve Board, December.

Gilchrist, Simon, and Charles Himmelberg (1991), Evidence on the Role of Cash Flow in Reduced Form Investment Equations, mimeo, Federal Reserve Board, December.

Greenwald, Bruce, and Joseph Stiglitz (1988), Information, Finance, Constraints and Economic Activity, in Meir Kohn and S. C. Tsiang, eds., *Finance Constraints, Expectations and Economic Activity*, Oxford: Oxford University Press, 141–65.

Kashyap, Anil, Owen Lamont, and Jeremy Stein (1992), "Credit Conditions and the Cyclical Behavior of Inventories: Evidence from the 1981–82 Recession," mimeo, Cambridge, MA, M.I.T., July.

Kashyap, Anil, Jeremy Stein, and David Wilcox (1991), The Monetary Transmission Mechanism, Evidence from the Composition of External Finance, mimeo, Cambridge, MA, M.I.T.

Kashyap, Anil, and Glenn Hubbard (1992), Internal Finance and the Investment Process: Evidence from U.S. Agriculture, *Journal of Political Economy*.

Kuttner, Ken (1992), Monetary Policy and External Finance: The Implication of Short Term Debt Flows, mimeo, Federal Reserve Bank of Chicago, May.

Milne, Alistar (1991), Financial Effects on Inventory Investment, mimeo, London Business School.

Milne, Alistar (1991), The Cyclicality of Employment, mimeo, London Business School, August.

Mishkin, Frederic (1991), Asymmetric Information and Financial Crises: A Historical Perspective, mimeo, Columbia University.

Morgan, Donald (1992), Are Bank Loans a Force in Monetary Policy? *Federal Reserve of Kansas City Review*.

Myers, Stuart C., and N. S. Majluf (1984), Corporate Financing Decisions When Firms Have Information That Investors Do Not Have, *Journal of Financial Economics* 13: 187–221.

Oliner, Stephen, and Glenn Rudebusch (1992), Sources of the Financing Decisions When Firms Have Information That Investors Do Not Have, *Journal of Financial Economics* 187–221.

Oliner, Stephen, and Glenn Rudebusch (1992), The Transmission of Monetary Policy to Small and Large Firms, mimeo, Federal Reserve Board, June.

Romer, Christina, and David Romer (1989), Does Monetary Policy Matter? A New Test in the Spirit of Friedman and Schwartz, *NBER Macroeconomics Annual* 4: 121–70.

Romer, Christina, and David Romer (1990), New Evidence on the Monetary Transmission Mechanism, *Brookings Papers on Economic Activity* I.

Sharpe, Stephen (1992), Debt and the Cyclicity of Employment, mimeo, Federal Reserve Board, January.

Stiglitz, Joseph, and Andrew Weiss (1981), Credit Rationing in Markets with Imperfect Information, *American Economic Review* 71 (June): 393–410.

Tobin, James (1970), Post Hoc Ergo Proctor Hoc, *Quarterly Journal of Economics* 84 (May): 310–17.

Whited, Toni (1991), Investment and Financial Asset Accumulation, *Journal of Financial Intermediation* 1: 307–34.

Whited, Toni (1992), Debt, Liquidity Constraints and Corporate Investment: Evidence from Panel Data, *Journal of Finance* 47 (September): 425–60.

Wiliamson, Stephen (1987), Costly, Monitoring, Optimal Contracts and Equilibrium Credit Rationing, *Quarterly Journal of Economics* 102 (February): 135–45.

CHAPTER 2

Identification and the Effects of Monetary Policy Shocks

Lawrence J. Christiano, Martin Eichenbaum, and Charles L. Evans

1. INTRODUCTION

In recent years there has been a resurgence of interest in constructing models of the monetary transmission mechanism. To evaluate these models and build better ones, we must know the historical facts about how monetary policy actions affect the economy. This chapter presents some of these facts and discusses some of the difficulties involved in arguing that they are in fact facts.

1.1. Some Recent Results

In a recent paper, Christiano, Eichenbaum, and Evans (1996) argue that the facts about the response of the economy to a contractionary monetary policy action can be summarized as follows. First, short-term interest rates, the value of the dollar, manufacturing inventories, and unemployment rise. Second, monetary aggregates, output, employment, profits, and retail sales fall. Third, the price level remains unchanged for roughly a year, before falling. Fourth, in the first half year or so after the contraction, net funds raised by the business sector in financial markets rise.

It is striking how, in many ways, these results conform with conventional wisdom regarding the empirical effects of money shocks. Some of these results are difficult to reconcile with important classes of monetary models. For example, the estimated price

Christiano and Eichenbaum acknowledge financial support from the National Science Foundation.

response is difficult to reconcile with most existing flexible price models. Also, the estimated response of borrowing by the business sector is difficult to reconcile with existing models of the monetary transmission mechanism (see Christiano, Eichenbaum, and Evans 1996 for a discussion). Because these facts can play such a useful role in discriminating among models, it is important to understand how they are determined.

1.2. The Role of Identification

The central problem in establishing the facts about the effects of monetary policy actions is that these actions often reflect policy-makers' responses to nonmonetary developments in the economy. We refer to the rule that relates policymakers' actions to the state of the economy as their *feedback rule*. To the extent that a policy action is an outcome of the feedback rule, the response of economic variables reflects the combined effects of the action itself and of the variables that policy reacts to. To isolate the effects of Fed policy actions per se, we need to identify the component of those actions that is not reactive to other variables. We refer to this as the exogenous component of a monetary policy action, or, as an exogenous monetary policy shock. With this definition, monetary policy actions are the sum of two components: the feedback rule and the exogenous shock. We interpret the question, How does the economy respond to a monetary policy action? as How does the economy respond to an exogenous monetary policy shock?

It is important to distinguish between this question and a more interesting one, namely, What is the impact on the economy of a change in the monetary authority's feedback rule? We attack the less interesting question that is the focus of this chapter because we have to.

The reason for this is as follows. Assessing the effect of a systematic change in the monetary authority's feedback rule would be straightforward if we had data drawn from otherwise identical economies operating under the feedback rules that we are interested in evaluating. We don't. And real world experimentation is not an option. The only place we can perform experiments is in structural models. The problem is deciding on which structural model we should use. Before trusting a model's answers to hard questions, it should, at a minimum, give the right answer to simple questions. The simple question that we focus on is, How does the system respond to an exogenous monetary policy shock? Granted, giving the right answer to this question is not a sufficient condition for acting on the implications of a given model. But, this test does help narrow the field of choice and give guidance to the development of existing theory.

In this chapter, we explore two general strategies for measuring exogenous monetary policy shocks. The first involves making enough assumptions (in econometric terms, _identifying assumptions_) to allow us to estimate the Fed's feedback rule. These identifying assumptions include a specification of the functional form of the feedback rule, the variables in the rule, and the variable controlled by the Fed, that is, its policy instrument. To get the exogenous shocks that we seek, we simply subtract the action implied by the feedback rule from the actual action taken.[1] This is the type of strategy pursued in Christiano, Eichenbaum, and Evans (1996). Because their calculations are based on the use of vector auto-regressions (VAR), we refer to this general strategy as the "VAR based approach."[2]

The second general strategy for identifying exogenous monetary policy shocks is the so-called narrative approach, most recently associated with the work of Romer and Romer (1989). Under this method, one looks at a broad set of data, including, for example, the minutes of the Fed's policy deliberations. The idea is to isolate episodes in which the change in policy controlled variables was both purposeful and large, and to examine the behavior of the economy afterward. The identifying assumption needed to interpret the results of this procedure is that when the Fed makes a particularly big policy move, then all (or at least, _most_) of that move is exogenous: That is, the feedback component of the policy action is zero or very small.

It is difficult to judge on a priori grounds which approach is better. The VAR approach leads to misleading results if the wrong

---

[1] An alternative approach to measuring exogenous monetary policy shocks is pursued in Blanchard and Quah (1989), Gali (1992), and King and Watson (1992). In this approach, less weight is placed on estimating the Fed's feedback function, and more is placed on exploiting assumptions about the long-run effects of monetary shocks.

[2] There are many other examples of the VAR approach applied to the effects of monetary policy shocks. For a recent review, see Cochrane (1994).

identifying assumptions are made in specifying the Fed's policy rule.[3] A seeming advantage of the narrative approach is that one is not required formally to specify a Fed feedback function. But nothing is free. In our view there are two key problems associated with the narrative approach. First, the central identifying assumption – that large policy actions are primarily exogenous in nature – has little motivation. Indeed, Romer and Romer (1989) themselves argue that in *every* episode that they isolate, the Fed's policy action was motivated by a desire to lower inflation. Second, the narrative method – at least as applied to postwar monetary policy – yields relatively little information: It delivers a few episodes of large policy actions, with no indication of their relative intensity. In contrast, the VAR approach generates many "episodes," one for each date in the data sample, and a quantitative measure of the intensity of the exogenous shock for each date. Consequently, the VAR approach can, in principle, generate much more precise estimates of the effects of a monetary policy shock.

Although the primary purpose of this paper is to evaluate the sensitivity of the results obtained by Christiano, Eichenbaum, and Evans (1996) to alternative identifying assumptions, we also examine sensitivity of inference to using the narrative approach. In particular, we contrast the results obtained using the identifying assumptions in Christiano, Eichenbaum, and Evans (1996) with those obtained using the index of monetary policy contractions constructed by Romer and Romer (1989).

1.3. Our Results

Our key result is that the overall qualitative findings about the impact of monetary policy shocks reported in Christiano, Eichenbaum, and Evans (1996) are robust to the different identification assumptions that we consider. But on some dimensions there is some sensitivity.

---

[3] In practice, identifying assumptions are selected in part on the basis of whatever a priori knowledge one has about the sign or shape of the response of economic variables to a monetary policy action. For example, we know that a monetary contraction should be associated with a fall in the Fed's holdings of government securities and in the banking sector's holdings of nonborrowed reserves. If a particular identifying assumption leads to a policy shock measure that generated implications at variance with this, it would be deemed inadmissible.

Two examples illustrate the nature of the identification problems that we encounter and the nature of this sensitivity. First, disturbances in VAR equations for real gross national product (GNP) and the federal funds rate are positively correlated. When we treat the federal funds rate as the Fed's policy instrument, we must come to terms with the direction of causation underlying this correlation: Does it reflect (i) the endogenous response of policy to real GNP via the Fed's feedback rule, or does it reflect (ii) the response of real GNP to policy?[4] Christiano, Eichenbaum, and Evans (1996) assume that the answer is (i) and obtain the result that output falls after a policy induced rise in the federal funds rate. As we show later, if one assumes that the answer is (ii), then a policy induced rise in the federal funds rate drives real GNP up for about two quarters, before driving it down. We reject this implication and the underlying identifying assumption on the grounds that it is sufficiently at variance with standard models to be implausible.

Second, on several occasions in the postwar era, a rise in inflation was preceded by a rise in the federal funds rate and in commodity prices. An example is the oil shock episode in 1974. Identification schemes that treat the federal funds rate as the Fed's policy instrument and do not include commodity prices (as leading indicators of inflation) in the Fed's feedback rule imply that contractionary monetary policy shocks lead to a sustained rise in the price level. Eichenbaum (1992) and Sims (1992) viewed this implication as sufficiently anomalous relative to standard theory to justify referring to it as the "price puzzle."[5] We show that under identification assumptions that allow for feedback from commodity prices to policy, the price puzzle disappears. This resolution of the price puzzle is consistent with a conjecture advanced by Sims (1992).

The plan of the paper is as follows. In Section 2 we discuss our version of the VAR approach to measuring monetary policy shocks. In Section 3 we investigate the impact of alternative measures of shocks to monetary policy (including the Romer and Romer index) on various aggregate variables. Section 4 analyzes the impact of different monetary policy shock measures on the net flow of financial assets between sectors of the economy. In addition we consider

---

[4] There are of course intermediate possibilities under which causation is bidirectional. The version of the VAR approach that we work with excludes this possibility.

[5] There do exist some models that predict a temporary rise in the price level after a monetary contraction (see Beaudry and Devereux 1994; Fuerst 1992).

the impact on inference of an alternative detrending technique, and of the use of monthly rather than quarterly data. Section 5 contains some concluding remarks.

2. MEASURING EXOGENOUS SHOCKS TO MONETARY POLICY

In this section we discuss our strategy for estimating the effects of exogenous shocks to monetary policy. The basic problem that we must deal with is determining how to measure the shocks themselves. In previous work we pursued a particular identification strategy that led to a particular measure of policy shocks. To investigate the robustness of our findings, here we examine alternative measures. With one exception, these correspond to imposing particular Wold causal orderings across the monetary policy shocks and the other economic variables. In the exception, we identify policy shocks with the index proposed by Romer and Romer (1989).

2.1. Identification Assumptions under Wold Causal Orderings

Our basic strategy for identifying exogenous shocks to monetary policy is to focus on the disturbance term in a regression equation of the form[6]

$$S_t = \psi(\Omega_t) + \sigma\varepsilon_{st} \qquad (2.1)$$

Here S_t is the policy instrument; ψ is a linear function; Ω_t summarizes the information set that the monetary authority looks at when setting S_t; σ is a positive number; and ε_{st} is a serially uncorrelated shock that is orthogonal to the elements of Ω_t and has unit variance. The information set, Ω_t, includes the past history of all variables in the statistical model as well as the time t realizations of a subset of those variables. To rationalize interpreting ε_{st} as an exogenous policy shock, (2.1) must be viewed as the monetary authority's rule for setting S_t. In addition, the orthogonality conditions on ε_{st} correspond to imposing a particular Wold causal structure on the policy and other variables under which the time t policy shocks do not

---

[6] This discussion is based on section 2 of Christiano, Eichenbaum, and Evans (1996).

affect the variables in Ω_t.[7] The dynamic response of a variable to a monetary policy shock can be measured by the coefficients in the regression of the variable on current and lagged values of the fitted residuals in equation (2.1).

This procedure is asymptotically equivalent to one based on fitting a particular vector autoregression (VAR):

$$Z_t = A_0 + A_1 Z_{t-1} + A_2 Z_{t-2} + \ldots + A_q Z_{t-q} + u_t \qquad (2.2)$$

The VAR disturbance vector, u_t, is assumed to be serially uncorrelated and to have variance–covariance matrix V. The VAR disturbances are assumed to be related to the underlying economic shocks, ε_t, by

$$u_t = C\varepsilon_t \qquad (2.3)$$

where C is lower triangular and ε_t has covariance matrix equal to the identity matrix. To relate this to (2.1), suppose that S_t is the kth element in Z_t. Then, ε_{st} is the kth element of ε_t. In addition, Ω_t includes $Z_{t-1}, \ldots, Z_{t-q}$. If $k > 1$ then Ω_t also includes $Z_{i,t}$ for $i = 1, \ldots, k-1$.

Parsimony dictates that only a moderately large number of variables can be included in Z_t. In our empirical analysis of the quarterly data, the vector Z_t always includes at least the following variables: the log of real gross domestic product (GDP) (Y), the log of the GDP deflator (P), minus the log of nonborrowed reserves (NBRD), the federal funds rate (FF), and the log of total reserves (TR).[8] When we want to assess the effect of a monetary shock on some other variable, D_t, that variable too is included in Z_t. The reason we work with NBRD rather than with the log of nonborrowed reserves is to facilitate comparisons of different policy shock measures that are based on these policy instruments. Positive FF and NBRD policy shocks will both correspond to contractionary monetary policy shocks.

Given a specification of Z_t, our identification schemes differ along three dimensions. First, we consider two measures of the policy instrument, S_t: the log of nonborrowed reserves and the federal

---

[7] A different class of schemes for identifying monetary policy shocks does not impose this Wold casual structure, that is, does not impose the assumption that ε_{st} is orthogonal to Ω_t. See, for example, Bernanke (1986), Gali (1992), King and Watson (1992), and Sims (1986).
[8] For a detailed discussion of the sources of all the data used in this analysis, see the appendix in Christiano, Eichenbaum, and Evans (1994).

funds rate.[9] Second, we consider the effects of including a measure of commodity prices ($PCOM$) in Z_t. Third, we consider alternative specifications of the contemporaneous elements of the information set Ω_t. In conjunction with our orthogonality assumptions on ε_t, this amounts to adopting different Wold orderings of the elements of Z_t. We consider three orderings.

1. *Benchmark policy ordering* (the ordering used in Christiano, Eichenbaum, and Evans 1996): When the federal funds rate is specified as the policy instrument (S_t), ε_{st} is estimated using the ordering of the variables in Z_t given by (Y_t, P_t, $PCOM_t$, FF_t, $NBRD_t$, TR_t, D_t). This ordering assumes that the monetary authority looks at the contemporaneous state of real economic activity (Y_t) as well as prices (P_t, $PCOM_t$) before deciding on ε_{st}. We refer to this measure of a monetary policy shock as an *FF* policy shock. When *NBRD* is specified as the policy instrument, ε_{st} is estimated using the following ordering of the variables in Z_t: (Y_t, P_t, $PCOM_t$, $NBRD_t$, FF_t, TR_t, D_t). We refer to this measure of a monetary policy shock as an *NBRD* policy shock. There are two exceptions to this ordering. On two occasions in the following analysis, the variable D_t is an indicator of aggregate production activity: the unemployment rate and the log of employment. In those cases, we place D_t before the policy variable in the ordering. This is consistent with our assumption that monetary policy shocks do not affect prices and output in the current period.

2. *Monetary policy first* ordering: When the federal funds rate is specified as the policy instrument, ε_{st} is estimated using the following ordering of the variables in Z_t: (FF_t, Y_t, P_t, $PCOM_t$, $NBRD_t$, TR_t, D_t). We refer to this measure of a monetary policy shock as an *FF*1 policy shock. The *NBRD* specification is analogously defined and the resulting policy shock measure is referred to as an *NBRD*1 policy shock.

3. *D variable first* ordering: When the federal funds rate is specified as the policy instrument, ε_{st} is estimated using the following ordering of the variables in Z_t: (D_t, Y_t, P_t, $PCOM_t$, FF_t, $NBRD_t$,

---

[9] See Christiano and Eichenbaum (1995) and Strongin (1995) for a discussion of the role of nonborrowed reserves in monetary policy. See Bernanke and Blinder (1992) for a discussion of the federal funds rate.

TR_t). We refer to this measure of a monetary policy shock as an *FFD* policy shock. The *NBRD* specification is analogously defined and the resulting policy shock is referred to as an *NBRDD* policy shock.

2.2. The Romer and Romer Index

Our final measure of monetary policy shocks is motivated by results in Romer and Romer (1989), who use minutes of the Federal Reserve Open Market Committee meetings to isolate periods in which the Fed purposefully initiated monetary contractions. For our sample period, they isolate four such dates: December 1968; April 1974; August 1978; October 1979. We follow Kashyap, Stein, and Wilcox (1993) by adding the 1966 credit crunch (1966:2) to the index of monetary contractions. In addition we add the August 1988 episode identified by Oliner and Rudebusch (1992) as the beginning of a monetary contraction. For ease of exposition, we refer to all of these episodes as Romer and Romer episodes. We compute the response of a variable to a Romer and Romer episode using the following method. Consider a VAR for the vector of variables Z_t:

$$Z_t = A(L)Z_{t-1} + \beta(L)d_t + \varepsilon_t. \tag{2.4}$$

Here $A(L)$ and $\beta(L)$ are one-sided polynomials in the lag operator L. The variable d_t denotes the time t value of the Romer and Romer index. This variable equals one in the period of a Romer and Romer episode, and zero otherwise. The response of Z_{t+k} to a time t Romer and Romer episode is given by the coefficient on L^k in the polynomial $[I - A(L)]^{-1}\beta(L)$. For this analysis, the ordering of variables in the Z_t vector is not relevant.

As noted in the Introduction, there is room for skepticism that Romer and Romer episodes correspond to periods in which there were exogenous monetary policy shocks. For example, Romer and Romer (1989) emphasize that the periods they focus on correspond to times when the Fed was particularly concerned about inflation, suggesting that these are times when policy was tight not because ε_{st} was high, but because $\psi(\Omega_t)$ was high.

3. MONETARY POLICY SHOCKS AND AGGREGATE
MACROECONOMIC VARIABLES

This section accomplishes two tasks. First, we display the measures of shocks to U.S. monetary policy corresponding to the different identifying assumptions discussed in Section 2. Particular attention is paid to (i) comparing the Romer and Romer (1989) index with our VAR based policy shock measures and (ii) documenting the role that commodity prices play in resolving the price puzzle. Second, we assess the robustness of inference regarding the effects of shocks to monetary policy on various economic aggregates.

3.1. Comparing the Alternative Policy Shock Measures

Figure 2.1 graphs the different shock measures discussed in Section 2. Shock measures based on VARs were estimated using quarterly data over the sample period 1960:1 to 1992:4. On the whole, the various policy measures that we study behave similarly, though they do display some interesting differences.

Because the policy shock measures based on VARs are by construction serially uncorrelated, they are quite noisy. For ease of interpretation we report the centered, three-quarter moving average of the shocks, that is, $(\varepsilon_{s,t+1} + \varepsilon_{s,t} + \varepsilon_{s,t-1})/3$. Also for convenience we include shaded regions, which begin at a National Bureau of Economic Research (NBER) business cycle peak and end at a trough. The upper left panel displays moving averages of the *FF* and *FF*1 policy shock measures in which commodity prices were included in the VAR. The upper right panel displays the analogous shocks for the case where commodity prices were excluded from the VAR. The lower panels report the corresponding shocks for the nonborrowed reserves based measures. Finally, the Romer and Romer episodes are depicted in each panel by the vertical lines (the 1974 episode is not displayed because it falls within an NBER shaded region).

Regarding the VAR shock measures, we find it useful to characterize monetary policy as "tight" or "contractionary," when the smoothed policy shock is positive, and "loose" or "expansionary" when it is negative.

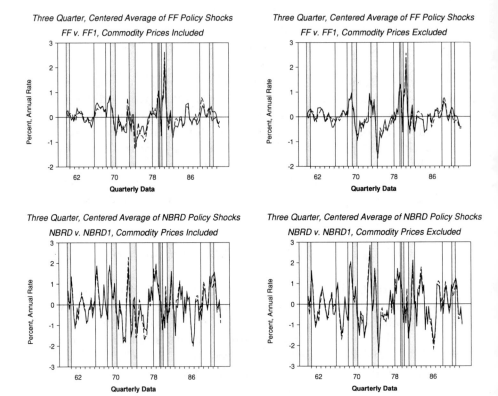

Figure 2.1. Alternative measures of monetary policy shocks.

According to Figure 2.1, all of the federal funds based shock measures indicate that policy tightened before each recession and eased around the time of each trough. With the exception of the 1981–82 period, a similar pattern is observed for the nonborrowed reserve based shock measures.

Notice that with some important exceptions, when commodity prices are included in the analysis, the federal funds and nonborrowed reserve based policy shock measures and the Romer and Romer episodes are in rough agreement. (There is a tendency for the VAR shocks to lag the Romer and Romer episodes by one or two quarters.) For example, the VAR based policy shock measures agree with the Romer and Romer assessment that 1979 and 1988 were periods of tight monetary policy. If we exclude *PCOM* from the analysis, then there is less agreement between the different measures. For example, in 1966:2 both the federal funds and non-borrowed reserve based shock measures indicate tight monetary policy when commodity prices are included. When commodity prices are excluded, then the exogenous component of policy is neutral, or slightly expansionary according to the federal funds measure.

There are three periods when there is significant disagreement between the policy shock measures: 1973, 1974, and 1981. First, Romer and Romer do not identify 1973 as a period of monetary tightening. Yet, the nonborrowed reserve based measures signal a monetary contraction. The federal funds based policy shock measures do too, but only if commodity prices are excluded from the analysis. When they are included (as they are in the benchmark specification), then the federal funds based policy shock measures indicate only a very small tightening in 1973.

Second, there is a Romer and Romer episode in 1974. This is the only such episode that occurs in the middle of a recession. The Romers make no explicit claim about whether this contraction was an exogenous policy shock (i.e., a positive realization of ε_{st}) or a systematic response to the oil shock (i.e., a rise in $\psi(\Omega_t)$.[10]) However, as we noted in the introduction, to interpret subsequent events as reflecting the effects of the contraction requires the assumption that it was exogenous. Our VAR based policy shock measures suggest that it was not. They indicate that the Fed's policy actions in this period reflect a predictable response to the rise in commodity prices associated with the oil shock. Figure 2.1 indicates that for both VAR based policy shock measures the contraction *does* look like a shock if commodity prices are excluded. But, when commodity prices are included, policy was not unusually tight. Since there was substantial inflation after this episode, this observation helps explain the result documented later that incorporating *PCOM* into the analysis helps resolve the price puzzle.

Third, the nonborrowed reserves based policy shock measures agree with the Romer and Romer measure that 1981 was not a period of tight monetary policy. By contrast, the federal funds based measure indicates very tight policy in 1981.

---

[10] For an elaboration of the Romers' view on this point, see their discussion on p. 149 of Romer and Romer (1989).

Relative to the Romer and Romer index, an important advantage of the VAR based policy shock measures is that they also identify periods of monetary expansion. For example, all of the VAR based shock measures indicate that monetary policy was expansionary at the end of the 1973–74 recession, up until 1976. This period also generates an important difference between nonborrowed reserves policy shock measures based on systems that do and do not include commodity prices. The inclusion of commodity prices makes policy look much more expansionary in 1976. Because inflation increased after this period, this suggests a reason why incorporating commodity prices into the analysis resolves the price puzzle for nonborrowed reserves based policy shock measures. Similarly, the fact that Fed funds based policy shock measures do not indicate that policy was tight in 1973 when commodity prices are included may explain why incorporating commodity prices helps those measures avoid the price puzzle.

With one exception, there is little noteworthy difference between VAR shocks computed on the basis of the benchmark policy ordering and those based on the monetary policy first ordering. The exception is the 1973 period for the federal funds policy shock measure based on the VAR that includes *PCOM*. According to the *FF*1 measure, which assumes policy does not feed back on the contemporaneous value of *PCOM*, policy was tight. According to the *FF* measure, which does allow contemporaneous feedback, it was not tight. This is consistent with the idea that Fed policy actions in that episode reflected the systematic response of policy to innovations in commodity prices.

3.2. Confronting the Price Puzzle

Figure 2.2 displays the impulse response of the GDP deflator (P) to ten different contractionary monetary policy shock measures. The solid line is our point estimate, and the dashed lines represent plus and minus one standard error bands.[11] The left-hand column displays the effects of policy shocks in VAR systems that include com-

---

[11] These were computed using the Monte Carlo method described in Doan (1990), example 10.1, using 100 draws from the estimated asymptotic distribution of the VAR coefficients and the covariance matrix of the innovations, u_t, in (2.3). The point estimates and standard errors of our coefficients are the average and standard deviation across draws of the simulated impulse responses.

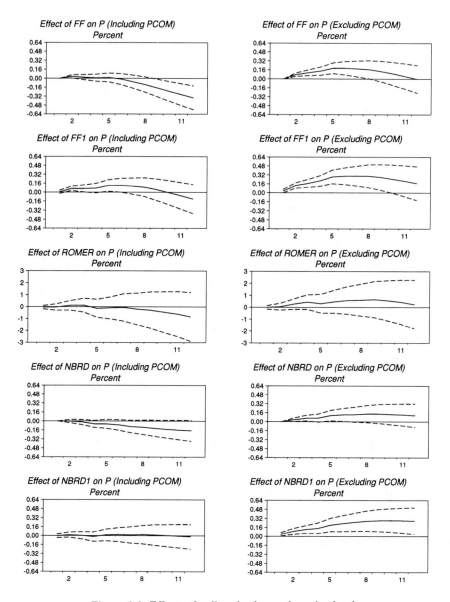

Figure 2.2. Effects of policy shocks on the price level.

modity prices, *PCOM;* the right-hand column displays the analogous effects from systems that exclude commodity prices. Five interesting results emerge here. First, impulse response functions based on VARs that do not incorporate *PCOM* imply a rise in the price level that lasts for several years after a contractionary monetary policy shock. This phenomenon is what we referred to previously as the price puzzle. Second, regardless of the identification used, the inclusion of *PCOM* either reduces or eliminates the puzzling behavior of *P* relative to VAR systems that exclude *PCOM*. Third, only for an *FF*1 policy shock is the price puzzle not eliminated by the inclusion of *PCOM*. Recall that the underlying identification assumption here is that the contemporaneous portion of the Fed's feedback rule for setting the period t federal funds rate does not include P_t, Y_t, or $PCOM_t$. The last two findings seem consistent with Sims's (1992) conjecture that the price puzzle emerges when the Fed has more information regarding inflation at its disposal than is allowed for in the identification scheme used to measure the policy shock.

Fourth, the findings regarding the implications of the Romer and Romer episodes for the price puzzle closely resemble those discussed previously. That is, a price puzzle emerges when *PCOM* is not included in the analysis, but there is no price puzzle when *PCOM* is included.

Fifth, when *PCOM* is included in the analysis, the price level hardly falls at all for several years after an exogenous monetary contraction. The greatest effect is the one implied by *FF*. There, the price level is essentially unchanged for the first year and a half, and is down by about 0.4 percent after three years. One way to assess the magnitude of the price effect is obtained by noting that it is much smaller than the monetary effect of a policy shock. In the next subsection we show that an *FF* policy contraction drives *M*1 down by about 0.4 percent after only about 1 year.

In the remainder of the chapter, unless specifically noted, we focus on the Romer and Romer and federal funds based policy shocks, allowing for commodity prices in the analysis. The analogue impulse response functions corresponding to the nonborrowed reserve based policy shocks are reported in the Appendix.

3.3. Effects on Monetary Variables

In order to assess the overall plausibility of our different policy shock measures we now turn to their effects on four short-term money market variables. Figure 2.3 displays the effects of *FF*, *FF*1,

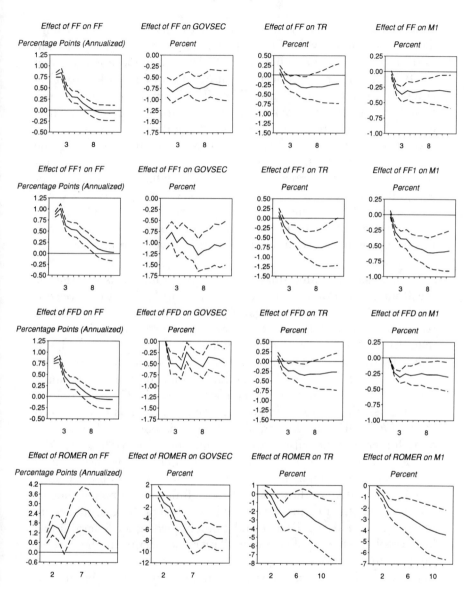

Figure 2.3. Effects of policy shocks on monetary variables.

and *FFD* policy shocks and Romer and Romer episodes on the federal funds rate, government securities held by the Federal Reserve (*GOV SEC*), total reserves (*TR*), and *M*1. Several interesting results emerge here. First, for each of the federal funds based policy shock measures the increase in the federal funds rate is persistent. The rise induced by an $FF1$ policy shock is more persistent than that induced by an FF policy shock.[12] The contemporaneous rise in the federal funds rate induced by an FF or an $FF1$ shock is roughly equal to about 80 basis points. The effect is similar for the nonborrowed reserve based shock measures (reported in the Appendix), except that the initial increase in the federal funds rate is smaller (about 40 basis points). Second, consistent with interpreting the federal funds based shocks as monetary policy shocks, the Federal Reserve's holdings of government securities fall after a contractionary policy shock: That is, a contractionary monetary policy shock coincides with open market sales of government securities. Third, total reserves and $M1$ fall for all of the policy shock measures. However, the response function of total reserves is imprecisely estimated.

Notice that the same qualitative response functions emerge for the Romer and Romer episodes: The federal funds rate increases, the Federal Reserve's holdings of government securities fall, total reserves fall, and $M1$ falls. There are differences pertaining to the magnitude and timing of the responses, however. Romer and Romer episodes coincide with periods in which there were large rises in the federal funds rate. The maximal impact on the federal funds rate after a Romer and Romer episode is roughly 250 basis points. In contrast, the maximal impact on the federal funds rate induced by an $FF1$ policy shock is equal to 100 basis points.[13] The Romer and Romer episodes also induce larger effects on $GOV\ SEC$, TR, and $M1$ (by factors of 5 to 8) than do the federal funds based policy shocks. Notice also that the impact of a Romer and Romer episode is delayed relative to those of the federal funds based policy shocks. For example, the maximal increase in the federal funds rate occurs seven quarters after a Romer and Romer episode; for federal funds based policy shocks, the maximal increase occurs in the second quarter after a shock.

For the subsequent analysis, it is important that we be able to

---

[12] Because the federal funds rate is included in Z_t, the federal funds rate impulse responses are reported from VARs that do not include a seventh variable D_t. Because of this, the FF and FFD policy shocks are the same here.

[13] These responses to a Romer and Romer episode are comparable to the 350 basis point effects that Eichenbaum and Evans (1992) estimated in monthly VAR systems that included international monetary policy reaction functions over the shorter sample period 1974–90.

rule out an alternative interpretation of VAR based policy shock measures, namely that they reflect shocks to money demand rather than to supply. According to this alternative view, (i) our policy shock measures reflect an unanticipated increase in the public's demand for money, and (ii) the subsequent reduction in economic activity is due to the interest rate effect. This interpretation runs into two difficulties. First, the response of *GOV SEC* is perverse if our policy shock measures actually reflect shocks to the demand for money. That is, in response to the public's heightened demand for money, the Federal Reserve would be draining liquidity from short-term money markets and driving up short-term interest rates even further. If anything, we expect that the Federal Reserve tries to accommodate the increased demand for reserves via increases in *GOV SEC*. Second, if the public is demanding more money, it seems very puzzling that broad aggregates like *M*1 would be falling. In light of these considerations, we conclude that the impulse response patterns displayed in Figure 2.3 strongly favor the interpretation that our benchmark policy shock measures reflect exogenous shocks to monetary policy.

3.4. Effects on Aggregate Variables

We now consider the effects of monetary policy shocks on various measures of aggregate economic activity and on commodity prices. Figure 2.4 displays the effects of *FF*, *FF*1, and *FFD* shocks, and Romer and Romer episodes on real GDP (*Y*), aggregate employment (*EMP*), the unemployment rate (*UNEMP*), and the change in commodity prices (*PCOM*). Recall that in the identification scheme underlying an *FF* policy shock, monetary policy responds systematically to the contemporaneous state of the aggregate economy. So *Y* and *PCOM* are always ahead of *FF* or *NBRD* in the Wold causal chain used to identify a shock to monetary policy. When employment and unemployment rates are included in the VAR, they too are assumed to be Wold causally prior to the federal funds rate. Consequently, in these benchmark VAR specifications, *FF* and *FFD* policy shocks are the same.

A number of interesting results emerge from Figure 2.4. First, real economic activity falls steadily after a contractionary *FF* policy shock. Specifically, both output and employment fall, while unem-

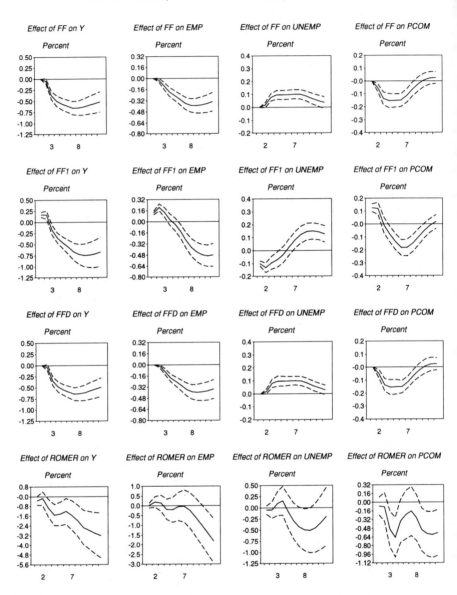

Figure 2.4. Effects of policy shocks on macroeconomic variables.

ployment rises. Second, after an *FF*1 policy shock, real activity initially appears to rise by a small amount and then begins a steady decline. One possible explanation for this pattern is that the *FF*1 policy shock measure fails to control adequately for contemporaneous movements in real activity that are driven by nonmonetary shocks to the system.[14] Third, *PCOM* falls in response to an *FF* policy shock. But, in response to an *FF*1 policy shock it rises initially, before falling. Again, this may reflect the presence of nonmonetary shocks that are not controlled for adequately in the *FF*1 policy shock measure. The analogue *NBRD* policy shock responses displayed in the Appendix give rise to similar response patterns.

As was the case for the money market variables, aggregate economic activity responds to a Romer and Romer episode as it does to federal funds based policy shocks, except with a delay. As can be seen in Figure 2.4, the initial drop in output after a Romer and Romer episode is negligible. Employment begins to fall substantially only after eight quarters, whereas unemployment rate begins its fall after about a year. This is not surprising in light of the fact that the maximal impact of a Romer and Romer episode on the federal funds rate occurs seven quarters after the shock.

Figure 2.5 displays the effects of a contractionary monetary policy shock on retail sales (*RSALES*), profits in the trade sector (*TR PROF*), profits in the nonfinancial sector, and inventories held in the manufacturing sector (*MFG INVT*). The results are quite robust across the federal funds based shocks and Romer and Romer episodes.[15] Retail sales fall in response to a contractionary monetary policy shock. Profits in the trade sector fall contemporaneously (except for the case of an *FFD* policy shock, where the identification restrictions preclude such a response). Profits in the nonfinancial business sector fall substantially across all of the policy shock measures, although the negative response is delayed for *FF*1 policy shocks and Romer and Romer episodes. Consistent with the preceding analysis, this may reflect (i) that the *FF*1 policy shock measures do not adequately control for nonmonetary impulses to real activity and (ii) that there is a general pattern of a delayed response to a Romer and Romer shock.

3.5. Summary

We conclude that although there are some differences across the alternative policy shock measures considered, the basic qualitative

[14] This explanation is similar to Sims's (1992) original explanation of the price puzzle.
[15] The Appendix documents the robustness of these results with respect to nonborrowed reserve based policy shock measures.

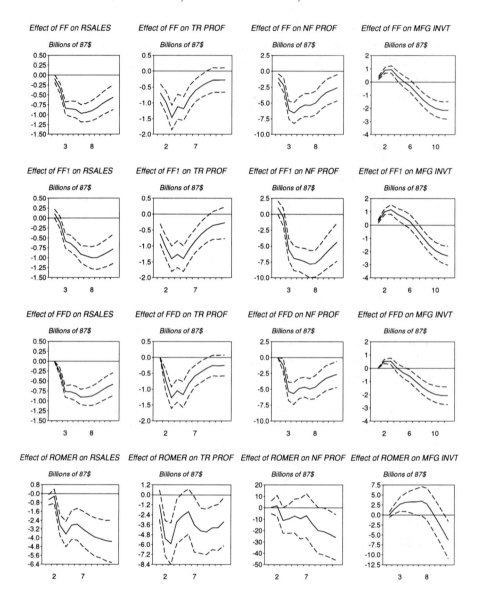

Figure 2.5. Effects of policy shocks on sectoral variables.

response of the system to different policy shock measures is quite robust. There is little to be gained by using the Romer and Romer index of monetary contractions. Using these episodes rather than the federal funds based policy shock measures amounts to throwing out a large number of interesting episodes as well as information about the intensity of each episode. Not surprisingly, the resulting response functions are estimated very imprecisely.

4. THE FLOW OF FUNDS

An important focus of the analysis in Christiano, Eichenbaum, and Evans (1996) is the response of net funds raised by different sectors of the economy to shocks in monetary policy. Our key findings were that after a contractionary policy shock (i) net funds raised by the business sector rise for a substantial period before falling and (ii) the initial response of net funds raised by the household sector is not statistically significant. In this section we assess the robustness of these findings to the different measures of policy shocks.

4.1. Sectoral Data Concepts

Sectoral data on *net funds raised* in financial markets are reported in the flow of funds accounts (FOFA). These data can also be computed from the national income and product accounts (NIPA) data.[16] The sectors that we consider are nonfinancial business, household, government (federal, state, and local), financial business, foreign, and the monetary authority. In this study we use both the FOFA and NIPA based measures of net funds raised for the business and corporate sectors; for the other sectors we report results only for the FOFA based measures of net funds raised.

4.2. Business and Corporate Sectors

Let *BNET* and *CNET* denote the FOFA based measures of real, net funds raised in the business and corporate sector, respectively. The corresponding NIPA measures are denoted by *BNET** and *CNET**. Figure 2.6 displays the dynamic response functions of *BNET, BNET*, CNET,* and *CNET** to the federal funds based

---

[16] The NIPA measure of net funds raised by a sector corresponds to tangible investment minus savings for that sector. Christiano, Eichenbaum, and Evans (1996) provide a more detailed comparison of the FOFA and NIPA measures.

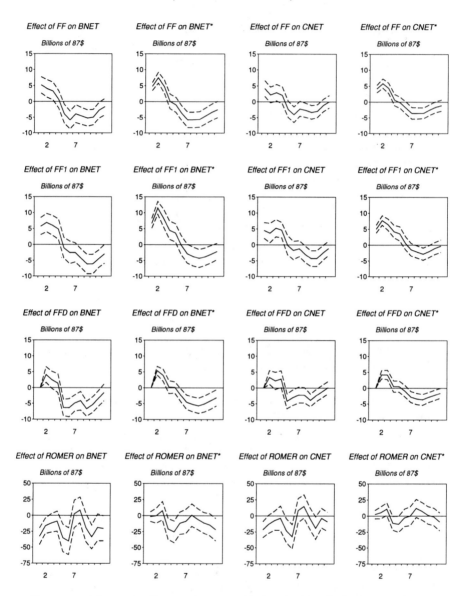

Figure 2.6. Effects of policy shocks on net funds raised by the business and corporate sectors.

policy shock measures and a Romer and Romer episode. Row 1 indicates that in response to an *FF* policy shock, net funds raised by the business and corporate sectors initially *rise*. This rise, which lasts for roughly six months to a year, is more persistent for the NIPA based measures of net funds raised.[17] Figure 2.6 also indicates that the initial rise in *BNET* and *CNET* generated by an *FF*1 policy shock is both more persistent and larger than the rise induced by an *FF* policy shock. The responses of *BNET** and *CNET** are also larger and somewhat more persistent. This finding may reflect the idea, discussed in Section 3, that *FF*1 policy shocks are contaminated by the effects of nonmonetary shocks.

Figure 2.6 indicates that our basic findings regarding the response of net funds raised by the business and corporate sector are robust to working with *FFD* policy shocks. The major difference is that here the policy shock cannot, by assumption, affect net funds raised contemporaneously. However, in the period immediately following the *FFD* policy shock, *BNET*, *BNET**, *CNET*, and *CNET** all rise for roughly a year. As with the *FF* and *FF*1 policy shock measures, the responses are more persistent for the NIPA than for the FOFA based measures of net funds raised. The Appendix shows that these conclusions are robust to working with nonborrowed reverse based policy measures.

Finally notice that because of sampling uncertainty, little can be said about the dynamic response functions of net funds raised by the business and corporate sectors to a Romer and Romer episode.

4.3. Other Sectors in the FOFA Data

Figure 2.7 displays the response of FOFA based measures of net funds raised by households (*HNET*), the government (*GNET*), financial institutions (*FINET*), and the foreign sector (*FONET*) to our different policy shock measures. A number of results are worth noting. First, none of the federal funds based policy shock measures generates statistically significant movements in *HNET* for roughly a year.[18] This finding is consistent with the limited participation

---

[17] In the Appendix we show that an *NBRD* policy shock generates a similar response function.

[18] The Appendix shows that this is also the case for the nonborrowed reserves based policy shock measures.

60 L. CHRISTIANO, M. EICHENBAUM, AND C. EVANS

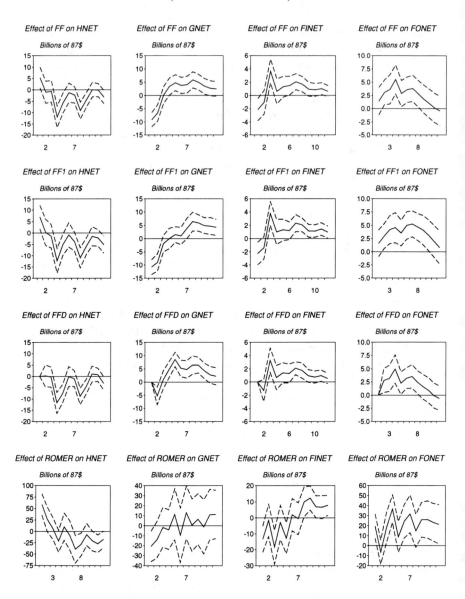

Figure 2.7. Effect of policy shocks on net funds raised by the household, government, financial, and foreign sectors.

assumption in Fuerst (1992) and Christiano and Eichenbaum (1995), namely, that households are slow to adjust their financial portfolios immediately after the realization of a monetary policy shock.[19] In contrast to the federal funds based shock measures, we find that the contemporaneous response of *HNET* to a Romer and Romer episode is significantly different from zero and positive. This is somewhat puzzling because the other variables we investigated (see Section 2) responded to a Romer and Romer episode with a substantial lag.

Second, *GNET* declines for about two quarters following a contractionary policy shock; that is, at the onset of a monetary contraction, net funds raised by the government fall. As the recession induced by the policy shock gains momentum, *GNET* rises. This is true regardless of which federal funds based policy shock measure we consider. Christiano, Eichenbaum, and Evans (1996) explore in more detail the components of the government deficit that initially fall following an *FF* policy shock. They report that the initial decline primarily reflects a rise in personal income tax receipts.

As it turns out, the initial decline in *GNET* is not robust to which policy shock measure we look at. For example, Figure 2.7 indicates that the decline following a Romer and Romer episode is not statistically significant. In the Appendix we show that the decline is also not significant for any of the nonborrowed reserve based policy shock measures. In this sense inference about the initial response of net funds raised by the government to a monetary policy shock is fragile.

Third, we do not find a systematic response of *FINET* to a policy shock. Fourth, for the first year, and across all of the policy shock measures that we consider, net funds raised by the foreign sector (*FONET*) rise. One interpretation of this result is that the monetary contraction in the United States is transmitted internationally. This could occur endogenously through international trade; or more directly, the foreign monetary authorities could respond systematically to the state of the U.S. economy and trigger a monetary contraction in their countries. Just as *BNET* rises in the United States at the onset of a monetary contraction, the foreign sector may be scrambling for additional funds as the resulting recession is

---

[19] This assumption applies to the underlying components of HNET, in addition to HNET itself. The behavior of the components is studied in Christiano, Eichenbaum, and Evans (1996).

transmitted abroad. Two recent studies provide some corroborating evidence on this point. Eichenbaum and Evans (1995) find that contractionary U.S. monetary policy shocks lead to an appreciation of the dollar and a rise in foreign interest rates. Evans and Santos (1993) find that measured productivity in the G-7 countries falls following a contractionary U.S. monetary policy shock. This response is consistent with the idea that a U.S. monetary contraction leads to a foreign monetary contraction, which drives down foreign output and – because of labor hoarding, variable capital utilization, or increasing returns to scale – foreign productivity.

To summarize, this section showed that net business borrowing initially rises after a monetary contraction. Because the flow of funds accounts form a closed system, it is in principle possible to answer the question, Which sectors fund this rise in borrowing? As it turns out, we do not have a robust answer to this question. For federal funds based policy shock measures, the answer seems to be that the rise in business borrowing is funded by an initial reduction in government borrowing due to a rise in personal income tax receipts. For nonborrowed reserves based measures, the answer is more ambiguous, because none of the other sectoral responses is statistically significant.

5. ANALYSIS OF MONTHLY DATA AND DETERMINISTIC TRENDS

In this section we establish the robustness of our results along two dimensions: (i) using monthly rather than quarterly data and (ii) detrending data assuming quadratic time trends.[20] The monthly data are of interest for a number of reasons. First, there is no reason to think that policy actions occur at the quarterly level. Second, on an a priori basis, it seems to us that recursive Wold casual identification schemes are more plausible the finer the time interval being considered. Unfortunately, the FOFA and NIPA measures of net funds raised by different sectors of the economy are not available at a monthly frequency. Consequently we look only at the robustness of our results concerning the effects of monetary policy shocks on

[20] Our results regarding robustness to time aggregation are consistent with the findings in Geweke, Miller, and Runkle (1994) and Owen (1994).

money market variables, aggregate economic activity, and price level.

5.1. Monthly Measures of FF Monetary Policy Shocks

In Section 2 we posited that the collection of variables, Ω_t, used by the Fed to set policy contains at least the past values of $\{Y, P, FF, NBRD, TR, PCOM\}$ assuming commodity prices are included in the analysis. The data on FF, $NBRD$, TR, and $PCOM$ are available at a monthly frequency. However, Y (real GDP) and P (the implicit GDP deflator) are available only at the quarterly frequency. Many researchers use industrial production in place of real GDP when working with monthly data (see for example Sims 1980; Eichenbaum and Singleton 1986). An important disadvantage of this measure is that it covers a narrow sector of the economy. For this reason, we chose to work with monthly nonagricultural employment. Coverage issues aside, it seems reasonable to think of the Fed's policy reaction function at the monthly level as depending on employment, because a large number of policy movements (systematic and nonsystematic) have occurred on the first Friday of the month when the employment report is released.[21]

This still leaves open the issue of how to measure P. Many analyses use the consumer price index (CPI) as a monthly measure of the price level. However, unlike the GDP deflator, the CPI is a fixed-weight deflator. An additional problem with the CPI is that for much of the sample period it measures the cost of shelter by including a mortgage cost component. Because this cost is directly related to interest rates, a "price puzzle" could arise simply as a result of the mortgage cost component of the CPI. To deal with this problem, we looked at three alternative measures of the aggregate price level: the implicit consumption expenditure price deflator (PCE), the CPI, and the CPI less shelter ($CPILSN$).

Figure 2.8 displays the dynamic response functions of various variables to a monetary policy shock computed using our benchmark identification strategy.[22] In particular, the monetary policy

---

[21] When we redo the analysis using industrial production in place of employment, we obtain very similar results.

[22] These were estimated from unconstrained VARs that included twelve lags of all variables.

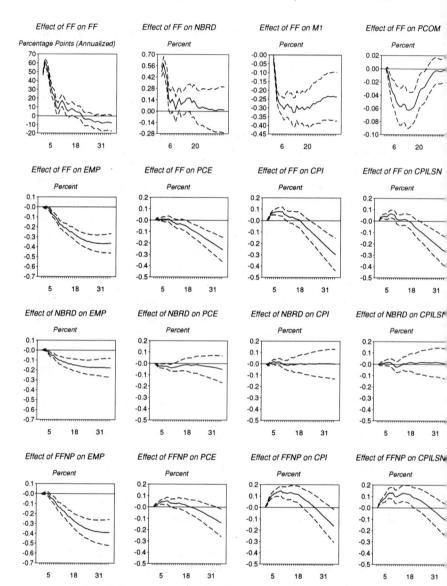

Figure 2.8. Effect of *FF* policy shocks in monthly data.

instrument is assumed to respond contemporaneously to employment and prices and these are assumed not to respond contemporaneously to policy shocks. Rows 1, 2, and 3 present dynamic response functions estimated from VAR systems that include *PCOM;* Row 4 reports dynamic response functions from systems where *PCOM* has been excluded from the analysis.

Consider first the effects of *FF* policy shocks when *PCOM* is included and the aggregate price level is measured using *PCE.* Row 1 indicates that the estimated dynamic response functions are very similar to the analogue response functions obtained using the quarterly data. The impact of a policy shock on the federal funds rate is persistent and induces a drop in nonborrowed reserves that lasts about six months, as well as a longer lasting decline in *M*1 and *PCOM.* From Row 2 we see that after a delay of a few months employment also drops.

Next we consider the price response to an *FF* policy shock. Notice that *PCE* does not respond for about six months, after which it begins a steady decline. This is qualitatively similar to the response of the implicit *GDP* deflator discussed in Section 3. Notice that when the *CPI* is substituted for *PCE* in the VAR, the price puzzle reemerges, with *CPI increasing* for about twelve months after a positive *FF* policy shock. Moreover, the initial rise is statistically significant. Consistent with the notion that the mortgage cost component of the CPI is playing a large role in this rise, when *CPILSN* is used rather than *CPI,* the rise in the price level induced by the policy shock is not as large or as significant. Still a small "price puzzle" remains. This may be due to the fact that *CPILSN* (like *CPI*) is a fixed-weight index, unlike *PCE* and the *GDP* deflator, which have time-varying weights.

Row 3 of Figure 2.8 displays the effects of an *NBRD* policy shock on employment and the three price levels when *PCOM* is included in the VAR system. As was the case for an *FF* policy shock, employment falls steadily following an *NBRD* policy shock. The response of *PCE* is negative throughout, whereas *CPI* and *CPILSN* rise for about six months before falling. Because all three response functions have very wide standard error bands, there is no interesting sense in which a price puzzle emerges. Similar results emerge when *PCOM* is excluded from the analysis.

To assess the role of commodity prices in resolving the price puzzle at the monthly level, Row 4 displays the effect of an *FF* policy shock on employment and the three price levels when *PCOM* is excluded from the VAR system. Notice that the price puzzle emerges for all three measures of the aggregate price level. The *PCE* response is borderline significant initially, rises for about six months, then falls below zero after about eighteen months. The initial rises in *CPI* and *CPILSN* are larger, more significant, and more persistent than the *PCE* response. We conclude that, as with the quarterly data, including *PCOM* plays an important role in eliminating or mitigating the price puzzle.

5.2. Allowing for Deterministic Trends

As a final check on the robustness of our results we reestimated the quarterly models, allowing for a quadratic time trend in the variables of interest. Figure 2.9 displays results for an *FF* policy shock. As can be seen, our basic results are quite robust.

6. CONCLUSIONS

This chapter has assessed the effects of shocks to monetary policy using alternative identifying restrictions to those used in Christiano, Eichenbaum, and Evans (1996). An important objective was to discover on what dimensions inference is sensitive to identification assumptions. With the exception of the Romer and Romer episodes, we have confined ourselves to identification schemes that correspond to imposing Wold causal orderings on the innovations in VARs. By no means does this exhaust the class of identifying assumptions that have been used in the literature. Alternative classes of identifying assumptions include those that involve restrictions on the long-run impact of shocks to monetary policy. (See, for example, King and Watson 1992.) An alternative class of identifying assumptions are nonrecursive schemes of the type considered by Bernanke (1986), Gali (1992), and Sims (1986), among others. These are sometimes referred to as "structural VARs." It would be of interest to investigate the sensitivity of inference to adopting these types of identifying restrictions, as well.

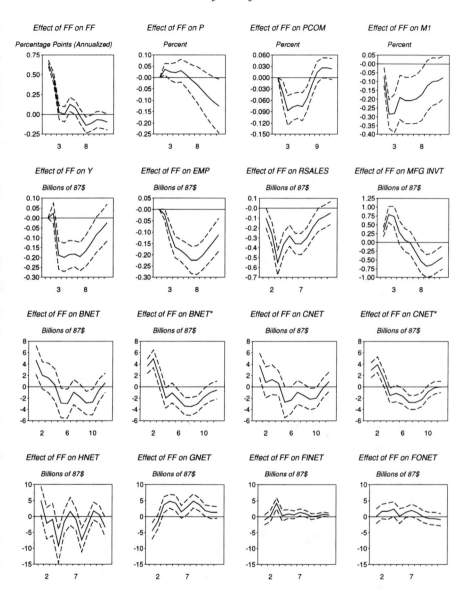

Figure 2.9. Effect of *FF* policy shocks in VARs with quadratic time trends.

APPENDIX

This Appendix displays the dynamic response functions of various variables to positive shocks in *NBRD*.

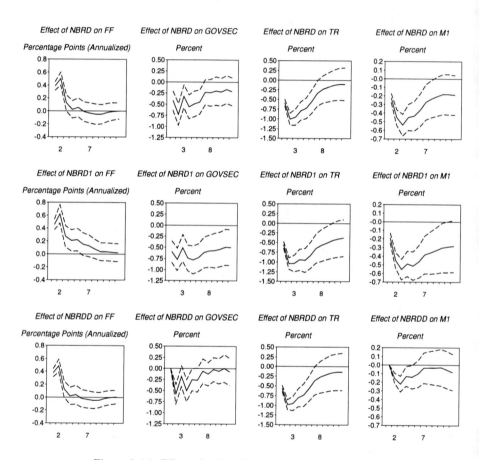

Figure 2.A1. Effect of policy shocks on monetary variables.

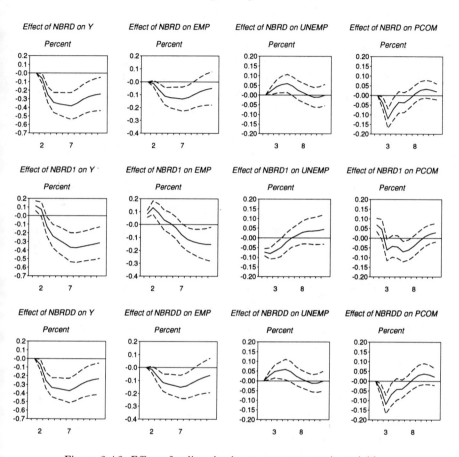

Figure 2.A2. Effect of policy shocks on macroeconomic variables.

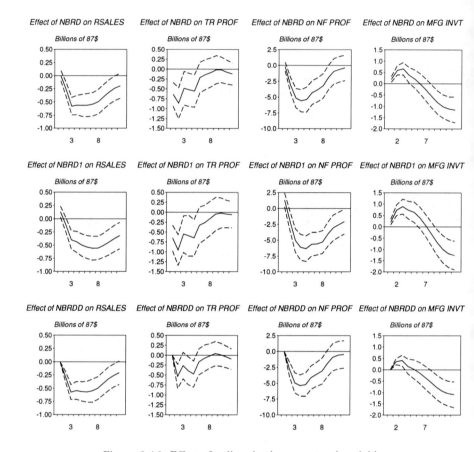

Figure 2.A3. Effect of policy shocks on sectoral variables.

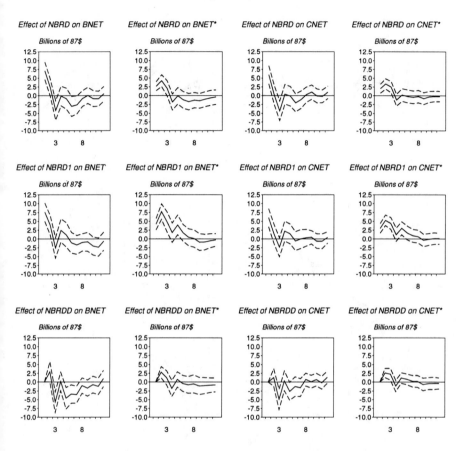

Figure 2.A4. Effect of policy shocks on net funds raised by the business and corporate sectors.

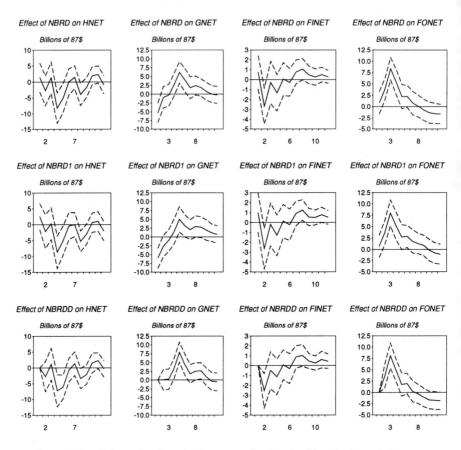

Figure 2.A5. Effect of policy shocks on net funds raised by the household, government, financial, and foreign sectors.

REFERENCES

Beaudry, and Mick Devereux (1994), Monopolistic Competition, Price Setting and the Effects of Real and Monetary Shocks, unpublished manuscript, University of British Columbia.

Bernanke, Ben (1986), Alternative Explanations of the Money Income Correlation, in Karl Brunner and Allan Meltzer, eds., *Carnegie Rochester Conference on Public Policy, Real Business Cycles, Real Exchange Rates and Actual Policies* 25 (Autumn), 49–100.

Bernanke, Ben, and Alan Blinder (1992), The Federal Funds Rate and the Channels of Monetary Transmission, *American Economic Review* 82(4): 901–21.

Blanchard, Olivier Jean, and Danny Quah (1989), The Dynamic Effects of Aggregate Demand and Supply Disturbances, *American Economic Review* 79(4): 655–73.

Christiano, Lawrence J., and Martin Eichenbaum (1992), Liquidity Effects, and the Monetary Transmission Mechanism, *American Economic Review* 82(2): 346–53.

Christiano, Lawrence J., and Martin Eichenbaum (1995), Liquidity Effects, Monetary Policy and the Business Cycle, *Journal of Money, Credit, and Banking* 27(4), 1113–36.

Christiano, Lawrence J., Martin Eichenbaum, and Charles L. Evans (1996), The Effects of Monetary Policy Shocks: Evidence from the Flow of Funds, (Forthcoming), *Review of Economics and Statistics*, February.

Cochrane, John (1994), Shock, manuscript, University of Chicago.

Doan, Thomas (1990), Users Manual, RATS Version 3.10, Evanston, IL: VAR Econometrics.

Eichenbaum, Martin (1992), Comment on Interpreting the Macroeconomic Time Series Facts: The Effects of Monetary Policy, *European Economic Review* 36 (June): 1001–11.

Eichenbaum, Martin, and Charles L. Evans (1995), Some Empirical Evidence on the Effects of Shocks to Monetary Policy on Exchange Rates, *Quarterly Journal of Economics*, 110: 975–1010.

Eichenbaum, Martin, and Kenneth J. Singleton (1986), Do Equilibrium Business Cycle Theories Explain Post-War Business Cycles? in S. Fischer, ed., *NBER Macroeconomics Annual 1986*, Cambridge, MA: MIT Press, 91–134.

Evans, Charles L., and Fernando Santos (1993), Monetary Policy Shocks and Productivity Measures in the G-7 Countries, Federal Reserve Bank of Chicago Working Paper WP-93-12.

Fuerst, Timothy (1992), Liquidity, Loanable Funds, and Real Activity, *Journal of Monetary Economics* 29(1): 3–24.

Gali, Jordi (1992), How Well Does the IS-LM Model Fit Postwar U.S. Data? *Quarterly Journal of Economics* 107 (May): 709–38.

Kashyap, Anil K., Jeremy C. Stein, and David W. Wilcox (1993), Monetary Policy and Credit Conditions: Evidence from the Composition of External Finance, *American Economic Review* 83(1): 78–98.

King, Robert, and Mark Watson (1992), Comparing the Fit of Alternative Dynamic Models, manuscript, Northwestern University, 2–3.

Oliner, Stephen D., and Glenn D. Rudebusch (1992), The Transmission of Monetary Policy to Small and Large Firms, manuscript, Board of Governors of the Federal Reserve System.

Romer, Christina D., and David H. Romer (1989), Does Monetary Policy Matter? A New Test in the Spirit of Friedman and Schwartz, in Olivier J. Blanchard and Stanley Fischer, eds., *NBER Macroeconomic Annual 1989*, Cambridge, MA: MIT Press, 121–70.

Sims, Christopher (1980), Macroeconomics and Reality, *Econometrica* 48(1): 1–48.

Sims, Christopher A. (1986), Are Forecasting Models Usable for Policy Analysis? Federal Reserve Bank of Minneapolis, *Quarterly Review,* Winter.

Sims, Christopher A. (1992), Interpreting the Macroeconomic Time Series Facts: The Effects of Monetary Policy, *European Economic Review* 36:975–1000.

Strongin, Steve, (1992), The Identification of Monetary Policy Disturbances: Explaining the Liquidity Puzzle, *Journal of Monetary Economics* 35(3), 463–98.

CHAPTER 3

Credit Market Imperfections and Low-Output Equilibria in Economies in Transition

Guillermo A. Calvo and Fabrizio Coricelli

1. INTRODUCTION

The output decline in economies in transition has been deep, sudden, and common to all economies that launched market reforms (Figure 3.1). These characteristics suggest a systemic nature of the output collapse (see also Kornai 1993). Specifically, the decline in output may have resulted from a change in regime consisting in a shift from a system of organization and coordination of production and exchanges based on central intervention or government tutelage to a decentralized system. Within this broad view we focus on the effects of credit policy in a system in which the role of credit markets has changed radically. In fact, most previously centrally planned economies (PCPEs) began their reforms lacking credit markets, namely lacking the information, trust, institutions, and rules that codified either in laws or in common practice define credit markets. In the prereform regime banks mainly served the role of accounting firms. The information capital necessary for the functioning of credit markets and the concomitant banking skills were absent in the prereform regime. Moreover, private credit markets did not exist in highly centralized economies. Besides legal restrictions, the lack of credible bankruptcy procedures was a major obstacle to the development of such private markets.

The reforms of 1990–91 implied a sudden break with the past. Credit policy was sharply tightened. The automatic extension of credit from the central bank was terminated. The full insurance guaranteed by the central bank as a lender of last resort was eliminated. Financial conditions of enterprises suddenly became a determinant of their output and wage payments. The central channels of organization and coordination of exchanges disappeared. Firms had to carry out their transactions in the market, at prices freely set

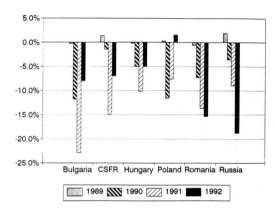

Figure 3.1. GDP growth (percentage changes over previous year).

by firms. Money became a fundamental instrument for transactions also with the enterprise sector, in contrast with the old regime, where the only relevant monetary exchanges were associated with the household sector.

In previous work we have explored whether such conditions in credit markets may help explain the output performance observed in the initial stages of reforms in PCPEs, focusing on the impact effects of a credit crunch.

In this chapter our focus shifts to the dynamic adjustment after the initial shock and, in particular, to the circular process of exchanges within the firm sector and the role of money and interenterprise credit in such a process. The chapter emphasizes the role of interenterprise arrears and possible externalities in the use of money in enterprise transactions. It is suggested that the initial liquidity crunch may push the system into a self-sustaining equilibrium of low liquidity and low output. The network of interenterprise arrears may contribute to such outcome, although it may soften the initial negative output effect of a liquidity crunch. Good and bad firms are linked through a chain of arrears.

Thus, the discussion raises doubts about the effectiveness of tight credit in inducing a more efficient allocation of resources across sectors and firms in the context of underdeveloped financial markets. In fact, one possible equilibrium outcome associated with the credit crunch is an explosion of arrears, the "demonetization" of enterprise transactions and the consolidation of the existing – likely inefficient – pattern of production and exchanges among enterprises.

The chapter is not a justification for lax credit policy, but rather a warning on the risks of an excessive contraction of liquidity in systems, like those in PCPEs, characterized by developed industrial structures combined with underdeveloped or completely absent financial markets.

Section 2 briefly discusses the impact effect of a liquidity crunch in a representative-firm setting with no frictions or externalities in the process of transactions among firms. A simple characterization of credit market imperfections is provided, and it is shown that with credit market segmentation a liquidity crunch leads, on impact, to a fall in output. Section 3 discusses some dynamics following a liquidity crunch, focusing on the role of interenterprise arrears. Section 4 reviews more closely the empirical relevance of the hypotheses developed in the analytical discussion of arrears, with particular attention to the case of Romania, for which an enterprise level data set was available. Section 5 concludes the chapter with a brief discussion of policy implications. Appendix 1 illustrates the simple analytics of three extensions to the basic model of Section 2, which can lead to low output persistence.

2. A SIMPLE MODEL OF LIQUIDITY-CONSTRAINED FIRMS

The model tries to capture some key institutional aspects of PCPEs, relating both to the underdevelopment of credit markets and to the structure of control of state enterprises based on a powerful role for workers.

To focus on the role of credit, we assume the economy is populated by competitive, identical firms that produce a final good using intermediate inputs and labor. Both final and intermediate goods are tradable. Thus, with constant international prices, their domestic price is determined by the exchange rate. To simplify further the analysis, we assume a system of fixed exchange rates. Consequently, prices are exogenous. In order to produce final goods firms must have a stock of inputs at the beginning of the production process, and inputs have to be paid in cash. The liquidity constraint is captured by assuming that firms face a liquidity-in-advance constraint

$$x \leq m \qquad (3.1)$$

where x stands for inputs of intermediate goods and m is real cash balances in terms of inputs. To account for the powerful role of the workers in state-owned enterprises, we assume that firms are managed by a workers' council. The council cares about the welfare of all the (identical) workers belonging to the coalition attached to the firm. Because our focus is on the initial impact of a liquidity squeeze, we assume that the size of the coalition, or membership, is fixed. Therefore, the council maximizes the expected utility of the representative member.[1]

To rule out dynamics of the labor market that would derail us from the main focus of the discussion, we assume that there are no unemployment benefits. As a result, the firm employs all its members, and thus employment becomes a fixed factor (its size is normalized to be equal to one). The production function can thus be written as $f(x)$, and f is assumed to satisfy the usual neoclassical conditions. Thus, if firms are liquidity-constrained, then condition (3.1) holds with equality, and output of final goods can be written as $f(m)$. Letting ω denote total labor income, and assuming an exogenous constant exchange rate, firms can accumulate liquidity over time according to

$$m_{t+1} = pf(m_t) - \omega_t \qquad (3.2)$$

where p stands for the price of output in terms of inputs. As noted, we assume that both goods are tradable and thus the relative price is exogenous.

Condition (3.2) highlights the fundamental role of wages in the process of liquidity accumulation of firms.

Let us consider the case in which households have perfect access to international capital markets. This justifies taking the (constant) world interest rate as the relevant discount factor for households.

---

[1] The outcome of the choice of the workers' council is optimal from the point of view of the coalition of workers and resembles the outcome of efficient contracts in capitalist firms, with the difference being that in the case we discuss, the income-sharing rule is trivial, as all the rents of the firm are appropriated by the workers. This setup contrasts sharply with the classical version of the labor-managed firm, which assumes that firms maximize income per worker (Ward 1958). That model implies the firm will fire workers even when there is no unemployment compensation.

Thus, the workers' council chooses the path of labor income that maximizes the present discounted value of labor income, that is,

$$\sum_{t=0}^{\infty} \omega_t \left(\frac{1}{1+r} \right)^t \tag{3.3}$$

subject to the liquidity-accumulation equation (3.2) and the initial stock of liquidity m_0. The linear specification of the workers' council objective function implies that the problem has a "bang-bang" type of solution (Shell 1967). Let m_∞ be such that it satisfies the following condition:

$$pf'(m) - 1 = r \tag{3.4}$$

If $m_0 = m_\infty$, it is optimal to set $m_t = m_0$ for all t. However, if $m_0 < m_\infty$, and thus the economy is in a liquidity crunch, then the optimal choice for the workers is to transfer to the firm an amount of money equivalent to $m_\infty - m_0$. Thus, the firm would borrow from its workers and circumvent the liquidity constraint. This situation can be defined as one in which credit markets work perfectly, as liquidity is transferred from the sector that has access to international credit markets – the workers' households – to the sector that is excluded from them – the firms. By contrast, credit market segmentation can be captured in a simple manner by assuming that wages cannot fall below a well-defined lower bound.

With credit market segmentation, if the firm operates initially in the liquidity-crunch region, the optimal choice would be to set wages at the minimum acceptable level until real monetary balances have attained their optimal steady-state level. The initial liquidity crunch may be determined either by a devaluation of the exchange rate – keeping the relative price p unchanged – or by a contraction of nominal balances. The liquidity crunch inevitably determines a contraction of output on impact. Note that this takes place even when the relative price of inputs does not increase and real wages decline; that is, there is no "supply shock" in the conventional meaning.

In sum, when facing a liquidity crunch firms "borrow from their workers" in order to achieve, at the maximum speed, the optimal level of real monetary balances. However, the segmentation of credit markets implies that output declines on impact.

This simple model provides an explanation for the puzzling behavior of wages during the early stages of reform, namely the fact that wages were set well below the ceilings established by the programs. Indeed, such a phenomenon is particularly puzzling, given the powerful role of workers in the decision making of enterprises.

There is a simple economic intuition behind these results. When the level of liquidity is below full capacity the inequality $pf'(m) - 1 > r$ holds.[2] The inequality states that the marginal return to liquidity used to purchase inputs $pf'(m) - 1$ is greater than the marginal return to liquidity left in the hands of the workers r. Thus, by lending to firms, workers get a rate of return larger than r.

The version of the model discussed previously adopts a series of simplifying assumptions that do not crucially affect the main results. Before pointing to some natural extensions of the model, it is worth noting that the preceding model focused on the case of fixed exchange rates and tradable inputs and output. With flexible exchange rates it is less obvious how the real stock of liquidity can fall below the full-capacity level. Indeed, the contraction of nominal liquidity would lead to an appreciation of the exchange rate, which could in turn maintain the real stock of liquidity at its full-capacity level. To generate the same result discussed in the text, the model has to be modified in one of two ways: (i) assuming some form of price-setting rigidity and/or (ii) assuming an asymmetric distribution of liquidity before the start of the program. In both cases a contraction in liquidity would lead to output effects. Rigidities in price setting may arise because of the presence of a significant share of input prices that is administered, or because of anachronistic cost-plus pricing in sectors not exposed to foreign competition. The asymmetric distribution of liquidity implies that the increase in the price level will determine liquidity constraints for liquidity-poor firms, whereas liquidity-rich firms would still be characterized by excess liquidity. To prevent the output decline, a reallocation of liquidity across firms would be necessary. Thus, the effects of a credit crunch are likely to be at work also in the case of flexible exchange rates, as long as there is segmentation in credit markets.

The main results of the model do not depend on the specific form of credit market segmentation, which was introduced by superimposing a lower bound on wages. In a richer – and perhaps more realistic – model the limits on enterprise borrowing from workers can arise from the fact that workers' households may face liquidity

---

[2] As a consequence of the assumption of strict concavity of the production function.

constraints as well. In addition, the main thrust of the preceding model carries over to a more realistic setting in which liquidity of firms can be altered by bank credit (see Calvo and Coricelli 1992 for such extensions).[3]

Finally, a more realistic model would incorporate inventories and interenterprise arrears. Indeed, the cash constraint may be loosened by the presence of these two elements. However, both the down loading of input inventories and the accumulation of arrears in payments to suppliers, although effective at the level of the single firm, may have negative aggregate effects on output as they create difficulties for inventory producing firms and for suppliers of inputs. Nevertheless, the introduction of inventories and arrears would not alter qualitatively the basic result relating to the impact effect on output of a liquidity contraction. Whether the use of inventories and the accumulation of arrears may eliminate the liquidity crunch is an empirical question. The definition of liquidity of the firm is modified, but not the nature of the constraint (3.1). Nevertheless, as discussed in the next section, the presence of interenterprise arrears may have important dynamic effects.

The model implies that output converges toward its full-capacity level as firms accumulate liquidity over time. The actual experience of PCPEs seems to indicate that the speed of recovery is rather low. Even in countries like Poland that had begun to grow during 1992, the level of output remains depressed (Figure 3.2). There are several possible channels of low-output persistence, some of which are explored in the next section. The simple model discussed previously obviously neglects the presence of exogenous shocks, for instance, the demise of the Council for Mutual Economic Assistance (CMEA), which may depress output. Although empirically relevant, these shocks do not alter the validity of the theoretical model. In fact, the CMEA shock itself could be seen as a case of trade implosion deriving from the destruction of a system of centralized credit and payment. In our model this can be characterized as a tightening of the liquidity constraint determined by a contraction of foreign credit.

---

[3] In the case of binding credit ceilings, the model is basically unchanged. When credit ceilings are not binding, the behavior of the stock of credit is demand-determined and depends on the path of interest rates on bank loans. However, in the relevant case in which interest rates are initially high and are expected to decline over time, the main results of the simple cash-in-advance model still hold.

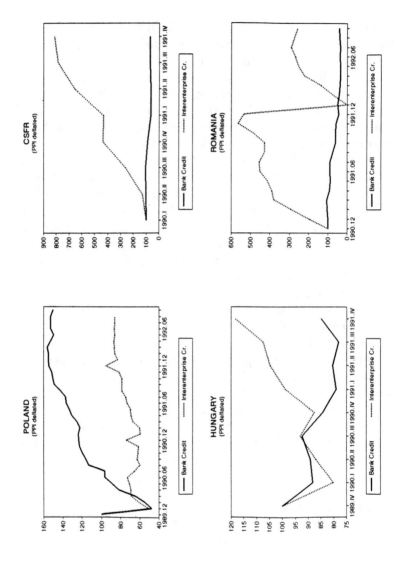

Figure 3.2. Interenterprise arrears.

Moreover, there are other channels accounting for a slower recovery that can be easily incorporated in the simple model exposed. These relate, for instance, to the horizon of the firms, endogenous inflation, and the effects of that inflation on money demand. These modifications, although altering the quantitative implications of the model in terms of speed of adjustment, do not change the main thrust of the simple model (see Appendix 1).

In contrast with these "incremental" changes of the simple model we discuss in the next section the possibility of a qualitative change in the properties of the dynamic adjustment implied by the simple model. In particular, we develop a model with multiple equilibria, with each equilibrium distinguished by different levels of output and liquidity. In this type of model the issue is not simply the speed of adjustment, as countries may get stuck into the initial state of depressed output.

3. LOW-OUTPUT PERSISTENCE: INTERENTERPRISE ARREARS

A salient characteristic of transformation programs has been the rapid development of interenterprise credit channels (see Begg and Portes 1992; Calvo and Coricelli 1992; Ickes and Ryterman (mimeo), The Inter-Enterprise Arrears Crisis in Russia; Clifton and Khan 1992; Daianu 1994; Rostowski 1994). It should be noted, however, that interenterprise credit is also large in market economies (see Rostowski 1993; Begg and Portes 1992). Therefore, the growth of interenterprise credit in PCPEs should, in principle, be a welcome development. Unfortunately, however, the rapid growth of that market has been accompanied by the emergence and, occasionally, ballooning of interenterprise arrears, that is, *involuntary* interenterprise credit. The latter is, in principle, undesirable because it occupies the place that shirking and stealing take in regular market economies.

To capture interenterprise arrears, let us assume that firms can acquire their inputs by paying with cash or by falling into arrears. Let θ indicate the share that is, in equilibrium, paid in cash. Taking the extreme case in which arrears are expected never to be paid back, the competitive nominal price of inputs and outputs (recall that inputs and outputs are fully tradable and their foreign currency price is unity while, in the simplest model, the exchange rate was set equal to unity) must be $1/\theta$.

In order to put a natural brake on arrears, we will assume that arrears are costly, and that the present discounted value of the cost (in terms of input) of additional arrears is proportional to the latter, where the factor of proportionality is denoted by $\varkappa > 1$. Hence, focusing exclusively on firms that sell to other firms, the analogue of cash accumulation equation (3.2), where now m is expressed in terms of input, becomes

$$\frac{\theta_t}{\theta_{t+1}} \, m_{t+1} = f(x_t)\theta_t - \varkappa(x_t - m_t) - \omega_t\theta_t \quad \text{for} \quad m_t \leq x_t \qquad (3.5)$$

New arrears per unit of time in terms of output (or input) are equal to $x - m$, which rationalizes the third term in equation (3.5). The first term, in turn, is net revenue in terms of input bought in the free market at home. To prove it, notice that nominal gross revenue is $\theta P f(m)$ where, as indicated, $P = 1/\theta$ = nominal price of output and input in the free market at home. Thus, θ remains as a factor in equation (3.5) because it is the relative price of *output in the firm* per unit of time to real cash balances in terms of input bought at home at time t, m_t. The presence of θ in equation (3.5) has nothing to do with the relative price of output with respect to input because, by previous considerations, the latter is always equal to unity. Finally, the factor θ_t/θ_{t+1} accounts for the change in the price of input between periods t and $t + 1$.

Given the linearity of the model, solutions will be, as a general rule, of the bang-bang variety. Therefore, to ensure well-defined solutions where arrears take place but where repudiation is not total, we will assume that θ cannot fall below some $\underline{\theta}$, such that $1 > \underline{\theta} > 0$. Notice that, by equation (3.5), optimal x_t will be chosen so as to maximize the right-hand side of that equation. Thus, at an interior maximum, we have

$$f'(x_t)\,\theta_t = \varkappa \qquad (3.6)$$

Moreover, the no-accumulation-of-arrears corner solution obtains if

$$f'(m_t) < \varkappa \qquad (3.7)$$

whereas the maximum-accumulation-of-arrears corner solution holds if

$$f'\left(\frac{m}{\theta}\right)\underline{\theta} > \varkappa \qquad (3.8)$$

Let us now turn our attention to optimality conditions for ω. To simplify, we will focus exclusively on steady states, where $\theta_t = \theta =$ constant through time. As in the previous sections, we will assume that the bounds on ω are wide enough for optimal ω to be inferior to its feasibility region. If $\underline{\theta} < \theta < 1$, then increasing the wage bill by 1 more unit at time t implies, by (3.5), θ fewer units of real monetary balances at the beginning of period $t + 1$, which, if used to pay input in period $t + 1$, saves ϰθ in cost of arrears. Thus, the wage bill in period $t + 1$ could increase by ϰ units. In view of expression (3.3), if the perturbation is taken at the optimal point, then a necessary condition for an interior optimum will be ϰ = 1 + r − a highly unlikely situation. Therefore, as expected, solutions will in general be at $\theta = 1$ or $\theta = \underline{\theta}$.

Consider the case in which θ = 1, that is, no accumulation of arrears. This case is similar to that in Section 2. Therefore, at optimum, $f'(m) = 1 + r$, which, combined with equation (3.7), implies that ϰ > 1 + r.

Finally, if $\theta = \underline{\theta}$ then, by (3.3) and (3.5), at optimum

$$f'\left(\frac{m}{\underline{\theta}}\right)\underline{\theta} = (1 + r)\underline{\theta} + \varkappa(1 - \underline{\theta}) \tag{3.9}$$

When the latter is combined with inequality (3.8), it implies that ϰ < 1 + r.

Consequently, we have shown that no arrears will take place if ϰ > 1 + r, whereas maximum accumulation of arrears will occur if the inequality is reversed.

Therefore, disregarding the possibility of an interior solution, the economy could exhibit a minimum-liquidity equilibrium (MLE) (i.e., $\theta = \underline{\theta}$), and a no-arrears equilibrium (NAE) (i.e., θ = 1), which corresponds to the equilibrium discussed in Section 2. Notice that, because when θ = 1, we have $f'(x) = 1 + r$, equation (3.9) implies that, as expected, output is lower at an MLE than at an NAE.

Given ϰ and r $(1 + r \neq \varkappa)$ one of the two equilibria will emerge. However, these variables are, to some extent, endogenous. First, as noted in Section 1, the *effective* interest rate (i.e., $r + W$) is affected by the firm's horizon. If the latter is short, the effective interest rate will be large, and a bad MLE is likely to materialize. Second, if as in Section 2 the model allows for inflation (i.e., nominal interest rate $i > r$), then one can show that all the preceding conditions hold with i substituting for r. Thus, when inflation increases beyond the critical point at which $1 + i = \varkappa$, the economy will suddenly shift from the NAE to the MLE. This reinforces the possibility that a "bad" equilibrium will take hold, because the shift from an NAE to an MLE represents a catastrophic decline in the demand for money.

In addition, the marginal direct cost of arrears, $\varkappa$, is likely to be affected by the amount of arrears. The larger the latter is, the smaller may be the marginal direct cost of arrears, $\varkappa$. Thus, an initial liquidity crunch, for example, may force firms into arrears. As the latter accumulate, firms realize that they are not the only ones in trouble and, therefore, that penalties cannot be so severe as in the case where just a few firms fall into financial difficulties. As a result, $\varkappa$ may decline so much that the bad MLE takes hold. In other words, *an initial credit crunch could generate a situation where interenterprise arrears accumulate without bound, and output is permanently lower than in the no-arrears situation.*

Obviously, much of the previous policy discussion applies to the present case. The present model, however, allows us to address the question of whether the clearing of arrears could be an effective policy to drive the economy to the good NAE. The model suggests two reasons for being skeptical. First, firms' horizons could be very short and, thus, $\varkappa$ would have to be very large to induce firms to avoid falling into arrears. Besides, large $\varkappa$'s may be hard to implement either because bankruptcy is nonexistent or because bankruptcy procedures are exceedingly slow. Second, $\varkappa$ may depend not only on past arrears but also on *expected* arrears. Thus, the MLE could be quickly regenerated if firms *expect* that the previous arrears situation will reemerge in the future.

Our skepticism is given support by experience in countries like Romania, where the elimination of arrears has quickly been followed by a buildup of new ones. Therefore, our discussion suggests that the solution in such cases must be found in massive privatization and effective bankruptcy regulations.

4. A CLOSER LOOK AT THE EVIDENCE ON INTERENTERPRISE ARREARS

The model of the "representative firm" provides an incomplete account of the dynamic adjustment of countries in transition. Indeed, independently of the incentives at the level of the individual firm, there could be problems in coordinating the recovery to the full-employment output in a system with interdependent firms. As shown in Section 3, when firms interact with each other, the "good" equilibrium with output recovering its full-employment level is only one of the possible equilibria. "Bad" equilibria with low output and low liquidity can arise. A main force determining this multiplicity of equilibria is associated with interenterprise arrears.

Arrears have grown in some countries from zero to amounts larger than overall bank credit or broad money (Table 3.1). Moreover, the heterogeneity of the behavior of arrears across countries may offer an important clue for understanding the different macroeconomic situation characterizing the various countries. Interestingly, the countries that we identified as unsuccessful in stabilizing their economies are those displaying explosive behavior of arrears.[4]

In the area of interenterprise arrears country experiences were remarkably heterogeneous (Daianu 1994; Rostowski 1994). Specifically, arrears have literally exploded in Romania and Russia, whereas they have increased much less in Hungary and Poland. Moreover, after "book cleaning" operations in Romania and Russia, arrears have rapidly grown again.[5]

In the model of Section 3 the main determinant of arrears was summarized by the parameter x, a proxy for the marginal cost of running into arrears for the individual firm. It was also suggested that such a cost is a decreasing function of the aggregate size of arrears. If firms cannot coordinate ex ante their behavior, there can be multiple equilibria with different levels of arrears.

If firms attach a positive probability to the government validation of the arrears through money creation, the likelihood of the high arrears equilibrium obviously increases. The cases of Romania and Russia clearly illustrate such a phenomenon of self-fulfilling prophecy. Indeed, in both countries the government response to the explosion of arrears has been a generalized cleanup effected

---

[4] The former Czechoslovakia is somehow an outlier. Indeed, arrears grew very rapidly in a context of low inflation. This suggests – contrary to what is argued in Rostowski (1993) – that credibility of the stabilization program is not the only factor affecting interenterprise arrears. Nevertheless, in relation to bank credit, arrears in the former Czechoslovakia remain much lower than in Romania and Russia.

[5] In Romania with the so-called global compensation scheme at the end of 1991 (see Clifton and Khan 1992 for a discussion), and in Russia in July 1992.

Table 3.1. *Interenterprise arrears (ratio of interenterprise arrears to bank credit)*

	Poland[a]	Romania	Hungary	Former CSFR	Russia
1989 IV	1.6	na	0.2	0.0	na
1990.I	1.7	na	0.1	0.0	na
1990.II	1.2	na	0.2	0.0	na
1990.III	0.9	na	0.2	0.1	na
1990.IV	1.0	0.1	0.2	0.1	na
1991.I	0.9	0.5	0.2	0.1	na
1991.II	0.9	0.7	0.2	0.2	na
1991.III	0.8	1.1	0.2	0.2	na
1991.IV	1.0	1.9	0.2	0.2	0.0
1992.I	0.9	0.0[b]	na	na	0.9
1992.II	0.9	1.1	na	na	2.3
1992.III	na	0.9	na	na	0.8[c]
1992.IV	na	na	na	na	na

[a] For Poland, the figures refer to interenterprise credit, whereas for the other countries the figures refer only to arrears, i.e., overdue credit.

[b] At the beginning of the year arrears were cleared through the Global Compensation Scheme.

[c] The figure is only for July. In July bank credit was injected into the system to clear the arrears.

through injection of bank credit. Not surprisingly, arrears have grown rapidly soon after the implementation of these cleanup operations, confirming the important role of the expectations of a bailout for the growth of arrears. In particular, as this expectation is likely linked to the size of aggregate arrears, the latter may be one of the channels through which K becomes a decreasing function of aggregate arrears.[6]

In addition to the issue of credibility of the no-bailout stance, institutional factors may affect the perceived individual cost of run-

[6] The time series behavior of arrears in Poland offers additional evidence on the importance of credibility of the stabilization program in affecting the accumulation of arrears. Indeed, at the beginning of the program, when credibility was likely high, interenterprise credit fell together with bank credit. As the credibility of the program weakened starting in the second half of 1990, interenterprise arrears began to move in opposite direction to bank credit. The correlation coefficient between interenterprise credit and bank credit, or enterprise money, is indeed negative after the first half of 1990. It is interesting to note that the change in the behavior of interenterprise arrears mirrors the change in wage behavior discussed.

ning into arrears. Ultimately, these institutional factors relate to unclear property rights and the consequent lack of credible bankruptcy threat, which in turn rules out the possibility of enforcing private contracts.

Finally, the possibility for suppliers to switch to different customers is another important factor affecting the expected cost of running into arrears. Given the highly concentrated structure of domestic markets and the rigid network of relations imposed by the central plan, in the initial stages of reform the flexibility of supplier-customers relations is likely to be associates with export opportunities. Hungary and Poland stand out as the countries with more rapid export growth to market economies. This may have implied a high x for these economies, which in turn can account for the moderate increase in interenterprise arrears.

In sum, the multiple equilibrium model of Section 3 helps to characterize the different country experiences as being largely associated with different perceived microeconomic costs of running into arrears (parameter x). However, the model also illustrates certain key features of interenterprise arrears. Specifically, the model generates a network, or chain, of arrears in a system in which all firms are viable – that is, have nonnegative profits. This condition is important because it permits a view of interenterprise arrears as a form of stable equilibrium. The presence of loss-making firms would imply that in the chain of arrears a group of firms is subsidized by other firms, an unlikely sustainable phenomenon. Of course we do not deny that arrears also reflect the presence of loss-making firms. However, we claim that this is not the dominant feature of arrears.

The empirical relevance of the view of arrears as an equilibrium network can be analyzed for the case of Romania, for which micro-data on all state-owned industrial enterprises are available for 1992.

4.1. The Case of Romania

Romania, together with Russia, is the country in which interenterprise arrears have been at center stage since the launching of the reform program in 1991. Targets on arrears have even featured in the conditionality of International Monetary Fund (IMF) and

World Bank programs. Moreover, Romania launched a global attempt to clean up arrears at the end of 1991. However, our focus on
Romania is determined also by the fact that Romania is the only
country for which we have detailed information at the enterprise
level.

Some caveats on this data set should be stressed at the outset.
First, the data set is available only for 1992, thus for the period
following the cleanup, called the global compensation (GC)
scheme. Second, the data provide a snapshot of the situation in the
first nine months of 1992 and are not time series. Despite these
limitations, the data set permits an analysis of the main features of
interenterprise arrears and of the correlation between enterprise
characteristics and arrears.

First, it is useful to summarize the behavior of gross arrears since
the start of reforms and relate them to bank credit. Figure 3.2 shows
that arrears grew rapidly after the launching of reforms in 1991,
they accelerated sharply in the months preceding the implementation of the GC scheme, and they grew up again after the cleanup,
although they did not recover the levels of pre-GC scheme. Figure
3.3 indicates the negative correlation between the level of arrears,
as a share of bank credit, and real bank credit to enterprises. It is
worth noting that the growth of arrears took place simultaneously
with a sharp and continuous decline in production and high persistent inflation.

The sharp initial contraction in real money and credit translated
into a persistent phenomenon of "demonetization," or fall in money
demand. Thus, prima facie, the case of Romania seems to correspond to the case of MLE identified in the previous section. Furthermore, the Romanian experience is an example of the limited
efficacy of cleanup operations not supported by macroeconomic
policies and microeconomic incentives.

We next analyze in more detail the characteristics of interenterprise arrears, using data on all state-owned industrial enterprises
for the first three quarters of 1992. These data permit analysis of (i)
the degree of "circularity" of the process, namely how important
the debts of firms that have a roughly balanced debt–credit (payables and receivables) position are and (ii) the role of loss-making
firms in the network of arrears. Finally, we report some suggestive
evidence from a small-scale enterprise survey which provides quali-

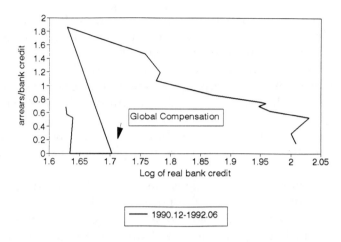

Figure 3.3. Romania (arrears and bank credit).

tative answers on the features and determinants of arrears in Romania.

One simple measure of the degree of circularity is given by the ratio of total net arrears, defined as the sum of net debt positions of net debtor firms, to total gross arrears. This ratio hovered between 25 and 30 percent during 1991 and 1992. This means that a large proportion of arrears appear to be a substitute for enterprise liquidity. Perhaps even more relevant are the number of firms involved in the network of arrears and the number of firms with significant net debt positions. For instance, in June 1992, of 1,692 state industrial firms, 1,455 displayed arrears in payments to suppliers, whereas most net arrears were concentrated in a handful of firms.[7] Therefore, the vast majority of Romanian firms have both debts and credits of similar magnitude, clearly illustrating the phenomenon of chain of arrears, whereas net arrears are not highly significant.

Regarding the importance of loss-making firms, only 200 firms, or 12 percent of the total, are loss-making, and they do not absorb a disproportionately large share of arrears – in relation to their sales,

---

[7] Indeed, 80 percent of net arrears was concentrated in 100 firms, accounting for 27 percent of sales, whereas the largest 10 debtors account for 50 percent of net arrears. This implies that arrears involve a significant transfer of liquidity from other firms only for a small number of firms.

for instance. Their share in total gross arrears is about 15 percent, and their share in total sales is about 10 percent.[8] Although loss-making firms are important recipients of net arrears, they do not play a crucial role in the whole chain of arrears.

Another element supporting the view of interenterprise arrears as a systemic phenomenon, associated with specific incentives and penalties, is given by the lack of any correlation between interenterprise arrears and tax arrears. In fact, although not statistically significant, the coefficient of correlation between the two types of arrears is negative.

We next try to assess in a regression analysis the robustness of the facts we identified on the basis of descriptive indicators.

Table 3.2 reports results of a cross-section analysis on the sample of state-owned enterprises in 1992. Estimates are derived for payables, receivables, and their difference, namely net arrears.[9]

The main objective of the regression analysis is to evaluate whether the high degree of circularity of arrears reduced the need for cash of enterprises. If the chain of arrears substituted for cash, one would expect a high correlation between receivables and payables, after adjusting for scale and other factors.

Regression results provide strong support for the preceding view. Indeed, a main determinant of payables (receivables) are receivables (payables). The coefficients on these variables are statistically significant even when other "structural" variables, sectoral dummies, and legal-form dummies are included in the regressions. The export orientation of firms is negatively correlated with both payables and receivables, indicating that linkages with foreign markets allow firms to escape the chain of arrears. This is consistent with Daianu (1994), who argues that exports allow firms to "escape the 'network-trap' and build new chains of reliable suppliers and customers." The role of financial variables, in particular the liquidity conditions of firms, is less clear-cut. Profits – defined on an accrual basis – appear to have a highly significant and large negative impact on payables, whereas they are not significantly related to re-

---

[8] The data refer to September 1992.

[9] As noted in studies of trade credit in market economies, the factors influencing payables and receivables can be quite different at the microeconomic level, where payables and receivables can differ (Nadiri 1969). Moreover, because we focus on manufacturing firms, payables and receivables are not even identical in the aggregate, as the manufacturing sector is net creditor to other sectors, especially to the trade sector.

Table 3.2. *Romania: regressions on interenterprise arrears, September 1992 (sample: 1,655 firms, OLS regressions)*

Variable	Coefficient	T-statistics	Coefficient	T-statistics
(2a) Dependent variable: arrears (payables)/sales				
Constant	0.08	4.68	0.10	4.97
Material/Total costs	0.11	4.65	0.11	4.41
Profits/Sales	−0.45	−8.32		
Exports/Sales	−0.07	−2.62	−0.17	−5.77
Receivables/Sales	0.28	20.84		
Change in deposits/Sales			−0.02	-1.63
Sd_1	−0.04	−1.18	−0.00	−0.06
Sd_2	−0.06	−2.86	−0.07	−3.14
Sd_3	−0.04	−1.07	−0.05	−1.36
Sd_4	0.19	6.81	0.29	9.44
Sd_5	0.07	3.33	0.11	4.90
Sd_6	0.01	−0.35	0.02	0.79
Sd_7	0.01	0.62	0.03	1.02
Sd_8	0.07	3.72	0.09	4.20
Sd_9	0.01	0.35	0.03	1.12
Sd_{10}	0.05	2.24	0.07	2.96
Sd_{11}	0.18	1.91	0.15	1.35
Sd_{12}	0.16	2.72	0.15	2.26
Fd_{11}	−0.02	−0.57	0.10	2.15
Fd_{13}	−0.10	−1.80	−0.10	1.60
Fd_{21}	0.19	2.42	0.13	1.44
Fd_{22}	0.12	3.11	0.04	0.96
Adjusted R-squared	0.34		0.12	
(2b) Dependent variable: arrears (receivables)/sales				
Constant	0.04	1.43		
Profits/Sales	0.05	0.59		
Exports/Sales	−0.09	−2.15		
Payables/Sales	0.73	20.82		
Sd_1	0.12	2.31		
Sd_2	−0.01	−0.38		
Sd_3	−0.01	−0.23		
Sd_4	0.18	4.16		
Sd_5	0.12	3.88		
Sd_6	0.12	3.41		
Sd_7	0.05	1.45		
Sd_8	0.04	1.22		

Table 3.2. *Continued*

Variable	Coefficient	T-statistics	Coefficient	T-statistics
Sd_9	0.08	1.94		
Sd_{10}	0.05	1.50		
Sd_{11}	−0.25	−1.62		
Sd_{12}	−0.01	−0.07		
Fd_{11}	0.41	5.93		
Fd_{13}	0.04	0.41		
Fd_{21}	−0.22	−1.72		
Fd_{22}	−0.11	−1.80		
Adjusted R-squared	0.29			
(2c) Dependent variable: net arrears (payables–receivables)/sales				
Constant	−0.02	−1.16		
Profits/Sales	−0.20	1.01		
Exports/Sales	0.06	0.75		
Material/Total costs	0.08	2.16		
Sd_1	−0.12	−2.35		
Sd_2	−0.01	−0.52		
Sd_3	−0.00	−0.03		
Sd_4	−0.11	−2.68		
Sd_5	−0.09	−3.10		
Sd_6	−0.12	−3.30		
Sd_7	−0.05	−1.48		
Sd_8	−0.02	−0.70		
Sd_9	−0.07	−1.85		
Sd_{10}	−0.04	−1.10		
Sd_{11}	0.29	1.87		
Sd_{12}	0.07	0.57		
Fd_{11}	−0.37	−5.42		
Fd_{13}	−0.07	−0.67		
Fd_{21}	0.26	1.97		
Fd_{22}	0.15	1.94		
Adjusted R-squared	0.04			

Note: Sd_i denote sectoral dummies; Fd_i denote firm-type dummies.

ceivables. Given the extremely low level of the stock of enterprise money, profits may represent a good proxy for enterprise liquidity. The fact that profits affect payables but not receivables suggests an asymmetric effect of enterprise liquidity on arrears. This is not surprising, as we are analyzing the phenomenon of arrears and not a regular trade credit market, in which liquidity is voluntarily transferred by "liquidity-rich" to "liquidity-poor" firms.

Directly using the change in bank deposits as a proxy for the liquidity conditions of firms leads to less robust results. Whereas a bivariate regression of payables on change in deposits yields a negative and significant coefficient (the coefficient is -0.02, with a T-statistic of -2.1), the introduction of the change in deposits in a multivariate regression yields a statistically insignificant, though still negative coefficient. Finally, several sectoral and legal-form dummies are significant, indicating the role of "structural" factors, related to the position of firms in the production and trade process.[10]

The results on receivables are similar to those on payables. We have already noted the insignificant coefficient on profitability, although it has the expected positive sign. The other two variables, export orientation and payables, are significant. The negative sign on the export variable seems to suggest that exports provide a more reliable source of cash for firms than domestic sales.

Results on net arrears are not easily interpretable. Indeed, net arrears are not an independent choice variable, at least within the approach outlined in the model of Section 3.[11] Because we did not use the same set of explanatory variables in the regressions on payables and receivables – as the ratio of material to total costs does not appear in the regression on receivables – the results on net arrears, namely the difference between arrears on payables and arrears on receivables, cannot be mechanically inferred by subtracting coefficients of the two regressions. However, results are in line with expectations, with technological factors such as the ratio

---

[10] The legal-form dummies indicate that the Regies Autonomes (RA) tend to have lower payable arrears, with respect to the control variable, commercial companies. This is interesting because usually the RAs are singled out as the firms still working under soft budget constraints, benefiting from large explicit and implicit subsidies. The low ratios of arrears to sales in these firms are of course also due to the fact that they produce primary goods and energy. Nevertheless, the result is an additional indication of the fact that the phenomenon of arrears is not predominantly associated with "bad" firms.

[11] In the literature on trade credit in market economies there is a debate on the relevance of net and gross credit (Meltzer 1960; Brechling and Lipsey 1963). Those who see trade credit as a transfer of liquidity from liquidity-rich to liquidity-poor firms emphasize the role of net credit. By contrast, those who see trade credit as credit for transaction purposes, and a mechanism for the enterprise sector as a whole to economize in the use of money, emphasize gross credit (Ferris 1981). Our view is closer to the latter approach.

of material costs on total costs, and sectoral dummies, affecting net arrears. In addition it is worth noting that the export orientation variable is positive, although not highly significant. Thus, exporters tend to be net debtors in the domestic market. This is consistent with the fact that they purchase inputs domestically, where arrears are tolerated and widespread, whereas they sell on foreign markets, where contracts tend to be enforced and thus payments be effected. Given the stronger effect of profitability – as a proxy for liquidity – on payables than on receivables, it should be expected that this variable will play a role as well on net arrears.

The main results of the preceding quantitative analysis seem to be supported by "qualitative" results obtained in a small-scale survey of Romanian industrial firms.[12]

Two main results of the survey stand out and strongly support the view of a chain of arrears determined by the low perceived cost of falling into arrears.

(i)   As reported in Table 3.3, the main cause of arrears is identified in the accumulation of overdue receivables, confirming the chain-of-arrears view repeatedly stressed here. Factors affecting the enterprise cash flow, such as the relative price of inputs with respect to final output and profit tax, are a distant second. The third factor is identified in high interest rates on bank loans, whereas availability of bank credit is not singled out as a main factor. Thus, credit constraints are felt more through the cost of credit than through credit rationing. Most firms perceived that the relative cost of arrears was much lower than the interest rate on bank credit, as they stated that no explicit, or implicit, interest rate was charged on arrears.[13]

(ii)   Another important item of information on the perceived cost of arrears comes from the ranking of payment priorities. Table 3.4 displays the ranking, which clearly indicates wages as first priority and payments to domestic suppliers as last. After wages, and with

---

[12] The survey was carried out at the end of 1992 by the World Bank, and it focused on questions on interenterprise arrears. The sample included twenty-nine state-owned firms covering all the main industrial sectors. Given the nonrepresentativeness of the sample, the survey provides mainly qualitative information on the phenomenon.

[13] It is worth noting that in 1992, when the survey was carried out, interest rates increased significantly with respect to 1991, and they were positive in real terms for several months (see World Bank 1993).

Table 3.3. *Romania: main causes of arrears*

Accumulation of overdue receivables	2.65
High interest rates	3.52
Increase in input over output prices	3.66
High profit tax	4.69
Loss of markets	5.38
Inventory accumulation	5.66
High turnover tax	5.66
Insufficient bank credit	5.76
High wage bill	7.86

Note: On a scale from 1 to 10, the lower the rating the more important is the cause.
Source: World Bank, "Fiscal Study on Romania," 1993.

similar ratings, one finds foreign suppliers, banks, and the budget. In the context of the model of Section 3, the ranking suggests that $\varkappa$ is lower than the return on using cash to pay wages. Another interesting aspect of this phenomenon is that those firms that reported having fallen into arrears in wage payments (three of twenty-nine) stated that they resolved their problem by collecting their receivables.

5. CONCLUSIONS

The chapter has emphasized the problems with credit tightening in a context of severely underdeveloped credit markets. It is shown that in such a context there can be multiple equilibria, with permanently different levels of economic activity. The analysis was developed from the perspective of interenterprise arrears.

The analysis provides theoretical and empirical support for the notion that interenterprise arrears in PCPEs do not simply reflect a situation in which winners make transfers to losers but, rather, reflect to a large extent a situation in which firms cannot comply with their contractual obligations, because other firms fail to do so. This chain-of-arrears situation complicates policy-making significantly. Straightforward solutions such as starting bankruptcy procedures on firms that fall into arrears may, under those circumstances, have high social costs. Good firms may be forced into

Table 3.4 *Romania: priorities of payments*

Payments to	Average Rating
Employees	1.45
Foreign suppliers	2.41
Banks	2.59
Budget	2.69
Domestic suppliers	3.28

Note: On a scale from 1 to 10, the lower the rating, the more important is the priority.
Source: World Bank, "Fiscal Study on Romania," 1933.

bankruptcy because their clients are unable or unwilling to pay their trade credit. On the other hand, massive interenterprise debt write-offs may present the wrong set of incentives. Even good firms may be induced to fall further into arrears in the expectation that they will eventually be bailed out.

The simple theory outlined here suggests that policy should aim at modifying the present set of incentives. Arrears have to be attacked before they have a chance to grow. Thus, policies should aim at increasing the marginal cost of falling into arrears. If there is a chain of arrears, and arrears have had a chance to grow, there is little the policymaker can do. Under those conditions, even sound policies such as tightening of bank credit may have no positive effect, given that firms may react by falling further into arrears with banks or the fiscal authority.

The analysis also suggests that PCPEs are not a homogeneous group. An explanation for this is that they have had widely different experiences with market institutions. Thus, an implication of the analysis is that macroeconomic policy must pay close attention to institutional characteristics. In particular, we have argued that when credit markets are dysfunctional a credit crunch can have long-lasting consequences.

APPENDIX

In this Appendix we present three extensions of the basic model discussed in Section 2, which help to explain low-output persistence.

SHORT ENTERPRISE HORIZONS

A salient characteristic of most transformation processes is the willingness to restructure and privatize a large portion of the originally socialized sector. In general, one would expect this type of expectation to have an effect on the firms' incentives. Thus, for example, if the firm were to be privatized at time T, the sum in expression (3.3) would have to run from 0 to T, thus lowering incentives for liquidity accumulation and depressing output. More interestingly, if privatization time, T, is unknown, and the probability of its occurring in the "next instant," if it has not occurred before, is δ (a constant), then one could argue that the optimal strategy for the enterprise is to maximize a sum like (3.3), where now the discount factor is $(1 - \delta)/(1 + r)$ (which corresponds to Yaari 1965 in discrete time). Consequently, the steady-state first-order condition (3.4) now becomes

$$pf'(m) = \frac{1 + r}{1 - \delta} \tag{3.4'}$$

Therefore, under privatization risk output will be permanently lower than the social optimum, where condition (3.4) holds, even if the system converges quickly to its steady state.

The insight from this model is straightforward. Either privatize quickly or make a credible announcement that privatization is unlikely to happen.[14]

ENDOGENOUS INFLATION

Our simple model in Section 2.1 assumes fixed exchange rates. However, it is easy to extend it to cases in which, for instance, the rate of devaluation is constant. Let the rate of devaluation be denoted by ε. Then one can prove that steady-state condition (3.4) becomes

$$pf'\ (m) = (1 + r)\ (1 + \varepsilon) \equiv 1 + i = 1 + \textit{nominal interest rate} \tag{3.4''}$$

Given exogeneity of relative prices, the domestic rate of inflation is also equal to ε. Thus, condition (3.4'') implies that the higher is the rate of inflation, the smaller is the demand for cash by enterprises (a perfectly conventional result). Besides, because output is given by $f(m)$, it follows that higher inflation is associated with smaller steady-state output.

Let us now consider the case of an economy that depends on seigniorage to finance (part of) its budget deficit. In such a case the rate of expansion of cash is a function of the price level: The higher the latter is, the higher

---

[14] A more complete analysis will, of course, have to take into account the inefficiencies involved in quick privatization as well as those associated with keeping enterprises in government hands.

the former will be. As is well known (see, e.g., Calvo 1992), such money-supply endogeneity may give rise to equilibria with different inflation rates. In other words, the same set of "fundamentals" may be associated with low or high inflation, depending on the state of expectations. Because, as noted, the level of output is inversely related to inflation, this extension of the model illustrates the possibility that the economy locks into a "bad" equilibrium with low output and high inflation.

There is more than one way in which an economy could lock into a "bad" equilibrium. One possibility is that, before the start of the transformation program, inflation was high. Thus, it would be perfectly normal for people to expect that it will take a while for inflation to come down – possibly forcing the monetary authority to validate expectations, undermining the program's credibility, and lengthening further the high-inflation–low-output period.

Another possibility, which is of even greater relevance for PCPEs, is that the "bad" equilibrium will be a *consequence* of the initial liquidity crunch. This is so because the latter increases nominal interest rates, an increase that could, in turn, be interpreted by individuals as a *signal* of higher future inflation. Higher inflationary expectations lower the demand for money; that, as argued, may induce the monetary authority to validate the high-inflation equilibrium.

The solution implied by the model is deceptively simple: Just push the economy to the high-liquidity equilibrium. However, an effective implementation of such a solution is not easy to come by. For example, a natural candidate would seem to be a one-step increase in money supply. However, for this policy to be effective, it is necessary for people to believe that it will result in *lower* inflation – an unlikely outcome given that the public observes an increase in the money supply. In fact, people may infer that the central bank is conducting "business as usual" by once again heavily relying on the inflation tax. Therefore, the *demand* for money may not increase – it may actually decrease – making high steady-state inflation even harder to overcome. In addition, in the period when the policy is implemented, the inflation rate may exhibit a very large spike (because money supply suffers a sizable jump, while money demand is constant or declines) – making a mockery of the stabilization plan.

Alternatively, the government could launch a propaganda campaign aimed at lowering inflation expectations. This could be accompanied by announcing, say, that the currency will be pegged to the U.S. dollar. However, this policy may backfire for the following reasons. First, it will unravel quickly if the public is not persuaded about the effectiveness of the stabilization program. The demand for money will remain low, forcing the government to resort to high money infusion in order to finance the budget deficit – thus eventually leading to a balance-of-payments crisis. Second, if in order to prevent a balance-of-payments crisis the exchange rate is allowed to float, then the low-inflation–high-output equilibrium can be achieved only if prices and nominal wages fall by, possibly, a substantial amount. Otherwise, in the absence of the dangerous one-step increase in nominal money discussed, real monetary balances will not be able to increase toward the "good" equilibrium. For this to work out, however, public sector prices and wages must also fall by, in principle, the same proportional rate. In fact, to enhance the credibility of the shift toward the "good" equilibrium, public sector prices and wages should take the lead. In the unlikely case in which there are no frictions and all prices and wages fall by the necessary amount, success will be granted. However, if private-sector prices and wages fall by less than what is necessary, then the relative position of government will be impaired. The fiscal deficit is likely to increase, the best workers in the public sector will be attracted to the private sector, and, those who remain may shirk more and be more willing to go on strike – all of which may push the economy back to the "bad" equilibrium.[15]

REFERENCES

Begg, D., and R. Portes (1992), Enterprise Debt and Economic Transformation: Financial Restructuring of the State Sector in Central and Eastern Europe, Centre for Economic Policy Research, Discussion Paper No. 695.

Berg, A., and O. Blanchard (1992), Stabilization and Transition: Poland 1990–1991, mimeo, National Bureau of Economic Research.

Berg, A., and J. Sachs (1992), Structural Adjustment and International Trade in Eastern Europe: The Case of Poland, *Economic Policy* 14 (April).

Brechling, F.P.R., and R. G. Lipsey (1963), Trade Credit and Monetary Policy, *Economic Journal* 73 (December): 618–41.

Bruno, M. (1992), Stabilization and Reform in Eastern Europe: A Preliminary Examination, International Monetary Fund, Working Paper, WP 92/30.

Calvo, G. (1992), Are High Interest Rates Effective for Stopping High Inflation? Some Skeptical Notes, *The World Bank Economic Review* 6: 55–69.

Calvo, G., and F. Coricelli (1992), Stabilizing a Previously Centrally Planned Economy: Poland 1990, *Economic Policy* 14 (April).

---

[15] Another interesting case of endogenous inflation is when prices are set at time t before knowing money supply at t. Under those conditions, an unemployment-averse government may ultimately validate more than one inflation level. A solution for this problem is sometimes sought in incomes policies. For a discussion of wage policy in the context of Poland, see Calvo and Coricelli (1992).

Calvo, G., and F. Coricelli (1993), Output Collapse in Eastern Europe: The Role of Credit. International Monetary Fund *Staff Papers* 40(1) (March), 32–52.

Calvo, G., and J. Frenkel (1991), From Centrally Planned to Market Economies: The Road from CPE to PCPE, International Monetary Fund *Staff Papers* 38(2): 268–99.

Clifton, E., and M. Khan (1992), Inter-Enterprise Arrears in Transforming Economies: The Case of Romania, IMF Paper on Policy Analysis and Assessment.

Coricelli, F., and T. Lane (1993), Wage Controls during the Transition from Central Planning to a Market Economy, *The World Bank Research Observer* 8(2) (July): 195–210.

Daianu, D. (1994), Inter-Enterprise Arrears in Post-Command Economies: Thoughts from a Romanian Perspective, International Monetary Fund Working Paper 94/54.

Ferris, S. (1981), A Transactions Theory of Trade Credit Use, *The Quarterly Journal of Economics* 94 (May): 243–70.

Frydman, R., and A. Rapaczynski (1993), Privatization in Eastern Europe: Is the State Withering Away? *Finance and Development* Washington, D.C., June.

Hrncir, M. (1993), Financial Intermediation in the Czech Republic: Lessons and Progress Evaluation, Discussion Paper on Economic Transition 9302, Department of Applied Economics, Cambridge University.

Kornai, J. (1993), "Transformational Recession," Collegium Budapest, Discussion Paper No. 1.

Mc Kinnon, R. (1991), *The Order of Economic Liberalization*, Baltimore: Johns Hopkins University Press.

Meltzer, A. H. (1960), Mercantile Credit, Monetary Policy and the Size of the Firm, *Review of Economics and Statistics* 42(2) (November): 429–97.

Nadiri, M. I. (1969), The Determinants of Trade Credit in the U.S. Total Manufacturing Sector, *Econometrica* 37(3) (July): 408–23.

Rostowski, J. (1994), The Inter-Enterprise Debt Explosion in the Former Soviet Union: Causes, Consequences, Cures, International Monetary Fund Working Paper (August).

Shell, K. (1967), Optimal Programs of Capital Accumulation for an Economy in Which There Is Exogenous Technical Change, in *Essays in the Theory of Optimal Economic Growth*, Cambridge, MA: MIT Press.

Ward, B. (1958), The Firm in Illyria: Market Syndicalism, *American Economic Review* 48: 566–89.

World Bank (1993), Romania: Fiscal Policy in Transition, Report no. 11878-RO (November).

Yaari, M. (1965), Uncertain Lifetime, Life Insurance, and the Theory of the Consumer, *Review of Economic Studies* 32 (April): 137–50.

PART II

International Financial Factors

CHAPTER 4

Transparency and the Evolution of Exchange Rate Flexibility in the Aftermath of Disinflation

Alex Cukierman, Miguel Kiguel, and Leonardo Leiderman

1. INTRODUCTION

Accumulated experience with exchange rate based stabilizations suggests the following typical prescription for successful disinflation: First fix the exchange rate (along with marked adjustment of fundamentals), produce a major disinflation, and shift to a more flexible exchange rate policy only at a later phase when disinflation has become persistent.

In broad terms, the foregoing pattern has been followed in at least three recent disinflations: Israel, Chile, and Mexico. These cases illustrate that fixing of the exchange rate at the start of stabilization, along with major adjustment of fundamentals, played a key role in producing quick disinflation. A fixed exchange rate was probably the simplest and *most transparent* system for the policymaker to make a credible antiinflation commitment and to have a strong impact on inflation expectations. As time progressed, substantial (yet not complete) disinflation was achieved, but it was associated with real exchange rate appreciation and a slowdown of economic growth. In all cases the shift toward increased flexibility of exchange rate policy was considered at that stage of the process when the antiinflation policy became reasonably credible and transparent – yet the consequences of the overvaluation of the currency were increasingly perceived as a serious risk to the ultimate success of the whole program. Increased flexibility was brought in by adopting a crawling peg and/or an exchange rate band. As a

Cukierman and Leiderman are at The Eitan Berglas School of Economics, Tel Aviv University, and Kiguel is at the Policy Research Department, the World Bank. This chapter was prepared for presentation at the conference Financial Aspects of the Transition from Stabilization to Growth, Tel Aviv University, June 6–7, 1993. The views expressed in the chapter are those of the authors and do not necessarily represent those of the World Bank.

matter of fact, all three countries are now operating under variants of exchange rate bands with crawling central parity rates. Similar trends toward increased flexibility of exchange rates are observed in Eastern European countries that are well after the initial stages of stabilization, such as Poland.

In this chapter, we deal with these characteristics of the evolution of exchange rate policy in the aftermath of exchange rate based stabilization. Throughout the analysis we stress two key factors that play an important role in determining the timing and form of the policy shift toward flexibility: transparency and changing policy objectives. Consider first transparency. It is plausible that immediately after a stabilization, when the memories of high inflation and previous failed stabilizations are fresh in the public's mind, the transparency of the commitment embodied in flexible exchange rate systems is lower than that of a fixed peg. However, we argue that after a sustained period of low inflation the transparency advantage of a fixed peg is reduced. At moderate rates of inflation more individuals are able to recognize when the commitment to a more flexible regime, such as an exchange rate band, has been broken than under high and variable inflation. Put somewhat differently, more individuals recognize the commitment embodied in an exchange rate band some time after stabilization than at its inception.

Turning to policy objectives, at the inception of stabilization the major concern of policymakers is the restoration of price stability. Fixing the exchange rate can help achieve quick disinflation, which is critical in raising political support for the continuation of the program. But after a while, if and when major disinflation has been achieved, the economic–political resistance to overvaluation of the currency becomes stronger and consequently the emphasis shifts away from price stability to external competitiveness. This shift, we argue, may increase the incentives for moving toward increased flexibility of the exchange rate regime.

The analysis focuses on the policy choices of dependable policymakers in an environment in which the public is uncertain about their dependability. As in Cukierman and Liviatan (1991) the public's uncertainty is modeled by postulating that there are two policymaker types, dependable policymakers who incur a (political) cost when they renege on a preannounced exchange rate regime and "weak" policymakers who do not incur such a cost. As in chapter 6 of Cukierman (1992) and in Lohmann (1992), the preannouncement of an exchange rate system precommits dependable policymakers, but only over some range of shocks. Weak policymakers are never really precommitted, but they have an incentive to make themselves, at least initially, indistinguishable from their dependable counterparts.

The better transparency of the commitment embodied in a peg is modeled by assuming that a lower fraction of individuals recognizes the commitment under a more flexible system such as a band than under a fixed peg. In more technical terms some individuals, such as those who routinely operate in financial markets, have fully rational perceptions even under a band. Others who are less sophisticated do not recognize the partial commitment embodied in the band even when it exists. The notion that some individuals may have rational perceptions whereas others have naive perceptions is not new. Haltiwanger and Waldman (1985), for example, analyze a situation in which some individuals have a better capacity for processing information than others.

Whereas most previous research has focused on the initial stage of exchange rate based stabilization, our main objective here is to provide a framework for the analysis of the evolution of exchange rate policy in the postdisinflation era. After presenting a basic set of stylized facts for Israel, Chile, and Mexico, in the next section, we develop in Section 3 a model that characterizes policymakers' choices between a fixed peg and an exchange rate band. The choice of the exchange rate regime is modeled as the outcome of an optimization problem by a dependable policymaker whose objective function weighs the level of the real exchange rate against the level and variability of the nominal exchange rate. We believe this formulation captures an important real world aspect of exchange rate policy determination in the countries mentioned (as well as others) in which the authorities are concerned about the external competitiveness of domestic products and the current account position but are also worried about the possible inflationary consequences of nominal exchange rate depreciation. As in Cukierman, Kiguel, and Leiderman (1993), the determination of exchange rate policy involves a trade-off between credibility and flexibility. Whether an announced regime is maintained or not depends on the realization of shocks and on the costs to dependable policymakers of reneging on their announcements. These costs imply the existence of a range of effective commitment in which the preannouncement is respected.

In Section 4, we use the analytical framework to characterize the conditions under which increases in the transparency of policy and in the relative importance of price stability give rise to a shift toward increased exchange rate flexibility. Whereas the analysis in Sections 3 and 4 deals with the choice between a fixed peg and a band, Section 5 discusses another possible form of enhanced flexibility: the shift from a fixed-central-parity band to a crawling-central-parity band. We do so by extending the analysis to a two-period framework in which the policymaker effectively chooses ex ante the location of the band and its width. In the case of a fixed band, the location of the band is the same in both periods, whereas it may differ across the two periods in the case of a crawling band. We then show that an increase in the relative transparency of a crawling band could give rise to a move toward this system. Section 6 presents brief concluding remarks.

2. MOTIVATION: THREE CASE STUDIES

In this section we briefly discuss the evidence on increased exchange rate flexibility in the aftermath of stabilization for three programs that are well known for their success at disinflation: Israel, Chile, and Mexico.[1] In all cases the shift toward increased flexibility took place when the antiinflation policy became reasonably transparent, but the consequences of overvaluation of the currency were increasingly becoming a serious risk to the ultimate success of the whole program.[2]

2.1. Israel

Israel's exchange rate policy followed a number of phases in the late 1980s and early 1990s. The policy evolved from a fixed exchange rate in mid-1985 to a crawling band in 1992–93; see Figure 4.1.

[1] For a detailed discussion of Israel's exchange rate bands, as well as those of Chile and Mexico, see Helpman, Leiderman, and Bufman (1994). Most of the evidence in the following three subsections draws heavily on that source.
[2] On increasing flexibility of exchange rate policy after stabilization, see also Dornbusch (1992).

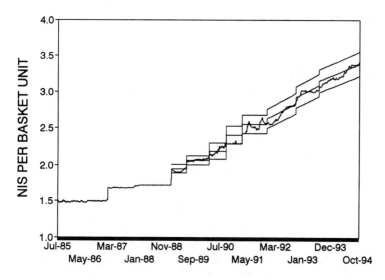

Figure 4.1. Israel's exchange rate vis-à-vis the currency basket. *Note:* For the period July 1985–July 1986 the exchange rate shown is that of the NIS against the U.S. dollar. From August 1986 onward the exchange rate shown is that of the NIS against the Israeli currency basket.

Following the stabilization program of July 1985 the new Israeli shekel (NIS) was pegged to the U.S. dollar. This exchange rate policy was a major building block of the stabilization program. In August 1986 the dollar peg was replaced by a peg to a basket of currencies. Following a sequence of devaluations of the NIS–basket exchange rate in 1987, 1988, and early January 1989, the government adopted an exchange rate band on January 3, 1989. The band consisted of an NIS–basket central parity fixed in nominal terms and a ±3 percent fluctuation zone around this parity. The band's width was enlarged to ±5 percent in March 1990. In December 1991, after an upward adjustment of the central parity rate, the authorities relaxed the fixity of the central parity and announced an upward crawl of the central parity at the rate of 90 percent per annum. The announced rate of crawl for the central parity rate was reduced to an annual rate of 8 percent per year starting from November 1992.

Figure 4.1 provides a plot of the daily NIS–basket exchange rate after the 1985 stabilization. Notice that starting in early 1989 various exchange rate bands are plotted. Each exchange rate band is identified by three lines: its central parity and its upper and lower limits. The figure exhibits a number of features:

First, the exchange rate followed an average upward trend throughout that period. The trend prevailed within bands and was supported by upward adjustments of the central parity.

Second, there existed frequent realignments of the central parity: There were six devaluations in less than four years. The entire period can be subdivided into seven exchange rate bands. The first five bands featured a fixed central parity. The first two among these had a width of ±3 percent around the central parity, and the bands that followed featured bounds of ±5 percent around the central parity. The last two bands exhibit increased flexibility in the form of a preannounced crawling central parity rate. There is evidence that indicates that these frequent realignments resulted in substantial interest rate volatility.[3] Domestic interest rates tended to rise when a realignment was anticipated, and they fell only when these expectations were adjusted downward following a realignment.

Third, some of the upward adjustments of the central parity were not necessarily associated with speculative attacks on the currency. Put differently, some of these adjustments were made when the exchange rate was not close to the upper limit of a band, for example, the realignments of March 1990 and 1991. Similarly, the move to a crawling band in December 1991, and the adjustment of its parameters in November 1992, took place when the actual exchange rate was very close to the central parity. Thus, the move toward increased exchange rate flexibility could possibly reflect, not so much a policy response to short-term speculative attacks, as a response to broader macroeconomic considerations, such as the underlying appreciation of the real exchange rate and the slowdown in economic growth (see later discussion).

Accordingly, in order to understand policymakers' motivation for gradually shifting toward increased exchange rate flexibility it is useful to consider the behavior of key macroeconomic indicators for the first few periods after the stabilization program. On the one

[3] See Helpman, Leiderman, and Bufman (1994).

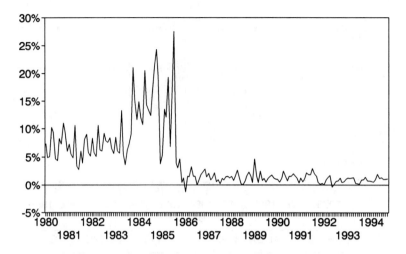

Figure 4.2. Israel: Rate of inflation (CPI, monthly terms).

hand, there were early (and mounting) signals that the program was reaching its main goals. In particular, a rapid reduction in inflation was observed already in the first few months after the implementation of the program; see Figure 4.2. From annual rates of inflation in the triple-digit range, the program quickly lowered inflation to about 16–20 percent per year in the period from 1986 to 1991, and to the single-digit figure of 9.6 percent in 1992. The major adjustment in fiscal fundamentals that was taking place in the context of the program probably contributed to the perception that disinflation was becoming increasingly credible through time. The domestic government budget deficit fell from 16 percent of GDP in 1984 to 1.3 percent of GDP in 1986–88; this was the result of both an increase in domestic revenues and a reduction in government expenditures. The stronger fiscal stance was reflected in a reversal in the time path of domestic and foreign public debt ratios, from increasing trends before 1985 to marked reductions after 1985.

On the other hand, as time progressed these signals of success in disinflation were accompanied by increasingly negative signals about the performance of real economic variables.[4] Real exchange rate appreciation was one such signal. Figure 4.3 plots the evolu-

---

[4] Obviously some of these developments could be explained by factors not necessarily associated with the stabilization policy per se.

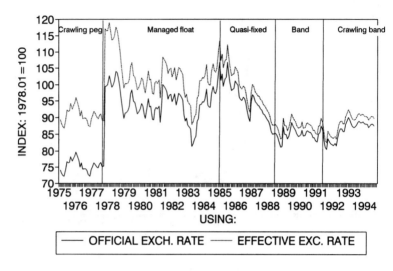

Figure 4.3. Israel: Real exchange rate of the NIS (using CPI).

tion of the real exchange rate, defined as the nominal exchange rate times the ratio of foreign to domestic consumer prices. The figure covers a relatively long time span during which Israel was under four different regimes: a crawling peg and a managed float before the 1985 disinflation, and the fixed peg and exchange rate bands after 1985. It can be seen that real exchange rate appreciation was the rule after 1985. The real exchange rate of the NIS against the basket of foreign currencies appreciated at about 8 percent in 1986, 2 percent in 1987, and 9 percent in 1988. The considerable real exchange rate appreciation that followed the program is evident in other measures of relative prices as well. The cumulative increase in the relative price on nontraded to traded goods over 1986–88 was 32 percent; the relative price of exports against domestic uses decreased by 20 percent over that period; and the relative price of services to manufacturing goods rose by 48 percent. At the same time, no major shifts were observed in Israel's terms of trade. From Figure 4.3 it appears that the exchange rate policy based on currency bands was apparently able to check, at the very least, the previous trend toward real exchange rate appreciation without resulting in an acceleration in the rate of inflation (see Figure 4.2). At the end of 1990 the real exchange rate was about 15 percent lower (i.e., more appreciated) than in the early eighties. However, a partial reversal took place under the crawling and in 1992, at which time there was a real exchange rate depreciation.

As far as economic growth indicators are concerned, the first two years after the program featured a consumption boom that resulted in rates of growth of gross domestic product (GDP) of about 5 percent per year in 1986–87. However, there was a marked slow-down of growth in 1988–89. On average, GDP growth reached about 2 percent per year over that period, and there was a decline in output of the traded goods sector of about 1 percent per year, led by a decline in the industrial sector's production of about 2.4 percent per year. Some of these changes clearly reflected a process of restructuring and rationalization of operations in business and industry, especially of those sectors that relied heavily on public sector funds during the high-inflation period.

To sum up, Israel's experience illustrates the costs and benefits of exchange rate based stabilization and the evolving nature of exchange rate policy after disinflation. The fixed exchange rate at the outset of the 1985 stabilization program, and the accompanying adjustment of fundamentals, probably played a key role in rapid disinflation and served as a transparent anchor to the nominal system and to inflation expectations. However, when low inflation became more credible and persistent, there was a growing incentive to increase the degree of flexibility of exchange rate policy in order to attenuate the underlying loss of competitiveness. It is likely that these considerations led to the shift toward exchange rate bands, which initially featured a fixed central parity rate but later on evolved into bands with a crawling central parity at a preannounced rate. In contrast to what was feared, the move toward enhanced flexibility was not associated with a rise in the rate of inflation. In fact, annual inflation reached a single-digit figure in 1992, and this was the lowest rate since the adoption of the 1985 stabilization program.

2.2. Chile

Like Israel's, Chile's exchange rate evolved from a fixed peg to a crawling band. Chile's first stabilization effort began after September 1973, at which time the government adopted a set of orthodox policy measures consisting mainly of tight fiscal and monetary policies.[5] Several devaluations were effected in the program's initial phase – a phase that featured major deregulation of prices, elimination of subsidies and of nontariff restrictions to trade, and other structural reforms. In spite of the major changes, disinflation was slow. That is, the rate of inflation remained at a three-digit figure up until 1977, four years from the change in policy. This prompted the next stage of the process, which consisted of exchange rate based stabilization. In February 1978 the authorities established a "tablita," that is, a preannounced schedule of nominal exchange rate depreciation. But in 1979 they shifted to a fixed exchange rate against the U.S. dollar, which was maintained until 1982. The fixed exchange rate, along with the accompanying policies, resulted in a sharp reduction in the rate of inflation (to approximately less than 30 percent per year); see Figure 4.4. As in Israel, the fixed peg was associated with considerable real exchange rate appreciation, as shown in Figure 4.5. The consequences of real appreciation together with the adverse external shocks at that time contributed to the debt crisis that resulted in a collapse of the fixed peg. Next came a shift from a fixed peg to a managed float, which was accompanied by substantial exchange rate depreciation and fears of renewed inflation.

The next stage in Chile's exchange rate policy was the adoption of an exchange rate band in 1985, following two steep devaluations of the domestic currency. The band features a crawling central parity in the form of daily adjustments in the peso–U.S. dollar reference exchange rate. At the start of each month, the authorities announce the size of the daily exchange rate adjustments for that month, which are based on the estimated difference between domestic inflation in the previous month and a forecast of foreign inflation. The changing behavior of the band's parameters over time indicates shifts toward increasing exchange rate flexibility. This is especially visible with respect to the width of the band. Whereas the width of the band was ±2 percent around the central parity in the initial phase, it was increased to ±3 percent in January 1988, and it was further widened to ±5 percent in June 1989. On January 23, 1992, there was a discrete revaluation of 5 percent in the central parity and the band's width was increased to ±10

---

[5] On the Chilean case, see, for example, Edwards and Edwards (1987) and Corbo and Solimano (1991).

CHILE: RATE OF INFLATION (CPI)
12 MONTH CHANGE

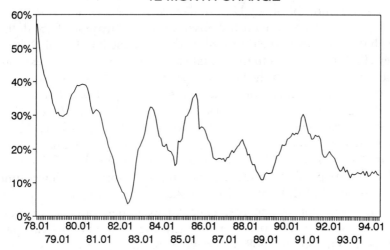

Figure 4.4. Chile: Rate of inflation (CPI) (12-month change).

CHILE: REAL EXCHANGE RATE
INDEX 1978.01=100

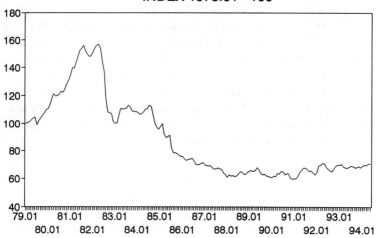

Figure 4.5. Chile: Real exchange rate (index 1978.01 = 100). *Note:* Increase means real appreciation.

percent around the reference rate. Since July 6, 1992, the band policy has been defined in terms of a basket of foreign currencies (as in Israel) and not of the U.S. dollar as in the earlier periods.

Figure 4.6 depicts monthly observations of the peso–U.S. dollar exchange rate from the inception of the crawling band until December 1992. In addition to the actual exchange rate the figure exhibits the central parity and the band's upper and lower limits. The enlargements of the band's width, and the tendency toward increased exchange rate flexibility, are clearly shown in this figure. In addition, as in the case of Israel, there is a marked upward trend in the exchange rate, which shows a sizable depreciation over the entire period. It is also interesting that there were several episodes in which the exchange rate persistently stayed at either the upper or the lower limit – episodes that did not lead to a collapse of the regime.

The behavior of the real effective exchange rate of the peso against the U.S. dollar under the crawling band exhibits two patterns: From 1985 to 1988 the crawling band regime was associated with considerable real effective depreciation of about 20 percent. From 1988 to 1992, however, there was a real appreciation of the peso, in part associated with large and persistent capital inflows. Overall, the real effective exchange rate returned in 1992 to the 1985 level, which was rather competitive relative to that of the early 1980s. All in all, the economy's performance since the inception of the crawling band (and the adoption of other policies) in 1985 has been impressive. Furthermore, the shift toward increased flexibility of the exchange rate within the band was not associated with a rise in inflation. During the seven years 1986–1992 GDP grew at more than 6 percent per year, inflation averaged 16 percent per year, and there were substantial decreases in the rate of unemployment and the ratio of external debt to exports. Underlying these developments was a strong fiscal stance; the budget deficit was only about 1 percent of GDP between 1985 and 1992.

2.3. Mexico

The adoption of an exchange rate band in Mexico in November 1991 is another example of a shift toward enhanced exchange rate flexibility upon achievement of major disinflation.[6] The Mexican

---

[6] The discussion that follows was written much before Mexico's crisis in 1994. Hence, we do not discuss this crisis.

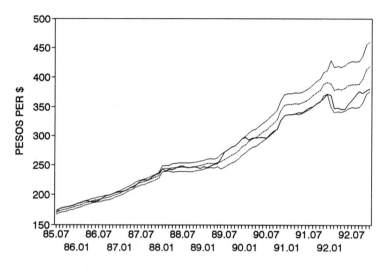

Figure 4.6. Chile: The exchange rate (monthly data).

economy was at the edge of a major crisis in the mideighties, with growing inflation (which reached a level of 143 percent in 1987), a high and rising public sector external debt, and limited access to international capital markets. The Economic Solidarity Pact, signed in December 1987, aimed at breaking the inflationary spiral. The pact consisted of a social–economic accord among workers, government, and entrepreneurs, and it was supported by deep fiscal and monetary adjustments, as well as major structural reforms.

These changes resulted in sharp disinflation; see Figure 4.7. The rate of inflation reached 18.8 percent in 1991 and 11.9 percent in 1992 (i.e., the lowest rate in seventeen years); a single-digit figure (i.e., 7–8 percent) was forecast for 1993. The fiscal deficit was sharply reduced from 16.1 percent of GDP in 1987 to a surplus of 0.4 percent of GDP in 1992. The ratio of external debt to GDP fell from 92.5 percent in 1987 to 24.4 percent in 1992. Similarly, the ratio of internal debt to GDP was reduced by about 20 percent of GDP during that period.

As far as the exchange rate policy is concerned, the stabilization program began with a fixed exchange rate as in Israel. After an initial devaluation of 38.9 percent, the pact established a fixed peso–U.S. dollar rate. Then, starting in January 1989, the authorities introduced more flexibility by shifting to a preannounced

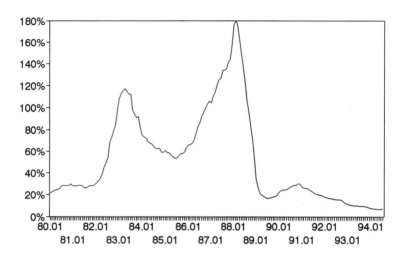

Figure 4.7. Mexico: Rate of inflation (CPI) (12-month change).

crawling peg.[7] Concretely, the peso was allowed to depreciate at one peso per day in 1989, eighty cents per day in 1990, and forty cents per day in 1991. Interestingly, the depreciation figures were preannounced in nominal terms (i.e., one Peso per day), which is perhaps the most transparent form of announcement of a crawl, and not in percentages (as in Chile or Israel). In addition, on November 11, 1991, the authorities introduced an exchange rate band. Exchange rate behavior under the band is plotted in Figure 4.8. The band differs from those of Israel and Chile in three main respects. First, it provides for asymmetric behavior of the band's upper and lower limits. Although the band's ceiling is subject to daily preannounced depreciation at a fixed amount, the band's floor remains fixed. The latter implies that a fixed exchange rate, as an outcome of market forces and intervention, could well be accommodated within the existing band. Second, as indicated earlier, the rate of crawl of the band's upper limit is specified in nominal terms, a fixed number of cents per day, rather than in percentage points. The band's upper limit was depreciated at the rate of twenty cents per day in 1992, and the band's width automatically increases through time. Thus, total width increased from 1.2 percent in November 1991 to 4.3 percent in December 1992.

Although the adoption of the exchange rate band provided for

[7] See Liviatan and Oks (1993) for recent developments in Mexico's exchange rate policy.

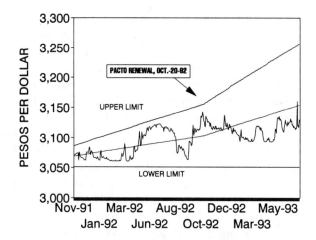

Figure 4.8. Mexico: The exchange rate band.

increased flexibility of the exchange rate, macroeconomic concerns about the consequences of the authorities' previous tendency to reduce the rate of crawl of the exchange rate emerged. Toward the end of 1992 it became clear that there were marked trends of slow-down of economic growth, rising current account deficits, and a real exchange rate appreciation of about 20 percent between 1989 and 1992. Thus, at renewal of the pact in October 1992 the rate of crawl of the upper limit was increased to forty cents per day in order to allow for an annual deprecation of 4.6 percent in 1993. The band's width will gradually increase throughout 1993 and will reach 8.7 percent at the end of 1993 – a width that is not very different from the 10 percent width in Israel.

Like that of Israel and Chile, the Mexican experience shows that a more flexible exchange rate policy in the form of a crawling band need not lead to an acceleration of inflation and may in fact be associated with a downward trend in the inflation rate, provided that fiscal and monetary fundamentals are properly controlled.

3. TRANSPARENCY AND THE CHOICE BETWEEN A FIXED PEG AND A BAND

A fixed peg and an exchange rate band are both partial commit-ment devices. They commit the policymaker to maintain the (nom-

inal) exchange rate within the preannounced range for some realizations of economic shocks. The commitment embodied in these
arrangements is only partial, in that there are also realizations of
underlying shocks that may lead policymakers to renege on their
commitment even when this entails a political cost.[8] In both cases
the main benefit of the commitment derives from its impact on
economic agents' expectations of devaluation.

The obvious difference between a peg and a band is with respect
to the form of the commitment. In the first case policymakers commit to a fixed exchange rate. In the second case they commit to
maintain it within a preannounced range. A less obvious difference,
which is sometimes mentioned but has not been analyzed explicitly,
is that the transparency of the commitment in a peg is likely to be
stronger than in a band. Although a fixed peg and a band are
probably equally transparent commitment devices for economic
agents who operate routinely in financial markets, other (less sophisticated) agents are likely to recognize more easily the commitment implicit in a fixed peg than in a band. Thus, other factors
equal, it is plausible that the impact of a fixed peg on the average
value of expected devaluation is stronger than that of a band.

As explained in the Introduction, the difference in transparency
between a peg and a band is likely to be especially large immediately after the adoption of a stabilization program, and in particular when such a program was preceded by a period of high and
variable inflation. This difference probably diminishes over time, as
disinflation is achieved. Moreover, it is likely that the relative importance assigned by policymakers to price stability diminishes
once the goals of stabilization are reached.

In what follows, we investigate whether such changes in the
relative transparency of a peg and a band and in the relative importance of price stability can explain the shift from initially fixed pegs
to exchange rate bands in economies where the stabilization of
inflation proved to be of a lasting nature. We do so by examining
how the expected values of policymakers' objectives under the two
exchange rate regimes change in response to the changes in transparency and in the relative importance of price stability discussed.
Throughout the analysis the authorities determine the rate of de-

---

[8] This conception of a partial commitment underlies the discussions in Lohmann (1992);
Cukierman, Kiguel, and Liviatan (1992); Cukierman (1992, chapter 6); and Cukierman,
Kiguel, and Leiderman (1993).

preciation of the domestic currency on the basis of an objective function that weighs the level of the real exchange rate against the level and variability of the nominal exchange rate. Accordingly, policymakers are assumed to choose π so as to maximize

$$V(\pi, \pi^e) = x(\pi - \pi^e) - h\frac{\pi^2}{2} \tag{4.1}$$

where π and π^e are the actual and the previously expected rates of depreciation of the domestic currency. For simplicity, we assume that these are also equal to the actual and expected rates of inflation, respectively. As shown by Cukierman, Kiguel, and Leiderman (1993; see especially appendix 1), $\pi - \pi^e$ is directly related to the real exchange rate. In order to capture the persistent trend toward nominal exchange rate depreciation that is evident in the three case studies of Section 2, we assume that x is a stochastic variable with positive realizations. Given h, a higher x implies that policymakers would be more inclined toward bringing about real exchange rate depreciation than toward maintaining a low rate of inflation. Given a realization of x, a higher h implies the reverse – policymakers are then relatively more concerned with price stability than with the real exchange rate.

The timing of moves is modeled as follows. First, before knowing the realization of x, the policymaker announces the type of exchange rate regime: a peg or a band. In the latter case, the width of the band is also announced. This is followed by the realization of the stochastic variable x. Then expectations of exchange rate depreciation are formed and embodied in wage contracts. Lastly, the policymaker chooses the actual rate of depreciation of the currency. If this choice involves reneging on the announcement made previously, the policymaker could incur a fixed cost denoted by c. The timing of moves is summarized in Figure 4.1.

In the absence of a commitment to either a peg or a band policymakers choose the rate of depreciation, π, in stage 4 so as to maximize their objectives. In doing that they take expectations as given. This yields the well-known discretionary solution

$$\pi = \frac{x}{h} \tag{4.2}$$

Even when a peg or a band is announced in stage 1 the public is unsure, at that stage, about the extent to which it will be respected in stage 4. This happens for two reasons. First the public is uncertain as to whether policymakers intend to stick to their announcement or not. Second, even dependable policymakers who take their announcements seriously may renege on them if shocks on the economy are such that producing a large change in the exchange rate becomes sufficiently important.

The first source of uncertainty is modeled by assuming that there are two possible policymaker types. One, labeled D (for dependable), incurs the cost c whenever he or she reneges on a preannounced peg or exchange rate band. The other W (for weak) does not incur such a cost. The second source of uncertainty is due to the fact that even if a dependable type is in office, he or she sticks to (or reneges) on the preannounced exchange rate regime depending on the realization of the shock x.

The first type of uncertainty affects the formation of expectations in stage 3. However, the second does not, because the realization of x is already known when expectations and nominal wage contracts are concluded in that stage. However, because x is not known in the first stage the uncertainty about it generally affects the choice of exchange rate regime by the policymaker.

Let α be the probability assigned by the public to the event that a dependable policymaker is in office. Because x is known when expectations are formed, the expected rate of depreciation is

$$\pi^e(x) = \alpha\pi_D(x) + (1 - \alpha)\frac{x}{h} \qquad (4.3)$$

where $\pi_D(x)$ is the rate of depreciation chosen by a dependable policymaker when a shock of size x is realized. The precise functional dependence of π_D on x depends on the type of exchange rate regime chosen and is derived later in this section for a peg and for an exchange rate band. Note that x/h is the *actual* rate of depreciation chosen by a weak policymaker because independently of the stage 1 announcement he or she always prefers to pick the discretionary rate x/h. The expectation in equation (4.3) reflects the public's understanding of the motives of both policymaker types as well as imperfect information about the identity of the type in office.

3.1. A Fixed Peg

Even when a fixed peg has been preannounced, the dependable policymaker may decide to breach this commitment if a subsequent positive realization of x is such that the importance of maintaining the real exchange rate is sufficiently high in comparison to price stability. More precisely, D decides to renege on the fixed peg if and only if

$$V\left(\frac{x}{h}, \pi^e\right) - V(0, \pi^e) > c \qquad (4.4)$$

The condition in (4.4) states that, given expectations, D prefers to revert to discretion if the difference in the value of the objectives when he or she does that and their value when he or she sticks to the ped is larger than the cost of reneging on the peg. Using (4.1) in (4.4) and rearranging we obtain

$$\pi_D(x) = \left\{ \begin{array}{ll} 0 & x \leq \sqrt{2hc} \equiv d \\ \dfrac{x}{h} & x > d \end{array} \right\} \qquad (4.5)$$

The following proposition verbally summarizes the result in equation (4.5).

Proposition 1: When a peg has been preannounced, a dependable policymaker respects it if $x \leq \sqrt{2hc}$. If $x > \sqrt{2hc}$ the dependable policymaker reneges on the peg and devalues at rate x/h.

Thus, when x is smaller than d the dependable policymaker is effectively committed to the peg. This is formalized by defining the set[9]

$$REC \equiv \left(x \mid 0 \leq x \leq \sqrt{2hc}\right) \qquad (4.6)$$

Note that the range of effective commitment *(REC)* is wider the higher the cost of reneging and the higher the relative concern of the policymaker for price stability as measured by h.

Using (4.5) in (4.3) we obtain an expression for inflation expectations

$$\pi^e(x) = \left\{ \begin{array}{ll} (1 - \alpha)\dfrac{x}{h} & x \in REC \\ \dfrac{x}{h} & \text{otherwise} \end{array} \right\} \qquad (4.3a)$$

Thus the stronger the reputation of policymakers, as measured by α, the stronger the downward impact of a peg on expected deprecia-

---

[9] Because the realizations of x are restricted to the positive orthant, only the range above zero is relevant. In the absence of this restriction the range of effective commitment is $-d \leq x \leq d$.

tion when x belongs to the *REC*. When $x \notin REC$ there is no impact
on expectations because both the dependable and the weak policymaker are known to act in a discretionary manner in this case.

How are the objectives of the dependable policymaker affected by
the realizations of x under a fixed peg? This question can be an-
swered by using (4.5) and (4.3a) in equation (4.1). The outcome is

$$V[\pi_D(x), \pi^e(x)] = \begin{cases} -(1-\alpha)\dfrac{x}{h} & x \in REC \\ -\left[\dfrac{x^2}{2h} + c\right] & x \notin REC \end{cases} \tag{4.7}$$

The decision about the exchange rate regime has to be made in
stage 1 before the realization of x is known. We will assume that the
dependable policymaker makes this decision by comparing the expected value of the objectives across alternative exchange rate regimes. The expected value (EV) of losses (defined for convenience
as minus the expected value of objectives) for the case of a peg is
given by

$$L^P \equiv -EV[\cdot] = \frac{1-\alpha}{h}\int_0^d x^2\, dF(x) + \int_d^{\bar{x}}\left[\frac{x^2}{2h} + c\right] dF(x) \tag{4.8}$$

where $\bar{x}$ is the largest possible realization of x that has positive
probability and $dF(x) \equiv f(x)$ is the probability density of x. Note
that the expected losses from a peg for a dependable policymaker
are lower the higher his or her reputation. If the policymaker's
reputation is lower than $1/2$, an increase in his or her relative
concern for price stability also lowers the expected losses.

How does the weak policymaker behave in office? Although the
policymaker ultimately behaves in a discretionary manner for all
values of x he or she always has an incentive to mimic the dependable counterpart in stage 1. The reason is that if the weak policymaker does not announce the same exchange rate regime as the one
that would have been announced by a D type, W is revealed as
weak at the outset. As a result, expected depreciation in the *REC*
increases from $(1-\alpha)(x/h)$ to x/h and this reduces the expected
value of objectives in comparison to the case in which W does not
reveal his or her type until stage 4.

It follows that the exchange rate regime that will be chosen by
both types is the one that minimizes the expected value of losses of
the dependable policymaker. The following subsection characterizes the expected value of an optimal band.

3.2. An Exchange Rate Band

The obvious difference between an exchange rate band and a peg is that in the first case policymakers commit to maintaining the exchange rate within some bounds rather than at a fixed value. We also highlight the possibility that the transparency of the commitment to the band is not as good as that of a pegged exchange rate. This is modeled by assuming that a fraction $1 - \delta$ ($0 \leq \delta \leq 1$) of individuals in the economy do not perceive the band as a commitment.

The timing of events is the same as in the case of a peg. Let π_m be the maximum rate of depreciation that can be implemented within the band. The basic formal difference between a peg and a band is that for $x \leq h\pi_m$ even the dependable policymaker can behave in a discretionary manner without incurring the cost of reneging c; that is, the band gives the dependable policymaker added flexibility. Hence, within the band both types choose the discretionary rate of depreciation x/h. When $x > h\pi_m$ there are, as was the case with a peg, two possibilities. If x is above $h\pi_m$ there are, as was the case with a peg, two possibilities. If x is not far away from $h\pi_m$ the dependable policymaker depreciates the currency but only at rate π_m rather than at the higher discretionary rate x/h. This yields a *range of effective commitment* in which D depreciates the currency only at rate π_m though tempted to devalue at a higher rate. If x is sufficiently above $h\pi_m$ the dependable policymaker reneges on the commitment to the band in spite of the political cost of reneging, c. We will refer to the values of x for which D chooses to abandon the band as the reneging range (RR).

Both the REC of a band and the RR are characterized by the condition $x \geq h\pi_m$. They are distinguished by the fact that in the range of effective commitment the difference in the value of objectives between a situation in which the rate of depreciation is x/h (and the commitment to the band is breached) and a situation in which it is π_m (and the commitment is not breached) is smaller than the cost of reneging, c. In the RR the opposite holds. More precisely:

$$x \in REC \Leftrightarrow V\left(\frac{x}{h}, \pi^e\right) - V(\pi_m, \pi^e) < 0 \tag{4.9a}$$

$$x \in RR \Leftrightarrow V\left(\frac{x}{h}, \pi^e\right) - V(\pi_m, \pi^e) > c \tag{4.9b}$$

By using equation (4.1) in equations (4.9) and rearranging, it can be shown that these conditions are equivalent to

$$REC \equiv \{x \mid h\pi_m \leq x \leq h\pi_m + d\} \qquad (4.10a)$$

$$RR \equiv \{x \mid x \geq h\pi_m + d\} \qquad (4.10b)$$

where it will be recalled that $d \equiv \sqrt{2hc}$. Thus, the range of effective commitment is wider the higher the cost of reneging c and the larger the concern of the policymaker for price stability (the larger h).

Since the band is less transparent than a fixed peg, it has a weaker impact on expectations in the REC.[10] This can be seen more precisely by noting that when x is in the range of effective commitment the mean expected rate of depreciation, even with perfect reputation ($\alpha = 1$), is

$$\pi^D(x, \alpha = 1) = \delta\pi_m + (1 - \delta)\frac{x}{h} \quad \text{for} \quad x \in REC \qquad (4.11)$$

Thus, the lower the transparency of the band as measured by the fraction, δ, of individuals who recognize it as a commitment, the lower is mean expected inflation in the REC. But, in general, reputation is not perfect. Hence in the REC, mean expected inflation is a weighted average between $\pi^D(x, \alpha = 1)$ and the discretionary rate x/h. It follows that, *for any* α

$$\pi^e(x) = \alpha\pi^D(x, \alpha = 1) + (1 - \alpha)\frac{x}{h} = q\pi_m + (1 - q)\frac{x}{h} \quad x \in REC \qquad (4.11a)$$

where $q \equiv \alpha\delta$. In all other ranges, including the range of x's for which the discretionary rate falls within the band, all individuals expect the discretionary rate x/h. Using this fact and equation (4.11a) in equation (4.1) we can calculate the value of D's objective function, given that he or she behaves optimally in stage 4, for each value of x. The outcome is

$$v[\pi^D(x), \pi^e(x)] = \begin{cases} -\dfrac{x^2}{2h} & 0 \leq x \leq h\pi_m \\[2mm] -\left[x(1 - \delta\alpha)\left(\dfrac{x}{h} - \pi_m\right) + \dfrac{h}{2}\pi_m^2\right] & x \in REC \\[2mm] \left(\dfrac{x^2}{2h} + c\right) & x \in RR \end{cases} \qquad (4.12)$$

[10] Because in other ranges *both* policymakers behave in a discretionary manner, the preannouncement of a band has no impact on expectations.

We have shown elsewhere how the dependable policymaker chooses the width of the band (Cukierman, Kiguel, and Leiderman 1993). Since the policymaker has to commit to a band width before the realization of x is known he or she chooses B so as optimally to trade off the benefits of lower expectations against the cost of real appreciation due to imperfect reputation[11] and the cost of occasional reneging on the band. Formally the choice of B by the dependable policymaker amounts to setting it at a value that maximizes the expected value of his or her objectives, or, equivalently, minimizes the expected value of his or her losses.

Let B be the width of the band measured as a percentage deviation from the central parity rate of exchange e_c, and let e_{-1} be the actual value of the exchange rate in the previous period. By definition

$$\pi_m = (1 + B)\frac{e_c}{e_{-1}} - 1 \tag{4.13}$$

so that, other factors being equal, π_m is larger the wider is the band, B. Assuming that when he or she chooses the band width in stage 1 the policymaker sets the center rate at the historically given nominal exchange rate, $e_c = e_{-1}$ and $\pi_m = B$. In view of this and equations (4.10) and (4.12) the choice of B reduces to the minimization of expected losses in (4.14):

$$L^B(B) \equiv -EV[\cdot] = \int_0^{hB} \frac{x^2}{2h} dF(x) + \int_{hB}^{hB+d} \left[(1 - \delta\alpha)x \left(\frac{x}{h} - B \right) + \frac{h}{2}B^2 \right] dF(x)$$

$$+ \int_{hB+d}^{\bar{x}} \left[\frac{x^2}{2h} + c \right] dF(x) \tag{4.14}$$

At an internal maximum for B

$$\frac{\partial L^B(B)}{\partial B} = 0 \tag{4.15}$$

It can be shown that if the peg and the band are equally transparent ($\delta = 1$), a fixed peg will never emerge as the solution to the minimization problem in equation (4.14).[12]

---

[11] Because of imperfect reputation, actual depreciation is lower than expected in the *REC*. As a consequence the real rate appreciates when x is in the *REC*. The real appreciation is larger the lower are reputation, α, and transparency, δ.

[12] Formally a peg is a band, B, with zero width. By substituting $B = 0$ into the first-order condition (eq. 18 in Cukierman, Kiguel, and Leiderman 1993), it can be shown that $\partial L^B(0)/\partial B < 0$ for all possible parameter values. Hence in the absence of differences in transparency (or possibly other differences) a fixed peg is never preferred to a band.

3.3 Comparison of Expected Losses under a Peg and Under a Band

Our presumption is that a dependable policymaker chooses the exchange rate system that produces smaller expected losses. To evaluate the factors determining the relative desirability of an exchange rate band and an exchange rate peg, we examine the difference in expected losses between the two systems. Subtracting equation (4.8) from equation (4.14) and rearranging, the difference in expected losses between a band and a peg can be expressed as

$$DL \equiv L^B - L^P = \int_0^{hB} \frac{x^2}{2h}\, dF(x) + \int_{hB}^{hB+d}\left[(1-\delta\alpha)\frac{x^2}{h} + \frac{1}{2}hB - (1-\delta\alpha)x\right] dF(x)$$

$$- \int_0^d (1-\alpha)\frac{x^2}{h}\, dF(x) + \int_{hB+d}^{\bar{x}}\left(\frac{x^2}{2h}+c\right)dF(x) - \int_d^{\bar{x}}\left(\frac{x^2}{2h}+c\right)dF(x) \qquad (4.16)$$

where the value of B is the value satisfying the first-order condition in equation (4.15). For any B, and in particular for the B that minimizes losses under a band, the sign of the difference in expected losses is generally ambiguous.

The reason for this is that there are several elements that operate in opposite directions. Under a band, even when it is optimally set, the policymaker incurs the additional cost of the devaluation bias whenever the realizations of x are such that the discretionary rate of devaluation is within the band. These additional costs of the band are reflected by the first term on the right-hand side of equation (4.16). The fact that the band is less transparent than the peg ($\delta < 1$) also tends to make the expected losses of the band higher than those of the peg.

On the other hand, because the range of reneging of the band is narrower than that of the peg, the expected value of the devaluation bias and of the cost of reneging is higher under a peg than under a band. This is reflected in the difference between the last two terms on the right-hand side of equation (4.16), which is negative.

4. HOW DO CHANGES IN TRANSPARENCY AND IN THE RELATIVE IMPORTANCE OF PRICE STABILITY AFFECT THE CHOICE OF EXCHANGE RATE REGIME?

It was shown in Section 2 that during some disinflations (such as those in Israel, Chile, and Mexico) the exchange rate was pegged initially and then, as the success of the stabilization became evident, the peg was replaced by a band or a crawl or a combination of these two more flexible systems. This section investigates whether such changes can be explained as being the consequence of an increase in the relative transparency of the band or an increase in policymakers' relative concern for maintenance of a competitive real exchange rate.

As argued in the introduction, it is plausible that immediately after a stabilization the transparency of the commitment embodied in more flexible exchange rate systems is lower than that of a fixed peg. However, after a sustained period of disinflation the transparency advantage of a fixed peg is reduced. At low rates of inflation more individuals are able to recognize when the commitment to the band has been broken than at high and variable rates. We model this effect by assuming that the parameter δ increases some time after stabilization.

At the inception of stabilization the major concern of policymakers is the restoration of price stability. But after a while, when this has been achieved, and the costs of an overvalued currency become more evident, the emphasis shifts away from price stability to external competitiveness.[13] In terms of the objective function in equation (4.1) this can be modeled as a reduction in h.

How is the difference in expected losses under an optimally set band and a peg affected by a change in the transparency parameter δ? The answer can be obtained by totally differentiating the difference in losses (DL) in equation (4.16) with respect to δ. It is shown in part 1 of the Appendix that

$$\frac{d(DL)}{d\delta} = -\frac{\alpha}{h} \int_{hB}^{hB+d} x(x - hB)\,dF(x) \qquad (4.17)$$

Because only values of x above hB are summed, this expression is negative. This leads to the following proposition.

Proposition 2: As the transparency of the commitment embodied in the band rises (δ increases), the difference between expected losses under an optimally set band and under a peg is reduced.

Suppose now that at the onset of stabilization $DL > 0$ so that policymakers prefer a peg to a band. As the persistence of price

[13] Survey evidence indicates that most of the public considers inflation to be the number one economic problem at the inception of stabilization, but not after a while.

stability is proved and recognized, δ increases, and the difference *DL* is reduced and may even become negative. When it turns negative, rational policymakers switch from the peg to an optimally set band. Thus Proposition 2 supports the notion that the shift from fixed pegs to exchange rate bands in the aftermath of stabilization (see Section 2) is consistent with an increase in the relative transparency of the band that occurs along with a persistent slowdown in inflation.

We turn next to the effect of *h* on the relative desirability of a peg and of a band. At first sight, it would seem that as *h* increases (i.e., the relative concern for price stability rises) the relative desirability of the fixed peg should increase. However, contrary to this preliminary intuition, the effect of *h* on the relative desirability of a peg and of an exchange rate band is generally ambiguous. As can be seen by scrutinizing equation (4.16) there are several effects that may operate in opposite directions. What is the intuitive reason for such opposite effects? One reason is that although an increase in *h* increases the costs of a devaluation bias, it also reduces the discretionary rate of depreciation, x/h. The first effect increases the relative desirability of the tighter commitment embodied in the fixed peg. But the lower discretionary rate reduces the need for a tighter commitment. These two opposing forces pervade many of the expressions in equation (4.16). Their opposite effects appear already in the first term on the right-hand side of (4.16), which represents the additional expected costs due to the depreciation bias within the band. When *h* increases, the range over which these costs are applicable increases, too. This tends to increase the desirability of a peg. However, because the discretionary rate x/h in the integrand goes down, there is also an effect that reduces the relative desirability of the peg when *h* goes up.

The following proposition presents sufficient (but not necessary) conditions for a positive relation between the relative desirability of a peg and the relative emphasis of policy on price stability.

Proposition 3:

    i. If the density of *x* rises sufficiently fast at low values of *x* and then drops sufficiently fast in the band's range of effective commitment,[14]

---

[14] Cukierman, Kiguel, and Leiderman (1993) show that at least the upper part of the REC of an optimal band must be in a range of *x* where $dF(x)$ is decreasing in *x*.

ii. The cost of reneging c is sufficiently large,

iii. The optimal band width is relatively narrow,

then an increase in the relative concern for a competitive real exchange rate raises the relative desirability of an exchange rate band in comparison to that of a peg.

Proof: See Part 2 of the Appendix. Examination of equation (4.A4) in the Appendix reveals that there are obviously other sets of sufficient conditions producing the result of Proposition 3. When the conditions of Proposition 3 are satisfied, the replacement of fixed pegs by bands is consistent with the view that this was at least partly due to an increased concern for external competitiveness. Because the conditions of Proposition 3 are sufficient but not necessary, this conclusion is likely to be true for a wider range of parameter values.

5. TOWARD A SYSTEMATIC COMPARISON OF A FIXED BAND WITH A CRAWLING BAND

We have seen in Section 2 that from December 1991 Israel moved from a fixed band to a crawling band. The relative advantage of the crawling band is that it reduces the expected cost of reneging. In terms of our model, because the expected value of x is positive, even a dependable policymaker will eventually renege on a fixed band. By contrast this is not necessarily the case under a crawling band, provided the preannounced rate of devaluation is sufficiently large. Hence a crawl (with or without a band) reduces the cost of reneging to dependable policymakers.

This section presents a minimal framework needed for the systematic comparison of a fixed band and a crawling band. To capture the essential feature of a crawling band, which is that policymakers can commit to different bands in different periods, we consider a two-period model. Within each period the objective function is given by equation (4.1) and the timing of moves is the same as in Section 3 (see Figure 4.1). Under either a fixed or a crawling band the policymaker in office preannounces exchange rate bands for both periods at the beginning of the first period. The difference between the fixed and the crawling band is that under the first regime the policymaker announces the same band for both periods, whereas under the second he or she may announce different bands for each period.

As in Section 3 there are two policymaker types: a dependable policymaker who incurs a cost c if he or she devalues within a given period by *more* than a preannounced amount and a weak policymaker who does not incur such a cost. The policymaker type is drawn anew in each period from a distribution that assigns a probability α to the event that the policymaker type is D and a probability $1 - \alpha$ to the event that the policymaker is type W.

Let x_i be the realization of x in period $i(i = 1, 2)$. We assume that x_1 and x_2 have the same distribution, that they are mutually independent, and that the common distribution has positive support.

To capture the possibility that the commitment embodied in the crawling band is less transparent than that of a fixed band, we assume that the fraction of individuals who perceive the crawling band to be a commitment is lower than the fraction of those who perceive the fixed band to be a commitment. For simplicity, and without loss of generality, we normalize the second fraction to one and denote the first fraction by δ. The objectives of policymakers are to maximize

$$x_1(\pi_1 - \pi_1^c) - \frac{\pi_1^2}{2} + \beta \left[x_2(\pi_2 - \pi_2^c) - \frac{\pi_2^2}{2} \right] \tag{4.18}$$

where $\beta \leq 1$ is the (political) rate of time preference of policymakers. Note that the parameter h from equation (4.1) has been normalized to one for simplicity.

Let B be the width of the (fixed) band and let π_m be the maximum rate of depreciation within the band in the first period. We assume that when the width of the band is chosen at the beginning of the first period the center rate is set at the historically given rate e_0. Hence the upper bound of the band is

$$\bar{e} = (1 + B)e_0 \tag{4.19}$$

We also assume that when a realignment occurs the new center rate is set equal to the new actual exchange rate and the width of the band remains the same. If there is no realignment in the first period

$$\pi_m \cong B - \pi_1 \tag{4.20}$$

The discretionary rate of depreciation in period 2 is

$$\pi_2 = x_2 \tag{4.21}$$

The first-period discretionary rate in some range may not depend only on x_1. However, under a bounded rationality assumption of the policymaker, it is equal to x_1. Details are discussed later.

5.1. A Fixed Band

The behavior of the dependable policymaker in each period depends on the realization of the preference parameter in that period. Within the period there are three qualitatively different cases. If x_i falls within the band, D picks the discretionary rate without incurring the cost of reneging, c. If x falls within the range of effective commitment (REC), D depreciates the currency until it hits the upper limit of the fixed band. Finally if x falls in the range of reneging (RR), D devalues at the discretionary rate and incurs the cost of reneging. We will define, accordingly, three sets of values of x_i:

$$N_i - x_i \in \{\text{the rate of depreciation is within the band in period } i)$$
$$C_i - x_i \in \{REC \text{ in period } i\} \tag{4.22}$$
$$R_i - x_i \in \{RR \text{ in period } i\}$$

where $i = 1, 2$. Policy actions, expectations, and the value of objectives depend on the realizations of x_1 and x_2. The functional form for the value of objectives in period 2 depends on the range within which x_2 falls as well as on the maximum allowable rate of depreciation within the band. This rate and the boundaries between ranges depend in turn on whether there has or has not been a realignment in the first period. In the first case the maximum allowable rate is B and in the second it is π_m. The different possible cases are represented in Figure 4.2.

Because the structure of decisions in period 2 is the same as that of a single-period fixed band, the equilibrium values of objective in the three ranges are given by equation (4.12) with $h = 1$. This is reproduced as equation (4.23).

$$V_2 = \begin{cases} -\dfrac{x_2}{2} & x_2 \leq \pi_m \\[2mm] -\left[(1 - \alpha)x_2(x_2 - \pi_m) + \dfrac{\pi_m^2}{2} \right] & \pi_m < x_2 \leq \pi_m + d \\[2mm] -\left(\dfrac{x_2^2}{2} + c \right) & x_2 > \pi_m \end{cases} \tag{4.23}$$

If there has been a realignment in period 1, $\pi_m = B$. Otherwise it is given by equation (4.20). It follows from equation (4.23) that after x_1 has been realized but prior to the realization of x_2, the expected value of losses in period 2 is

$$L_2 \equiv -EV_2 = \int_0^{\pi_m} \frac{x_2^2}{2} dF(x_2) + \int_{\pi_m}^{\pi_m + d} \left[(1 - \alpha)x_2(x_2 - \pi_m) + \frac{\pi_m^2}{2} \right] dF(x_2)$$

$$+ \int_{\pi_m + d}^{\bar{x}} \left(\frac{x_2^2}{2} + c \right) dF(x_2) \tag{4.24}$$

Equation (4.24) implies that when $x_1 \in N_1$ the choice of π_1 affects the expected value of losses in period 2. The direction of this effect is generally ambiguous. We will assume that when picking π_1, the dependable policymaker disregards this additional effect either because of bounded rationality or because this effect is relatively small.[15] Under this assumption the discretionary rate in period 1 is x_1 and expected losses in that period (denoted L_1) have the same form as those in equation (4.24) with x_2 and π_m replaced by x_1 and B, respectively.

The width of the fixed band, B, is chosen prior to the realizations of both x_1 and x_2 so as to minimize the present discounted value of losses, $E(PVL)$. It is shown in part 3 of the Appendix that this expected value is given by

$$E(PVL) \equiv L_1(B) + \beta L_2(B) = \int_0^B f(x_1)dF(x_1) + \int_B^{B+d} g(x_1)dF(x_1) + \int_{B+d}^{\bar{x}} h(x_1)dF(x_1)$$

$$+ \beta \left[\int_0^B \left(\int_0^{B-x_1} f(x_2)dF(x_2) + \int_{B-x_1}^{B+d-x_1} g(x_2)dF(x_2) + \int_{B+d-x_1}^{\bar{x}} h(x_2)dF(x_2) \right) dF(x_1) \right.$$

$$+ \int_0^d g(x_2)dF(x_2) + \int_d^{\bar{x}} h(x_2)dF(x_2)$$

$$\left. + \int_0^B f(x_2)dF(x_2) + \int_B^{B+d} g(x_2)dF(x_2) + \int_{B+d}^{\bar{x}} h(x_2)dF(x_2) \right] \tag{4.25}$$

where

$$f(x_i) \equiv \frac{x_i^2}{2}; \qquad h(x_i) \equiv \frac{x_i^2}{2} + c, \qquad i = 1, 2$$

$$g(x_1) \equiv (1 - \alpha)x_1 - B) + \frac{B^2}{2}$$

[15] π_1 is generally determined only implicitly when the feedback from the second period to the choice of π_1 is taken into consideration.

$$g(x_2) \equiv \begin{cases} (1 - \alpha)x_2(x_2 + x_1 - B) + \dfrac{(B - x_1)^2}{2} & x_1 \in N_1 \\[2mm] (1 - \alpha)x_2^2 & x_1 \in C \\[2mm] (1 - \alpha)x_2(x_2 - B) + \dfrac{B^2}{2} & x_1 \in R_1 \end{cases} \qquad (4.26)$$

Minimization of the expression in equation (4.25) yields the first-order condition

$$L_1'(B) + \beta L_2'(B) = 0 \qquad (4.27)$$

which determines the width of the fixed band, B.

5.2. Comparison of a Crawling Band with a Fixed Band

The analysis of a crawling band is identical to that of the fixed band except for the following differences. First, the policymaker can choose a different band width in each period. But the policymaker must commit to these possibly different widths prior to the realizations of x_1 and x_2. Second, because of differences in transparency between the fixed and the crawling band, the expressions for $g(x_i)$ in the case of a crawling band differ from those expressions for a fixed band (see equation [4.26]) in that α is replaced everywhere by $\delta\alpha$. The choice of B_1 and B_2 is characterized by the solution to the following minimization problem:

$$\min_{\{B_1, B_2\}} L_1(B_1) + \beta L_2(B_2) \qquad (4.28)$$

When the transparencies of the crawling and of the fixed band are the same, $\delta = 1$ and the maximand in equation (4.28) is *identical* to the maximand in equation (4.25). Because in the first case there are more instruments, the value of equilibrium expected losses under a crawling band cannot exceed their value under a fixed band. Hence in the absence of differences in transparency a dependable policymaker always prefers (at least weakly) a crawling to a fixed band.

However, when the transparency of the crawl is smaller than that of the fixed band ($\delta < 1$) there is an effect that operates in the opposite direction.[16] Hence the ultimate choice between the two exchange rate systems depends on whether the advantage of the crawling band in

---

[16] This can be seen by comparing the expressions for $g(x_i)$ from equations (4.26) with those same expressions with α replaced by $\delta\alpha$.

reducing the expected costs of reneging is larger or smaller than its disadvantage in terms of transparency.

5.3. The Effect of a Change in Relative Transparency on the Choice between Band Types

Our presumption is that, as the success of stabilization gradually becomes more evident, the transparency of a crawling band rises in relation to that of a fixed band. In terms of the model, δ goes up. By the envelope theorem

$$\frac{dE(PVL^c)}{d\delta} = \frac{\partial E(PVL^c)}{\partial \delta} \tag{4.29}$$

where $E(PLV^c)$ is the expected value of losses under a crawling band. It is easy to see from the expressions for $g(x_i)$ under a crawling band that the sign of the partial derivative in equation (4.29) is negative. This leads to the following proposition.

Proposition 4: An increase in the relative transparency of a crawling versus a fixed band increases the relative desirability of the first system and may lead to the replacement of a fixed band with a crawling band.

In December 1992 Israel replaced a fixed band system with a crawling band. Proposition 3 provides a possible clue to the motivation underlying this change. As the persistence of nominal stability became more evident, the relative transparency of the more elaborate crawling band rose. As a result, the advantage of this system in terms of lower costs of reneging became the dominant factor in comparison to its disadvantage in terms of transparency. This led to the switch to the more flexible system.

6. CONCLUDING REMARKS

This chapter has attempted to rationalize the gradual but persistent trend toward more flexible exchange rate systems in the aftermath of stabilization by focusing on the different environments faced by policymakers immediately after stabilization and later on.

The main results of the analysis can be briefly summarized as follows. First, the gradual replacement of fixed pegs with more flexible systems is consistent with the view that this is due to the fact that, after the success of disinflation became evident, the relative transparency of the more flexible exchange rate arrangement gradually rose, too. Second, the chapter derives conditions under which this tendency is due also to an increased relative concern for maintenance of a competitive real exchange rate.

APPENDIX

1. DERIVATION OF EQUATION (4.17)

Totally differentiating (4.16) with respect to δ:

$$\frac{d(DL)}{d\delta} = \frac{\partial L^B}{\partial \delta} + \frac{\partial L^B}{\partial B}\frac{dB}{d\delta} - \frac{\partial L^P}{\partial \delta} \tag{4.A1}$$

From equation (4.15) $\partial L^B/\partial B = 0$ so the middle term drops (envelope theorem) and (4.A1) reduces to

$$\frac{d(DL)}{d\delta} = \frac{\partial L^B}{\partial \delta} - \frac{\partial L^P}{\partial \delta} = \frac{\partial DL}{\partial \delta} \tag{4.A2}$$

Equation (4.17) in the text is obtained by calculating the partial derivative of DL with respect to δ.

2. PROOF OF PROPOSITION 3

Totally differentiating equation (4.16) with respect to h

$$\frac{d(DL)}{dh} = \frac{\partial L^B}{\partial h} + \frac{\partial L^B}{\partial B}\frac{dB}{dh} - \frac{\partial L^P}{\partial \delta} = \frac{\partial DL}{\partial h} \tag{4.A3}$$

Using the fact that $\partial L^B/\partial B = 0$, and using a good deal of algebra, we obtain

$$\frac{d(DL)}{dh} = \frac{1}{2}\left[hB^3 f(hB) - \int_0^{hB}\left(\frac{x}{h}\right)^2 dF(x) \right]$$

$$+ \sqrt{\frac{c}{2h}}\,[2\alpha c f(d) - \delta\alpha\sqrt{2c}(\sqrt{2c} + \sqrt{h}\,b)f(hB + d)]$$

$$- B\left[\frac{h}{2}B^2 f(hB) + \delta\alpha\sqrt{2c}\,(\sqrt{2c} + \sqrt{h}\,B)f(hB + d)\right]$$

$$+ \frac{1}{2h^2}\left[\int_d^{d+hB} x^2 dF(x) + 2\left((1-\alpha)\int_0^d x^2 dF(x)\right.\right.$$

$$\left.\left. - \int_{hB}^{hB+d}\left((1-\delta\alpha)x^2 - \frac{(hB)^2}{2}\right)dF(x)\right)\right] \tag{4.A4}$$

There are four basic terms in brackets on the right-hand side of (4.A4). Because B is relatively small and $f(x)$ increases initially, the first term on the right-hand side of (4.A4) is positive. Because $f(\cdot)$ decreases sufficiently fast in the REC of the band, it is positive, too. The third term is negative. However, it does not dominate the other positive terms provided B is sufficiently small. Finally, the last term is positive because c, and therefore $d = \sqrt{2hc}$ is large in comparison to hB and because $f(x)$ decreases sufficiently fast in the REC of the band.

3. DERIVATION OF EQUATION (4.25)

The expected value of L_2 prior to the realization of x_1 depends on whether x_1 is in the set N_1, C_1, or R_1. Taking expected values of equation (4.24) conditional on each of these three sets and using (4.20) we obtain

$$E\left[\frac{L_2}{N_1}\right] = \frac{1}{P[N_1]}\int_0^B \left[\int_0^{B-\pi_1} f(x_2)dF(x_2) + \int_{B-\pi_1}^{B+d-\pi_1} g(x_2)dF(x_2)\right.$$

$$\left. + \int_{B+d-\pi_1}^{\bar{x}} h(x_2)\right] dF(x_1) \qquad (4.A.5a)$$

$$E[L_2/C_1] = \frac{1}{P[C_1]}\int_B^{B+d}\left[\int_0^d g(x_2)dF(x_2) + \int_d^{\bar{x}} h(x_2)dF(x_2)\right]dF(x_1) \qquad (4.A.5b)$$

$$E[L_2/R_1] = \frac{1}{P[T_1]}\int_{B+d}^{\bar{x}}\left[\int_0^B f(x_2)dF(x_2) + \int_B^{B+d} g(x_2)dF(x_2)\right.$$

$$\left. + \int_{B+d}^{\bar{x}} h(x_2)dF(x_2)\right]dF(x_1) \qquad (4.A.5c)$$

The expected value of the present discounted value of losses is, by definition

$$E[PVL] = L_1 + \beta[E[L_2|N_1]P[N_1] + E[L_2|C_1]P[C_1] + E[L_2|R_1]P[R_1]] \quad (4.A.6)$$

Equation (4.25) in the text is obtained by substituting equations (4.A5) into (4.A6) by using the bounded rationality assumption and by rearranging.

REFERENCES

Corbo, V., and A. Solimano (1991), Chile's Experience with Stabilization Revisited, in M. Bruno et al. eds., *Lessons of Economic Stabilization and Its Aftermath*, Cambridge, MA: MIT Press.

Cukierman, A. (1992), *Central Bank Strategy, Credibility and Independence: Theory and Evidence*, Cambridge, MA: MIT Press.

Cukierman, A., M. Kiguel, and L. Leiderman (1993), "The Choice of Exchange Rate Bands: Balancing Credibility and Flexibility," Working Paper No. 1-93, The Sackler Institute of Economic Studies, Tel Aviv University, February 1993.

Cukierman, A., M. Kiguel, and N. Liviatan (1992), How Much to Commit to an Exchange Rate Rule? Balancing Credibility and Flexibility, *Revista de Analysis Economico* 7 (June): 73–90.

Cukierman, A., and N. Liviatan (1991), Optimal Accommodation by Strong Policymakers Under Incomplete Information, *Journal of Monetary Economics*, 27 (January): 99–127.

Dornbusch, R. (1992), Lessons from Experiences with High Inflation, *World Bank Economic Review* 6 (January): 13–32.

Edwards, S., and A. Edwards (1987), *Monetarism and Liberalization: The Chilean Experiment*, Cambridge, MA: Ballinger.

Haltiwanger, J., and M. Waldman (1985), Rational Expectations and the Limits of Rationality," *American Economic Review* 75 (June): 326–341.

Helpman, E., Leiderman, L., and G. Bufman (1994), A New Breed of Exchange Rate Bands: Chile, Israel, and Mexico, *Economic Policy* 19, 259–306.

Liviatan, N., and D. Oks (1993), "Evaluation of Recent Developments in Mexico's Exchange Rate Policy," Unpublished draft, The World Bank, April 1993.

Lohmann, S. (1992), Optimal Commitment in Monetary Policy: Credibility Versus Flexibility, *American Economic Review* 82 (March): 273–286.

CHAPTER 5

Cross-Border Banking

Jonathan Eaton

1. INTRODUCTION

A number of multilateral, bilateral, and unilateral initiatives are
seeking to increase international financial integration: Liberalization of trade in financial services was an important topic in the
Uruguay Round; financial integration is a major component of such
regional integration arrangements as the European Community and
North American Free Trade Agreement (NAFTA); a number of
countries, such as Australia and Indonesia, have taken steps to open
their domestic financial markets to foreign banks.

The prospect of increased international competition in banking
services raises fundamental questions about sources of comparative
advantage and the potential gains from trade in banking services.
Because trade in banking services can take several fundamental
forms, the issues are complex and multifaceted.

At least three forms of international competition in banking services are worth distinguishing: (i) competition between banks in
different countries, (ii) competition between the currencies of different countries as the unit of account for loans and deposits, and (iii)
competition between the financial regulatory environments of different countries.

1.1. Firm Competition

One type of international competition is the entry of foreign banks
into domestic banking. In its pure form such competition is be-

This chapter was prepared for the presentation at the conference Financial Aspects of the
Transition from Stabilization to Growth at the David Horowitz Institute for the Research of

tween foreign banks and domestic banks in accepting domestic deposits and making loans domestically on the domestic banks' home turf. Foreign-owned banks are subject to the same reserve requirements and other regulatory constraints as domestically owned banks, with deposits and loans denominated in local currency (so that banks are not engaged in any "currency transformation" between deposits and loans). At issue here, then, is the relative productivity of individual banks, all operating in the same regulatory environment with the same currencies, in providing banking services to a domestic clientele.[1] Hence international competition of this type does not involve direct competition between different regulatory systems because customers continue to be served by banks that are subject to the same regulations. Nor is there any competition among different currencies. Competition of this form does not require significant flows of capital between the home and host countries of the banks in question.

1.2. Currency Competition

A second form of competition prevails between alternative currencies of denomination. Banks may offer loans or accept deposits denominated in foreign currencies. Examples are the dollar-denominated deposits introduced at various points in Mexico and Peru, and the array of deposit and loan denominations provided by banks in the Eurodollar market. The banks offering these deposits and loans may be foreign or domestically owned, and activity may be subject to the same regulations regardless of the currency of denomination. If the banks subject to the same regulations may offer loans and deposits in different currencies, the relative efficiency of individual banks or of alternative regulatory systems is not at issue. What is at issue is the relative attractiveness of different

Developing Countries, Tel Aviv University, June 6–7, 1993. I thank the conference participants, especially Benjamin Bental, Horst Bockelmann, and Mark Gertler, for many helpful comments. Akiko Tamura provided excellent research assistance.

[1] Several countries, such as Australia and Indonesia, have undertaken financial liberalizations with the hope of attracting entry by foreign banks. Market penetration by foreign banks has remained small, largely limited to serving the financial needs of multinational clients based in the home countries of the banks in question. See, for example, the discussions in Lewis and Davis (1987) and Garber and Weisbrod (1993).

currencies as units of denomination, which may derive, for example, from their stability of value or their use as currencies of denomination in international trade.

Unless individual banks exactly balance the composition of their assets and liabilities by denomination, currency competition, unlike foreign entry, does put banks in the role of "currency transformers." It does not, however, necessarily imply any cross-country capital flows, or "country transformation."[2]

1.3. Cross-Border Competition

A third form of international competition in banking is between banks operating in different regulatory environments: Banks subject to different regulations may compete to attract deposits, to make loans, or to do both. Because regulatory environments typically correspond to geographical regions, competition of this form is likely to create significant cross-border flows of bank deposits and liabilities. Moreover, such competition can create "banking centers," countries that act as net intermediaries for the rest of the world. To the extent that banks subject to different national regulatory systems have distinct ownership, an element of competition of this type also concerns the competitiveness of individual banks. For example, Switzerland may be a banking center because Swiss banks are, by their very nature, efficient intermediaries. Another source of comparative advantage, however, is the regulatory environment itself. Cross-border flows of deposits and loans have involved banks that have branches in the client's home country, suggesting that at least an element of competition derives from the bank regulations of the country where the banking activity occurs.

These conceptual distinctions among different pure forms of international bank competition help clarify the various determinants of comparative advantage in banking. But increased banking competition is likely to occur in hybrid forms. For example, the establishment of U.S. branch banks abroad (foreign entry) probably

[2] Lewis and Davis (1987) distinguish among three types of transformation that international banks can engage in. One, the usual focus of the domestic banking literature, is "maturity transformation," because bank assets and liabilities can be of different maturities. A second is "currency transformation," because the composition of the currencies of denomination of a bank's assets may differ from that of its liabilities. A third is "country transformation," because a bank's liabilities and claims may not match by country.

increased interbank loan activity (cross-border banking). Foreign entry may also occur precisely in order to provide loans and deposits in different currencies to a local "currency clientele" (to use Aliber's [1984] terms).

Moreover, even though foreign entry in principle subjects foreign and domestic banks to the same regulations, a foreign bank's ability to compete may derive from its regulatory environment at home. A foreign bank may benefit, for example, from an enhanced ability to raise funds abroad, or from the lender-of-last-resort function of the central bank in its home country.

Recognizing that international bank competition can take various forms, several of which may operate in any actual situation, in this chapter I focus more narrowly on competition of the second and third types. Banks located in different countries compete worldwide for deposits and loans but denominate deposits and loans in domestic currency and are subject to local banking regulations. Because I treat all banks as identical, and the banking sector as perfectly competitive, the issue of international competition at the firm level does not arise. The nationality of the ownership of a bank is irrelevant.

In the next section I discuss some basic data on cross-border bank positions, which I use to identify countries that serve as international banking centers. I then examine some key features of these countries that seem to distinguish them from those that are not banking centers.

In Section 3 I develop a simple model of a national banking system to identify factors that may be associated with a nation's ability to attract deposits or to make foreign loans. The model focuses on two instruments of monetary policy, money growth and reserve requirements. A key assumption is that bank claims and liabilities are nominally denominated in domestic currency. Monetary authorities undertake policy with multiple goals. One is to earn seigniorage. Another is to serve the competing interests of existing creditors and debtors, as well as those of new lenders and new borrowers, in its constituency.

In Section 4 I apply the model to examine some implications of cross-border banking, which can take the form of international integration of deposit markets, loan markets, or both.

Section 5 provides some concluding observations, discusses the limitations of the analysis, and suggests some extensions.

2. CROSS-BORDER BANKING AND INTERNATIONAL
BANKING CENTERS

The ability of a national banking system to attract foreign deposits,
and to make foreign loans, reflects its international competitiveness
as an intermediary. Appendix Tables 5.A1 and 5.A2, based on data
from the International Monetary Fund's (IMF's) *International Financial Statistics*, report net cross-border deposits of nonbanks and
net cross-border credit to nonbanks, by residence of the bank, for a
sample of European, Asian, and Western Hemisphere countries.
Countries were selected on the basis of the availability of data. Data
are averages of the available annual data for 1981–85 and 1986–90.
Column 3 reports net interbank liabilities. Data are in millions of
current U.S. dollars. I distinguish between countries identified by
the IMF as "industrial" and "developing."

On the basis of their net cross-border deposits from nonbanks
and their net cross-border claims on nonbanks, countries fall into
four categories. Table 5.1 assigns the countries for which I have
data to the four categories.

2.1. Banking Centers

Banking centers provide net intermediation services to the rest of
the world. These countries' banks are both net recipients of depos-
its from foreign nonbanks and net lenders to nonbanks abroad.
Among industrial countries this group contains, for example, the
Netherlands, Switzerland, and the United Kingdom (in both peri-
ods), and Japan (in the earlier period, indicated by "Japan I").
Among the developing countries this group includes the Cayman
Islands and Singapore for both periods.

2.2. The Disintermediated

Opposite to this group are countries that are on net disintermediated. Nonbank residents of this group are net depositors in banks
abroad and are net borrowers from foreign banks. Among industrial countries, membership in this group is more select and more

Table 5.1. *Banking transformation*

Positions	Net deposit inflow	Net deposit outflow
	Banking centers	*Outward transformers*
	Austria	United States I
	Belgium	Panama I
Net	France	Germany II
loan	Netherlands	Japan II
outflow	Switzerland	
	United Kingdom	
	Japan I	
	Cayman Islands	
	Singapore	
	Inward transformers	*The disintermediated*
	Denmark	Italy
	Norway	Australia I
	Sweden	United States II
Net	Canada	Argentina
loan	Greece	Colombia
inflow	Ireland	Jamaica
	Spain	Malaysia
	Germany I	Mexico
	Australia II	Philippines II
	Philippines I	Uruguay

unstable. Only Italy was disintermediated in both periods. Australia was disintermediated in the earlier period, as was the United States in the later period.

Among developing countries, however, this group includes all the South American countries for which data are available (in both periods), along with Mexico, Malaysia, and Jamaica (each in both periods) and Panama and the Philippines (each in the later period).

2.3. Inward Transformers

A third category of banking system receives net deposits from foreign nonbanks yet fails to supply all of the domestic demand for bank loans. For countries in this group, the banking system transforms all (net) foreign deposits into (net) domestic loans.

Among the industrial countries, Denmark, Norway, Sweden, Canada, Greece, Ireland, and Spain fall into this category in both periods, as does Germany for the first period and Australia for the second. Among the developing countries in the sample only Philippines, in the earlier period, belongs in this group.

2.4. Outward Transformers

Opposite to this group are countries whose nationals deposit more abroad than their banks receive in deposits from abroad, and whose banks are net suppliers of loans abroad. For this group of countries, banks transform (net) domestic deposits into (net) foreign loans. This group includes the United States and Panama in the earlier period and Germany and Japan in the later one.

2.5. How Important Are Cross-Border Positions?

To examine the importance of cross-border positions relative to the domestic banking sector, Appendix Tables 5.A3 and 5.A4 report net cross-border deposits from nonbanks, net cross-border claims on nonbanks, and net interbank claims as a share of domestic bank assets. Among the banking centers cross-border banking is especially significant for Singapore, Belgium, and Switzerland. For these countries net foreign deposits represent at least 30 percent of domestic assets. Among disintermediated countries net cross-border loans are especially large for Argentina and Panama. At the other extreme, net cross-border positions for Germany and Japan are small.

2.6. Banks and Nonbanks: What Are the Distinguishing Features?

Among the four categories of countries, membership in the group of banking centers appears to be more stable than membership in other groups. Are there financial characteristics of these countries that differ systematically from those of noncenters? To address this question, Columns 4 through 7 of Appendix Tables 5.A3 and 5.A4 report additional data on the financial systems of these countries. Column 4 reports annual average seigniorage as a share of gross domestic product (GDP), defined as the increase in reserve money between consecutive years relative to the GDP of the earlier year.[3] Column 5 gives the average annual ratio of quasi-money to gross domestic product. Column 6 indicates the average annual rate of inflation of the producer price index during the period. Column 7 provides the ratio of the monetary base to quasi-money.

Appendix Table 5.A5 reports averages of relevant statistics broken down between industrial and developing countries and between banking center countries and other countries. (Unfortunately, Singapore is the only nonindustrial banking center for which I have data.) The table indicates the following relationships:

1. Inflation rates are much lower in banking centers than elsewhere. (Inflation also tends to be lower in industrial countries than in developed countries.)
2. Quasi-money as a fraction of gross domestic product (GDP) is much larger in banking centers than in noncenters. (This ratio also tends to be larger in industrial countries than in developing countries.)
3. Banking centers generate less revenue from seigniorage (relative to GDP) than noncenters (as do industrial countries compared with developing countries).
4. The ratio of reserve money to quasi-money is lower in banking centers than in noncenters (and is lower in industrial countries than in developing countries).
5. There does not seem to be a stable relationship between a country's role as a banking center and net interbank deposits, at least among the industrial countries.

What determines why some countries become banking centers and others experience international disintermediation? Section 3 develops a simple model of a regulated intermediation system to identify some factors that may be important and to explain why banking centers have the features that they do.[4]

---

[3] I take this definition from Fischer's (1982) classic paper on seigniorage.
[4] Alworth and Andresen (1992) provide a systematic regression analysis of the determinants of deposit inflows and outflows using a much more comprehensive data set proprietary to

3. A MODEL OF REGULATED INTERMEDIATION

I adopt a variant of the Samuelson (1958) overlapping generations model. The analysis is complicated. At the expense of realism I have tried to make the simplest set of assumptions that allow an analysis of the issues at hand.

3.1. Endowments and Preferences

I consider a national economy in which individuals live for two periods. Some of these individuals (called lenders) receive an endowment while they are young, whereas others (called borrowers) receive their incomes when they are old. I assume that there are equal numbers of each type and normalize their populations to one each. (To facilitate exposition I refer to lenders as feminine and to borrowers as masculine.) I normalize a lender's (early) endowment at two and set the borrower's (late) endowment at $2y$.

Both lenders and borrowers want to smooth their consumption across the two periods of their lives. A simple way of introducing this motive is to assign each of them a lifetime utility given by

$$U = \ln C^y + \ln C^o \tag{5.1}$$

where C^y is what the individual consumes in youth and C^o is his or her consumption in old age.

This specification has two convenient implications for what follows: (i) Regardless of the interest rate, a lender will want to invest exactly half her income, or one, in her youth; (ii) at any (finite) interest rate, a borrower will want to borrow whatever will require a payment of half of his endowment, or y, in old age.

Naturally, lenders have a motive to make loans to youthful borrowers, who have a motive to borrow. If contracts were automatically enforceable and intermediation costless, in competitive equilibrium lenders would lend half their endowment to borrowers in their youth in exchange for half the borrowers' endowment in old age. The real interest rate in the economy would be y. (It's conve-

the Bank of International Settlements, which was not available to this author. One result supportive of the argument here is that countries with higher reserve requirements tend to have fewer foreign deposits.

nient to specify interest rates in terms of repayment of principal plus interest, or one plus the interest rate as conventionally defined.)

3.2. Financial Intermediation

I assume, however, that these individuals are unable to enforce direct loan contracts among themselves. Instead, they must lend and borrow through a banking system. To invest lenders must make deposits in banks and borrowers can only borrow from banks. Banks can enforce loan contracts and will honor deposit commitments.

Intermediation would be inconsequential if banking (i) were perfectly competitive, (ii) were costless, (iii) were not subject to reserve requirements or other taxes, and (iv) specified loan and deposit contracts in real terms. Competition among banks would then push the interest rate to y and resources would be allocated just as if lenders could deal directly with depositors.

The focus here is on banking policy, rather than on the competitiveness of individual banks or on market structure. Hence I treat intermediation as intrinsically costless and the banking system within each country as perfectly competitive. But I assume that banks (i) must hold a fraction λ of deposits as reserves, which take the form of reserve money issued by the local government, and (ii) specify loan and deposit contracts in terms of the currency of denomination of that money. Each period t the government specifies a reserve requirement λ_t and the nominal supply of reserves M_t.

In making both assumptions together I combine issues of "currency competition" with "cross-border" competition. In principle, I could allow banks to denominate loans or deposits in foreign currency, as they often do, even while they hold reserves in local currency. It would be interesting to investigate the consequences, but the analysis would be much more complicated. Banking systems do, however, tend to denominate loans and deposits in local currency and are sometimes required to do so. (The fact that the government is usually the ultimate enforcer of loan contracts gives it a great deal of power in determining what form contracts can take.)

Under these assumptions, a lender in her youth at time t will invest half of her endowment in bank deposits, which offer a nominal return R_t^D. The bank can lend a fraction $(1 - \lambda_t)$ to borrowers, whom it will charge a nominal interest rate R_t^L. The remaining deposits must be held as reserves, which I assume pay zero nominal interest. Denoting the ratio of the price level in a previous period to that in the current period (one over one plus the conventional inflation rate from last period to this) as Π_t, competition among banks will drive the real return on a period t deposit to

$$R_t^D = [(1 - \lambda_t)R_t^L + \lambda_t] \qquad (5.2)$$

Whatever the interest rate, a borrower demands a loan amount that requires a repayment of y in his old age. Because $1 - \lambda_t$ is the available loan amount, equilibrium in the loan market implies that the nominal interest rate on loans must satisfy

$$(1 - \lambda_t)R_t^L \Pi_{t+1}^e = y \qquad (5.3)$$

where Π_{t+1}^e is the period t expectation of Π_{t+1}.

The demand for reserves in period t is just λ_t, the reserve requirement times the deposit level. The government sets the nominal supply each period at M_t. Hence the price level in period t is

$$P_t = \frac{M}{\lambda_t} \qquad (5.4)$$

so that

$$\Pi_t = \frac{M_{t-1}/M_t}{\lambda_{t-1}/\lambda_t} \qquad (5.5)$$

The government's choice of the reserve requirement and money supply each period affects four important magnitudes: (i) Because deposits and loans made in the previous period were denominated in nominal terms, current monetary policy, by affecting the inflation rate, determines the ex post real return on bank loans and deposits due that period. (ii) Because reserves pay zero nominal interest, monetary policy, through the inflation rate, determines the real return on reserves held over from the previous period.[5] (iii) The current reserve requirement determines how much will be available for *new* loans that period. (iv) Money growth and the

---

[5] Together (i) and (ii) determine bank revenues. Competition among banks for deposits means that nominal deposit rates will leave banks zero anticipated profit. I assume that lenders are also the owners of bank equity. Hence, ex post, lenders earn the total return on bank loans either as interest on deposits or as bank profits (although in equilibrium bank profits are zero).

reserve requirement determine how much revenue the government earns from seigniorage that period, g_t, which will be

$$g_t = \lambda_t - \lambda_{t-1}\Pi_t \qquad (5.6)$$

3.3. Monetary Policy

I take the government's need for seigniorage as exogenous and constant at a level g. Taking into account its need for seigniorage revenue, the government must set M_t and λ_t each period to satisfy equation (5.6). Hence inflation in period t will be

$$\Pi_t = \frac{\lambda_t - g}{\lambda_{t-1}} \qquad (5.7)$$

Given the government's need for seigniorage, monetary policy each period can be summarized by the reserve requirement λ_t.

Two factors constrain the government's choice of λ_t. First, because bank reserves cannot exceed deposits, λ_t cannot exceed one. Second, because the price level cannot be negative, from equation (5.6), the reserve requirement must exceed the need for seigniorage. At the lower bound $\lambda_t = g$ inflation must be infinite to finance the government's seigniorage requirement.

As of period t, the nominal return on loans due is given, but the nominal return on new loans will take into account expected inflation as implied by (5.3), where the expectation will be consistent with anticipated future policy through (5.7).

Substituting these relationships into the expression for utility, the lifetime welfare of lenders and borrowers in each living generation at time t, as a function of monetary policy and predetermined variables, is

$$U^{YB} = \ln(1 - \lambda_t) + \ln y$$

$$U^{YL} = \ln(y + \lambda_{t+1} - g)$$

$$U^{OB} = \ln\left[2y - (1 - \lambda_{t-1})R^L_{t-1}\frac{\lambda_t - g}{\lambda_{t-1}}\right]$$

$$U^{OL} = \ln[(1 - \lambda_{t-1})R^L_{t-1} + \lambda_{t-1}] + \ln\left(\frac{\lambda_t - g}{\lambda_{t-1}}\right)$$

where U^i is the utility of individual of type i, where $i =$ YB, YL, OB, OL for young borrowers, young lenders, old borrowers, and old lenders, respectively.

Setting a higher reserve requirement allows the government to achieve its seigniorage objective with less monetary growth and hence less inflation. Given the nominal interest rate set the previous period and the government's current need for seigniorage, a higher reserve requirement, because it means lower inflation, is good for old lenders but bad for old borrowers. Setting a higher reserve requirement also harms young borrowers by restricting what is lent them. Because the nominal loan rate satisfies (5.3), young lenders are unaffected by current monetary policy, but they, of course, benefit from a higher reserve requirement in the future, because it implies less inflation and a higher real return on reserves.

I assume that the government chooses the reserve requirement λ_t each period to maximize a weighted average of the utilities of each type of living individual, taking the previous reserve requirement and nominal interest rate as given, but anticipating how its current choice of monetary policy may influence the nominal interest rate and future monetary policy. I denote the weight it places on individuals of type i as δ^i, where again $i = YB, YL, OB, OL$ for young borrowers, young lenders, old borrowers, and old lenders, respectively. Formally, then, each period t the government chooses λ_t to maximize

$$\Sigma \delta^i U^i, \qquad i = YB, YL, OB, OL \qquad (5.8)$$

The first-order condition for a maximum, assuming that the interest rate set the previous period correctly anticipated subsequent monetary policy, is

$$\frac{-\delta^{YB}}{1 - \lambda_t} + \frac{\delta^{YL}}{y - \lambda_{t+1}^e - g} \frac{d\lambda_{t+1}^e}{d\lambda_t} + \frac{\delta^{OL} - \delta^{OB}}{(\lambda_t - g)} = 0 \qquad (5.9)$$

Note that monetary policy in period $t - 1$ does not affect the optimal choice in t.[6] Hence I can treat $d\lambda_{t+1}/d\lambda_t = 0$. If exogenous parameters remain constant over time then the government will choose the same reserve requirement and inflation rate each period, so that individuals can reasonably expect that $\lambda_{t+1}^e = \lambda_t$.

In characterizing the policy outcome one must consider two cases: If $\delta^{OL} \leq \delta^{OB}$, then, to convey the maximum benefit to borrowers at the expense of lenders, the government will simply set λ at its lower bound of g and impose an infinite inflation tax. In this case the deposit rate is y and the loan rate $y/(1 - g)$.

---

[6] The second-order condition for a maximum is satisfied.

Alternatively, if $\delta^{OL} > \delta^{OB}$ then the government will choose an interior solution. Solving (5.9), the reserve requirement is then

$$\lambda = \frac{(\delta^{OL} - \delta^{OB}) + \delta^{YB}g}{\delta^{OL} - \delta^{OB} + \delta^{YB}}$$

and the consequent (simple) inflation rate is

$$i = \frac{(\delta^{OL} - \delta^{OB} + \delta^{YB})g}{(\delta^{OL} - \delta^{OB})(1 - g)}$$

Expressions for the real return on deposits and loans are, respectively;

$$R^D = y + \frac{(\delta^{OL} - \delta^{OB})(1 - g)}{\delta^{OL} - \delta^{OB} + \delta^{YB}}$$

$$R^L = \frac{\delta^{OL} - \delta^{OB} + \delta^{YB}}{\delta^{YB}(1 - g)} \cdot y$$

Three factors determine monetary policy: (i) the seigniorage requirement g, (ii) the welfare weight placed on old lenders relative to that on old borrowers $\delta^{OL} - \delta^{OB}$, and (iii) the welfare weight placed on young borrowers δ^{YB}. In addition, both interest rates are higher the larger the endowments of borrowers relative to lenders. The following matrix shows how monetary policy and the consequent interest rates respond to these variables:

	g	$\delta^{OL} - \delta^{OB}$	δ^{YB}	y
λ	+	+	−	0
inflation	+	−	+	0
R^D	−	+	−	+
R^L	+	+	−	+

(The sign in each element of the matrix indicates how the first item in that row responds to an increase in the top item in that column.)

The categorization of individuals into these four groups is of course very stylized, as is the characterization of monetary policy as an attempt to serve their respective interests and to raise revenue. This description does, however, capture some essential impacts of monetary policy: First, monetary policy can raise revenue for the government, and in some countries seigniorage revenue is significant. Second, to the extent that preexisting nominal contracts link individuals in the economy, inflation helps debtors at the expense of lenders. Third, more restrictive reserve requirements divert loanable funds from new borrowers to government liabilities.

An implication of the analysis is that governments with little need for seigniorage that place great weight on protecting the value of outstanding loan contracts (relative to the weight they place on debtors and new borrowers) will tend to have low inflation and restrictive reserve requirements. Countries with large seigniorage needs that place great weight on the interests of old and new borrowers will have higher inflation and less restrictive reserve requirements. Given its seigniorage needs, a country that places more weight on maintaining the real value of existing loan contracts will use monetary restrictions relatively more often than inflation (monetary growth) to raise seigniorage revenue. Even though lenders and borrowers establish nominal interest rates that perfectly anticipate the inflation that actually occurs, because some deposits are held in the form of reserves that pay a zero nominal return, inflation is not neutral in its distributional effects: Higher inflation puts more of the burden of raising seigniorage revenue on lenders.

3.4. Implications for Cross-Border Banking Flows

So far I have considered a single economy in isolation. In the next section I extend the analysis to consider the implications of various forms of integration. But the model of the closed economy foreshadows much of what happens.

Imagine a variety of countries that differ in terms of the four features described at the top of the matrix. A country is likely to attract deposits from abroad if its deposit rate is higher than elsewhere, and to borrow from abroad if its loan rate is higher than elsewhere.

Inward versus Outward Transformation. Not surprisingly (as in a purely real model), countries where borrowers (those with late endowments) have high endowments relative to lenders (with early endowments), that is, countries where y is relatively high, will attract capital from abroad, in both deposits and loans (the case of inward transformation). These countries have good investment opportunities relative to the domestic supply of loanable funds. More-over, countries whose governments weight the interests of (existing) lenders heavily relative to those of (existing and new) borrowers are, other factors equal, more likely to attract both deposits and loans. These countries impose higher reserve requirements both to reduce the need for inflation to finance seigniorage and to raise the interest rate on loans.[7] Because more of domestic lenders' savings is diverted toward holding reserves, less is available for borrowers. Conversely, countries where lenders have high endowments relative to borrowers or whose governments place greater weight on the interests of borrowers than those of lenders are likely to have lower interest rates on both deposits and loans, and to experience both deposit and loan outflows.

Banking Centers versus Disintermediation. Why do some countries be-come banking centers whereas others are disintermediated? The analysis points to the government's need for seigniorage as the determining factor. Countries whose governments seek to extract more resources from their financial systems will, other factors equal, have lower real deposit rates and higher real rates on loans. Deposits will tend to flow out of these countries to countries with lower seigniorage needs, and borrowers will seek to borrow from these countries to take advantage of lower loan rates. This result is consistent with the observation that banking centers in the sample of countries examined earn much less seigniorage, relative to their GDPs, than other countries, and have lower reserves relative to deposits.

4. MARKET INTEGRATION

Say that monetary policy remains a national concern, but that financial markets become integrated internationally. Financial inte-gration could mean that deposits, bank claims, or both, become traded internationally.

---

[7] Under the assumptions here, a higher reserve requirement benefits depositors by improv-ing their terms of trade vis-à-vis borrowers. This result does not generalize to borrower preferences that exhibit much more intertemporal substitutability, or, as shown later, to situations in which the loan market is internationally competitive.

4.1. Deposit Trade

Say that banks compete internationally for deposits but continue to lend only at home. This may be the outcome, for example, with no legal restrictions at all on capital flows, if banks maintain a unique ability to monitor the creditworthiness of local borrowers.[8]

Opening a national economy to trade in deposits would mean that banks and lenders in that economy would face a given world real deposit rate, which I will denote R^{*D}. I ignore possible inflation, exchange, and default risk and treat this rate as constant. In order to attract deposits, domestic banks must offer a deposit rate competitive with the world rate. Competition among domestic banks for deposits implies the zero profit condition

$$R^D = [(1 - \lambda_t)R_t + \lambda_t]\Pi^e_{t+1} = R^{*D}$$

That is, the anticipated real return on domestic loans and reserves, appropriately weighted by the reserve requirement, must equal the world rate.

To the extent that a country attracts or loses deposits, its seigniorage base rises or falls. I use ω_t to denote the ratio of period t deposits invested locally to the total deposits of lenders that period. Hence a value of ω_t above one means that the country has attracted net deposits from the world that period, and a value below one means that it has lost deposits to the world. I also make the assumption, which turns out to have consequence, that net and gross deposit positions coincide, that is, that deposits flow only one way. I discuss the significance of this assumption later.

Taking into account potential deposit trade, the expression for the price change needed to finance a given level of seigniorage revenue becomes

$$\Pi_t = \frac{\lambda_t \omega_t - g}{\lambda_{t-1} \omega_{t-1}} \tag{5.10}$$

---

[8] Comments by some observers suggest that this is the likely outcome of financial integration. Gerber and Weisbrod (1993), for example, argue that financial integration between the United States and Mexico will have little effect on U.S. bank lending to Mexican nonbanks because U.S. banks lack familiarity with Mexican loan customers. Stiglitz and Weiss (1981) formally model the role of informational advantages in lending. Equivalent arguments with respect to deposit activity are less prevalent. In fact, cross-currency bank claims and bank deposits are of roughly comparable magnitude. This similarity may, however, simply reflect artificial barriers to financial integration rather than the intrinsic tradability of the two types of financial instruments.

Because young lenders can earn the world deposit rate by investing abroad, their welfare is unaffected by domestic monetary policy. that is, if investors make local deposits, they must expect the domestic return to match the foreign return. The utility levels of the other factions in the economy now become

$$U^{YB} = \ln(1 - \lambda_t) + \ln\omega_t + \ln y$$

$$U^{OB} = \ln\left[2y - (1 - \lambda_{t-1})R_{t-1} \frac{\lambda_t \omega_t - g}{\lambda_{t-1}\omega_{t-1}} \right]$$

$$U^{OL} = \ln[(1 - \lambda_{t-1})R_{t-1} + \lambda_{t-1}] + \ln\left(\frac{\lambda_t \omega_t - g}{\lambda_{t-1}\omega_{t-1}} \right)$$

Investors will choose to invest an amount ω_t that satisfies

$$R^{*D} \geq \frac{y - g + \lambda_{t+1}^e \omega_{t+1}^e}{\omega_t} \tag{5.11}$$

where the right-hand side of the inequality denotes the domestic real return as a function of current deposit investment ω_t, y, g, and the reserve requirement λ_{t+1}^e and deposit investment ω_{t+1}^e expected in the *future*. This expression must hold with equality if $\omega_t > 0$. Note that *current* monetary policy does not affect *current* portfolio investment. Note also that, at an interior equilibrium, investment rises with borrower's income, the expected future reserve requirement, and future deposit investment and falls with the seigniorage requirement.[9]

I assume that monetary authorities set λ_t each period before depositors decide where to place their funds. Because monetary policy does not affect current investment, however, I assume that monetary authorities correctly anticipate the subsequent portfolio decision. In order to satisfy the seigniorage requirement authorities must set λ_t at least at g/ω_t (at which point generating the needed seigniorage requires infinite inflation).

The first-order condition for the reserve requirement becomes

$$\frac{-\delta^{YB}}{1 - \lambda_t} + \omega_t \frac{\bar{\omega}_{t-1}\delta^{OL} - \delta^{OB}}{(\lambda_t - g)} \leq 0 \tag{5.12}$$

where $\bar{\omega}_{t-1} = \max(\omega_{t-1}, 1)$. The expression holds with equality if the consequent $\lambda_t > g/\omega_t$.[10]

---

[9] An interior investment allocation is locally stable, because, given expectations about the future, the domestic real return decreases in the amount invested locally.

[10] Again, the second-order condition for a maximum is satisfied.

If the solution is interior, having more domestic deposits raises the optimal reserve requirement and thereby lowers the inflation needed to meet the seigniorage requirement.

A steady-state equilibrium comprises a portfolio position ω and a reserve requirement λ that jointly satisfy expressions (5.11) and (5.12), with $\omega_t = \omega^e_{t+1} = \omega$, $\lambda_t = \lambda^e_{t+1} = \lambda$.

Because the analytic expressions for the equilibrium values of λ and ω are complicated to the point of intractability, I rely on some numerical solutions to illustrate the results. This model is too stylized for any of the parameter values and solutions to be considered indicative of any actual economy. The only purpose is to suggest the direction of the effect of a change in circumstances and in government preferences on monetary policy and on deposit flows.

Appendix Table 5.A6 presents steady-state value of λ (the reserve requirement), ω the share of domestic deposits held domestically, and the consequent inflation rate for the values of δ^{YB} and δ^{OB} indicated on the first and second columns (with δ^{OL} normalized at one) and for the values of y, g, and R^{*D} indicated on the top row. I consider values of δ^{YB} of .95, 1, and 1.05 and of δ^{OB} of .90 and .93.

The Base Case. As a base case I set $y = 1$ (meaning that borrowers and lenders have the same endowment), a seigniorage requirement of .005 (or .25 percent of the aggregate endowment), and a world deposit rate of 7.5 percent. Note that the inflation rate is very sensitive to the weight placed on old borrowers. For each value of δ^{YB}, the inflation rate is between 5 and 6 percent when δ^{OB} is at its lower value and several hundred percent when it is at its higher value. Accompanying higher inflation is a lower reserve requirement. The low inflation regime is associated with deposit inflow ($\omega > 1$) and the high inflation regime with deposit outflow ($\omega < 1$).

The simulations suggest, then, that countries that place relatively more weight on maintaining the real value of loan contracts will attract more deposits. Because the base of the inflation tax is higher, a given amount of seigniorage revenue can then be raised with a lower inflation rate.

Increasing the social weight on the interests of new borrowers affects these magnitudes in the same direction as increasing the weight on existing debtors, but the magnitudes involved are much smaller.

Future Endowments. Say that the endowment of borrowers is instead 1.01, meaning that borrowers have higher endowments relative to lenders. For all the welfare weights considered, the implications are greater deposit inflow and lower inflation. Inflation is negligibly lower in cases where existing creditors have a higher welfare weight (when the country initially imports deposits) but dramatically lower in cases where existing debtors have a heavier weight (and the country initially exports deposits). In two of these three cases raising the value of y converts the country from a deposit exporter to a deposit importer.

Seigniorage. Doubling the seigniorage demands of the government approximately doubles the consequent inflation rate. This change also increases the reserve requirement. These two changes have offsetting effects on the net deposit position, which is virtually unchanged.

The World Deposit Rate. Lowering the world deposit rate from 7.5 to 7 percent has the same effects as increase in y. Either change makes this country a more attractive place to invest relative to the rest of the world, so the country attracts more deposits from abroad. Hence, a lower world interest rate means more foreign deposits, lower inflation, and a lower reserve requirement. Again the effects are negligible when existing debtors have a lower welfare weight (so that inflation is already low in the base case), but they become significant when existing debtors have more clout.

Simulations in which higher weights were placed on the interests of borrowers lacked interior solutions. In these cases either the inflation rate was infinite or the country was unable to attract any demand deposits at all.

Net and Gross Deposit Positions. I have assumed that net and gross deposit positions coincide. In this case the net deposit position determines how much national depositors suffer from inflation. To the extent that deposits flow in two directions, national deposits in local banks fall short of what the net position would imply. There is consequently greater incentive for the government to use the inflation tax as a source of revenue, because national lenders are less adversely affected. If gross and net positions can differ, the model makes no prediction about the magnitude of two-way flows. But what they turn out to be affects the equilibrium net position: As more domestic depositors invest abroad, the government has greater incentive to raise the inflation rate. In anticipation of higher inflation, fewer *net* deposits flow in.[11]

4.2. Loan Trade

A mirror exercise allows international trade in bank loans but treats deposits as nontraded. I do not undertake it here. A difference is that, because new *borrowers* can tap loans from the world market, monetary policy has no effect on their welfare. Lenders rather than borrowers thus bear the full incidence of the reserve requirement and the inflation tax.

4.3. Full Financial Integration

Consider now a country that faces open competition in world markets both for deposits and for loans. I continue to call (one plus) the world real deposit rate R^{*D} and the world real loan rate (plus one) R^{*L}. In order to compete in international loan markets, the national banking system cannot charge interest on loans that borrowers expect to exceed R^{*L} in real terms and must offer depositors interest rates that they expect to yield at least R^{*D} in real terms. Hence, to maintain an internationally competitive banking system, given public expectations about future inflation, the monetary authority must impose a reserve requirement that satisfies

$$R^{*D} = \lambda_t \Pi^e_{t+1} + (1 - \lambda_t) R^{*L}$$

The change in the price level as a function of the reserve requirement λ, seigniorage g, and the share of national deposits invested

---

[11] This result suggests a reason why capital flight might be associated with high inflation. The standard explanation is that capital flees to avoid the inflation tax. Another suggested here is that capital flight, by reducing the tax base, forces the government to inflate at a higher rate to achieve its seigniorage objective.

locally continues to be given by expression (5.10). Hence λ_t must satisfy

$$R^{*D} = \frac{\lambda_{t+1}^e \omega_{t+1}^e - g}{\omega_t} + (1 - \lambda_t)R^{*L} \qquad (5.13)$$

Note that, given anticipated future magnitudes, the return on domestic deposits falls with the *current* amount of demand deposits invested locally and with the current reserve requirement.[12]

Consider a steady-state situation in which the government expects to receive the same in bank deposits in the future as now, so that $\omega_t = \omega_{t+1}^e = \omega$. In this case everyone will expect the same monetary policy in the future as now, so that $\lambda_{t+1}^e = \lambda_t = \lambda$. The government will then have to set

$$\lambda = \frac{(R^{*L} - R^{*D}) - g/\omega}{R^{*L} - 1}$$

in order to remain competitive in deposit and loan markets (as it must be in order to attract deposits to earn any seigniorage whatsoever). In order to earn an amount g in seigniorage the price change must be

$$\Pi = \frac{\omega(R^{*L} - R^{*D}) - R^{*L}g}{\omega(R^{*L} - R^{*D}) - g}$$

I continue to assume that the government chooses its current reserve requirement each period before depositors decide where to invest, but that the government anticipates the subsequent deposit allocation correctly.

Depending on ω, there are two cases to consider:

1. If $\omega \geq R^{*L}g/(R^{*L} - R^{*D})$, then the government can collect its entire seigniorage requirement and continue to offer competitive interest rates. Given g, the inflation rate will be lower (and the reserve requirement higher) the larger the deposit base ω. As g rises, so does the inflation rate.
2. If $\omega < R^{*L}g/(R^{*L} - R^{*D})$, then the government cannot, even with infinite inflation, collect its entire seigniorage requirement and still offer competitive terms. The best that the government can do is to set $\lambda = (R^{*L} - R^{*D})/R^{*L}$, in which case it can collect

---

[12] The first relationship implies that an interior outcome, if it exists, is stable.

at most $(R^{*L} - R^{*D})\omega/R^{*L}$ in seigniorage. (In this case the reserve requirement is equivalent to an outright tax on deposits at rate λ.)[13]

The value of ω is itself not determined. Wherever depositors invest they earn the same rate of return. If a country *happens* to receive a large amount of deposits, then it can meet its seigniorage needs with a low inflation rate. Because it has more deposits it will have more funds available to lend, so it is more likely to become a net lender internationally. Countries that receive fewer deposits will have to impose higher inflation in order to raise a given amount of seigniorage and to impose a lower reserve requirement in order to remain internationally competitive. If the level of deposits falls below $R^{*L}g/(R^{*L} - R^{*D})$, then the government cannot earn the seigniorage that it wants even with infinite inflation.

This result suggests a fundamental indeterminacy about what countries emerge as banking centers. There may be myriad equilibria depending upon where lenders decide to put their funds. Nevertheless, a country that is trying to generate a lot of seigniorage revenue is going to need a larger level of deposits in order to remain internationally competitive. This result suggests why banking center countries as a group rely less on seigniorage revenue to finance government expenditure than other countries do.

The analysis of the closed economy case suggested the direction in which deposits and loans would flow between countries whose financial systems are initially closed if some trade were then allowed. However, once financial markets become totally open, the allocation of deposits and loans may be arbitrary. But monetary authorities concerned with maintaining their seigniorage base may not be indifferent among alternative outcomes. This result suggests why international financial markets may be as subject to restrictions on capital flows as they are: Countries experiencing large deposit outflows may, for example, seek to prohibit them in order to maintain their seigniorage base.

---

[13] If, instead, the government established the reserve requirement after depositors chose where to put their funds, then the government would be able to offer a competitive return and finance its seigniorage needs only if existing deposits met or surpassed the critical minimum. Otherwise, any small number of depositors in the country would see that there were not enough of them to allow the government to achieve its revenue objectives and leave them with a competitive return. Presumably they would also then seek to invest

5. CONCLUSION

Certain countries export the intermediation services of the banks subject to their jurisdiction, receiving deposits from abroad and making loans abroad. These countries typically have lower inflation, collect less seigniorage, and have lower reserves relative to bank assets than other countries, particularly those that are disintermediated internationally.

This chapter has developed a simple model of bank intermediation that attempts to identify factors that may be important in determining which countries become banking centers. The analysis points to the following factors as important:

1. A country is more likely to become a banking center if its political system is responsive to the interests of existing creditors relative to those of existing debtors. Such a country has less incentive to impose a high rate of inflation in order to transfer resources from creditors to debtors.
2. Because seigniorage is a tax on financial intermediation, a country that is less reliant on revenue from seigniorage is more likely to become a financial center.
3. An element of indeterminacy may be involved in that countries that *happen* to have more deposits can earn more in seigniorage with less inflation.

The analysis is meant to suggest some fundamental relationships rather than to identify all factors that are likely to be relevant. Some particularly critical omissions are the following:

1. I have identified cross-border competition with currency competition, ignoring the fact that banking systems can and do issue deposits and make loans that are denominated in foreign currencies. In principle the analysis could be extended to allow for foreign currency loans and deposits.
2. I have treated monetary policy as the outcome of the day-to-day incentives of the monetary authority. The outcome may suffer

elsewhere. Hence there are two types of equilibrium for each country, one with deposits above the threshold, and another with no deposits.

from the well-known problem of time inconsistency. For example, everyone in a country may benefit from a commitment to low inflation rate in the future even though the government may benefit from a high current level of inflation. I assume that the government responds only to its current incentives. Monetary institutions may exist, however, that make commitment to the long-run optimal policy credible.

3. Although it simplified the analysis enormously, the assumption of Cobb–Douglas preferences is special. A number of specific results would not generalize to arbitrary sets of preferences.

4. I have ignored several other factors that play an important role in international competition for banking services.

   a. In assuming that banking services do not require resources I ignore the possibility that comparative advantage in intermediation, or factor abundance in resources used intensively in banking, is a reason for trade. Comparative advantage in my model is "artificial," that is, determined by government policy, rather than the "natural" consequence of relative productivities and factor endowments.

   b. By assuming that banking is perfectly competitive I ignore the role of oligopolistic and monopolistic competition as a reason for international trade in banking services. Recent developments in international trade suggest how imperfect competition by itself can lead to cross-border trade.[14]

   c. In considering a situation of perfect certainty I ignore international diversification as a reason for cross-border intermediation.

   d. I have not considered the role of the central bank as a provider of deposit insurance and lender of last resort. Recent developments in the theory of domestic banking have suggested the contribution of insurance mechanisms to banking efficiency.[15]

Some extensions to the analysis may prove fruitful. For example, one extension would no longer treat countries as price takers in international markets for deposits and bank loans, allowing for market power and strategic interaction among the monetary author-

---

[14] Helpman and Krugman (1985) survey this literature.
[15] Diamond and Dybvig (1983) is the classic reference.

ities in different countries. The framework may usefully address the effects of harmonization of monetary policies or the integration of national monetary systems, as opposed simply to international trade in bank assets and liabilities.

The indeterminacy of the location of intermediation with fully integrated financial markets suggests how international trade in bank deposits and loans may be harmful as long as the framing of monetary policy remains a national concern. The services that banks provide are inherently connected to the policies of the monetary authorities who manage the currencies in which bank assets and liabilities are denominated. Exploiting the potential gains from international trade in financial services may require not only greater integration of financial markets, but greater integration of monetary policies as well.

APPENDIX

Table 5.A1. *Net bank cross-border positions, 1981–1985*

	Claims on foreign nonbanks	Liabilities to foreign nonbanks	Net interbank liabilities
Industrial countries			
Australia	−14,679	−130	−1,521
Austria	12,111	5,904	9,630
Belgium	66,491	23,293	49,423
Canada	−2,617	13,821	4,178
Denmark	−12,153	213	−909
France	51,035	28,343	34,183
Germany	−1,932	5,616	−343
Greece	−4,733	772	2,617
Ireland	−4,964	1,406	−2,746
Italy	−20,523	−8,237	17,104
Japan	23,172	853	31,755
Netherlands	10,017	5,782	−1,956
Norway	−4,632	2,600	−1,088
Spain	−6,934	5,080	−8,308
Sweden	−6,178	696	7,109
Switzerland	25,433	84,291	−104,203
United Kingdom	133,220	125,631	34,890
United States	42,223	−102,724	−56,626
Developing countries			
Argentina	−16,101	−5,063	4,916
Bolivia		−301	524
Brazil		−4,049	25,424
Cayman Islands	47,988	45,901	49,793
Colombia	−4,624	−2,326	−235
India		−1,425	−19,312
Indonesia		−569	−26,002
Jamaica	−418	−79	−19,187
Korea		68	11,395
Malaysia	−6,299	−606	−2,091
Mexico	−54,892	−9,389	24,464
Panama	16,486	−11,461	10,306
Peru		−1,280	−20,816
Philippines	−5,334	3,206	3,180
Singapore	29,610	20,136	8,655
Uruguay	−924	−1,141	−15,944

Note: Annual averages in millions of current U.S. dollars.

Table 5.A2. *Net bank cross-border positions, 1986–1990*

	Claims on foreign nonbanks	Liabilities to foreign nonbanks	Net interbank liabilities
Industrial countries			
Australia	−24,059	459	15,581
Austria	23,289	14,831	15,667
Belgium	127,990	93,376	29,929
Canada	−12,024	17,497	662
Denmark	−24,288	299	−3,267
France	92,396	65,344	48,057
Germany	12,483	−27,001	−79,532
Greece	−6,957	2,319	6,372
Ireland	−11,036	823	−2,135
Italy	−37,664	−8,282	54,650
Japan	58,143	−4,319	148,141
Netherlands	6,588	4,619	−19,270
Norway	−4,755	8,139	4,395
Spain	−3,715	9,556	−20,062
Sweden	−1,906	4,533	29,782
Switzerland	44,678	147,337	−204,371
United Kingdom	182,418	206,052	42,467
United States	−84,675	−155,666	47,015
Developing countries			
Argentina	−21,730	−9,989	9,895
Bolivia		−386	78
Brazil		−12,938	53,339
Cayman Islands	111,870	98,838	147,321
Colombia	−5,488	−3,460	−628
India		−2,104	−42,880
Indonesia		−2,099	−17,069
Jamaica	−383	−306	−15,865
Korea		−314	4,468
Malaysia	−6,890	−957	−6,020
Mexico	−51,628	−6,774	16,155
Panama	−9,144	−28,943	−33,489
Peru		−2,443	−17,117
Philippines	−4,610	−296	969
Singapore	75,119	46,329	16,195
Uruguay	−609	−1,847	−34,913

Note: Annual averages in millions of current U.S. dollars.

Table 5.A3. Cross-border positions and financial characteristics, 1981–1985

	Net claims on foreign nonbanks	Net liabilities to foreign nonbanks	Net interbank liabilities	Seigniorage/ GDP	Quasi-money/ GDP	Producer price inflation	Reserve money/ Quasi-money
Industrial countries							
Australia	-0.199	-0.002	-0.020	0.006	0.299	0.054	0.191
Austria	0.121	0.059	0.097	0.004	0.681	0.036	0.162
Belgium	0.543	0.189	0.407	0.001	0.239	0.089	0.389
Canada	-0.012	0.065	0.020	0.001	0.348	0.053	0.135
Denmark	-0.410	0.005	-0.029	0.011	0.289	0.083	0.148
France	0.079	0.044	0.053	0.006	0.437	0.096	0.149
Germany	-0.003	0.007	0.000	0.003	0.400	0.041	0.238
Greece	-0.223	0.036	0.123	0.038	0.449	0.210	0.461
Ireland	-0.492	0.147	-0.216	0.006	0.269	0.091	0.391
Italy	-0.061	-0.025	0.051	0.020	0.329	0.117	0.461
Japan	0.015	0.001	0.022	0.005	0.637	-0.001	0.147
Netherlands	0.057	0.033	-0.011	0.004	0.537	0.044	0.133
Norway	-0.137	0.076	-0.036	0.004	0.381	0.070	0.172
Spain	-0.041	0.029	-0.047	0.034	0.503	0.124	0.396
Sweden	-0.087	0.009	0.101	0.004	0.518	0.096	0.131
Switzerland	0.118	0.390	-0.481	0.002	0.850	0.029	0.236
United Kingdom	0.189	0.179	0.048	0.001	0.243	-0.020	0.175
United States	0.023	-0.055	-0.031	0.003	0.433	0.029	0.130

Developing countries

Argentina	-0.703	-0.222	0.218	0.160	0.205	3.930	0.996
Bolivia		-0.848	1.250	0.090	0.061		2.472
Brazil		-0.113	0.660	0.022	0.043	2.330	1.227
Cayman Islands							
Colombia	-0.581	-0.299	-0.026	0.018	0.086	0.229	1.273
India		-0.019	-0.295	0.018	0.248	0.073	0.526
Indonesia		-0.024	-1.050	0.008	0.090	0.105	0.820
Jamaica	-0.347	-0.068	-15.964	0.030	0.317		0.378
Korea		0.001	0.219	0.003	0.253	0.054	0.242
Malaysia	-0.275	-0.026	-0.101	0.010	0.405	-0.041	0.308
Mexico	-1.290	-0.221	0.581	0.059	0.199	0.624	0.847
Panama	0.604	-0.437	0.437	0.003	0.313	0.030	0.151
Peru		-0.327	-5.590	0.066	0.129		0.996
Philippines	-0.358	0.206	0.217	0.011	0.200	0.221	0.348
Singapore	1.258	0.838	0.344	0.015	0.457	-0.052	0.373
Uruguay	-0.252	-0.315	-3.064	0.031	0.411	0.528	0.226

Note: Cross-border positions as a ratio to total commercial bank assets. All data are annual averages.

Table 5.A4. Cross-border positions and financial characteristics, 1986–1990

	Net claims on foreign nonbanks	Net liabilities to foreign nonbanks	Net interbank liabilities	Seigniorage/GDP	Quasi-money/GDP	Producer price inflation	Reserve money/Quasi-money
Industrial countries							
Australia	-0.165	0.001	0.096	0.004	0.380	0.031	0.145
Austria	0.104	0.065	0.070	0.004	0.734	-0.006	0.135
Belgium	0.474	0.332	0.127	0.001	0.278	-0.018	0.269
Canada	-0.039	0.061	0.000	0.002	0.304	0.021	0.138
Denmark	-0.241	0.005	-0.034	-0.001	0.320	0.008	0.160
France	0.068	0.047	0.035	0.001	0.417	0.022	0.149
Germany	0.007	-0.014	-0.043	0.008	0.421	0.002	0.245
Greece	-0.180	0.058	0.168	0.027	0.503	0.131	0.370
Ireland	-0.528	0.047	-0.094	0.006	0.294	0.011	0.329
Italy	-0.055	-0.012	0.080	0.008	0.421	0.002	0.490
Japan	0.015	-0.001	0.035	0.010	0.807	-0.019	0.131
Netherlands	0.022	0.014	-0.045	0.007	0.584	0.002	0.148
Norway	-0.057	0.096	0.051	0.001	0.338	0.464	0.168
Spain	-0.009	0.023	-0.051	0.021	0.419	0.022	0.505
Sweden	-0.017	0.024	0.167	0.008	0.511	0.035	0.139
Switzerland	0.097	0.315	-0.436	-0.003	0.932	0.004	0.159
United Kingdom	0.112	0.123	0.024	0.004	0.474	0.015	0.097
United States	0.444	-0.056	0.016	0.004	0.442	0.025	0.133

Developing countries

Argentina	−0.988	−0.448	0.455	0.084	0.192	10.080	0.710
Bolivia		−0.472	0.083	0.019	0.108		0.629
Brazil		−0.111	0.511	0.057	0.075	5.820	1.039
Cayman Islands							
Colombia	−0.703	−0.444	−0.105	0.026	0.085	0.260	1.115
India		−0.019	−0.388	0.022	0.298	0.076	0.514
Indonesia		−0.054	−0.366	0.008	0.211	0.090	0.346
Jamaica	−0.212	−0.166	−7.538	0.034	0.330		0.563
Korea		−0.002	0.064	0.015	0.290	0.015	0.253
Malaysia	−0.225	−0.028	−0.186	0.017	0.486	0.039	0.295
Mexico	−1.250	−0.174	0.391	0.021	0.146	0.743	0.493
Panama	−1.001	−2.645	−1.818	−0.001	0.319	−0.019	0.090
Peru		−0.704	−4.480	0.073	0.080		1.384
Philippines	−0.339	−0.024	0.087	0.018	0.218	0.108	0.430
Singapore	1.567	1.011	0.307	0.016	0.631	0.012	0.291
Uruguay	−0.125	−0.351	−8.205	0.040	0.448	0.737	0.219

Note: Cross-border positions as a ratio to total commercial bank assets. All data are annual averages.

Table 5.A5. *Financial characteristics of banking center and nonbanking center countries*

	Net interbank position ($billion)	Seigniorage/ GDP	Quasi-money/ GDP	Producer price inflation	Reserve money/ Quasi-money
1981–85					
Industrial countries					
Banks	7,674	0.003	0.517	0.039	0.199
Nonbanks	−3,685	0.012	0.383	0.088	0.259
Developing countries					
Banks	29,224	0.015	0.457	−0.052	0.373
Nonbanks	−1,670	0.038	0.211	0.735	0.772
1986–90					
Industrial countries					
Banks	−14,587	0.003	0.569	0.003	0.159
Nonbanks	16,800	0.008	0.421	0.029	0.246
Developing countries					
Banks	81,758	0.016	0.631	0.012	0.291
Nonbanks	−5,934	0.031	0.235	1.632	0.577

dYB	dOB	dOL=1	$y = 1$, $g = .005$, $R*D = 1.075$	$y = 1.01$, $g = .005$, $R*D = 1.075$	$y = 1$, $g = .010$, $R*D = 1.075$	$y = 1$, $g = .005$, $R*D = 1.070$
.95	.90	res. req. (l)	.100	.100	.100	.100
		dom. dep. (w)	1.02	1.03	1.02	1.03
		inflation	.05	.05	.10	.05
.95	.93	res. req. (l)	.008	.073	.013	.056
		dom. dep. (w)	.93	1.003	.93	.98
		inflation	2.08	.07	4.40	.10
1	.90	res. req. (l)	.095	.095	.100	.095
		dom. dep. (w)	1.02	1.03	1.02	1.02
		inflation	.05	.054	.11	.05
1	.93	res. req. (l)	.007	.070	.012	.038
		dom. dep. (w)	.93	1.00	.93	.96
		inflation	3.24	.08	6.73	.16
1.05	.90	res. req. (l)	.091	.091	.100	.091
		dom. dep. (w)	1.01	1.02	1.01	1.02
		inflation	.06	.06	.11	.06
1.05	.93	res. req. (l)	.007	.054	.012	.030
		dom. dep. (w)	.93	.98	.93	.96
		inflation	4.40	.100	9.06	.21

174 J. EATON

REFERENCES

Aliber, R. Z. (1984), International Banking: A Survey, *Journal of Money, Credit, and Banking* 16: 661–78.

Alworth, J. S., and S. Andresen (1992), The Determinants of Cross-Border Non-Bank Deposits and the Competitiveness of Financial Market Centres, *Money Affairs*.

Diamond, D., and P. E. Dybvig (1983), Bank Runs, Deposit Insurance, and Liquidity, *Journal of Political Economy* 91: 401–9.

Fischer, S. (1982), Seigniorage and the Case for a National Money, *Journal of Political Economy* 90: 295–313.

Garber, P. M., and S. Weisbrod (1993), Opening the Financial Services Market. In P. M. Garber, ed., *The Mexico–U.S. Free Trade Agreement*, Cambridge, MA: MIT Press.

Helpman, E., and P. R. Krugman (1985), *Market Structure and Foreign Trade*, Cambridge, MA: MIT Press.

Lewis, M. K., and K. T. Davis (1987), *Domestic and International Banking*, Cambridge, MA: MIT Press.

Samuelson, P. A. (1958), An Exact Consumption-Loan Model with or without the Social Contrivance of Money, *Journal of Political Economy* 66: 467–82.

Stiglitz, J. E., and A. Weiss (1981), Credit Rationing in Markets with Imperfect Information, *American Economic Review* 71: 393–411.

CHAPTER 6

Immigration and Growth under Imperfect Capital Mobility: The Case of Israel

Zvi Hercowitz, Nirit Kantor, and Leora Rubin Meridor

1. INTRODUCTION

An influx of immigrants from the Soviet Union began to arrive in Israel in 1989. By the end of 1992 approximately 450,000 had arrived, comprising 10 percent of the 1989 population, and more are expected in the next few years. This wave was triggered by glasnost, and therefore, from the point of view of the Israeli economy, the *occurrence* of this immigration is clearly an exogenous event. However, its *magnitude* can be considered related to the domestic macroeconomic conditions.

Because the immigrants possess practically no physical or financial capital, the direct effect of the immigration is a decline in the capital/labor ratio. This implies lower real wages and higher unemployment during the first few years, which in turn diminish the potential immigrants' benefits from immigration. The degree of international capital mobility is an important factor in this context: Less capital mobility implies slower capital accumulation, and hence lower real wage and higher unemployment paths.

The aim of this chapter is to analyze and quantify the implications of the degree of capital mobility for immigration and growth, in the face of an open window of emigration abroad (from the Commonwealth of Independent States [CIS]) for a given period. The framework of the present analysis is a neoclassical small-open economy growth model, where imperfect capital mobility is represented by an upward sloping supply curve of foreign funds. The shape of this curve is parametrized empirically and it is exogenously given. Therefore, the cost of borrowing is not derived from the model itself, as in Eaton and Gersovitz (1981). The basic notion here is that the supply schedule of foreign funds is subject to exogenous changes, which may follow from special loans granted by

175

international organizations or other governments. A recent example is the $10 billion loan guarantees extended by the United States government to Israel in 1992.

The decision to immigrate in this framework depends on expected income flows. Although there is no aggregate uncertainty in the model presented here, the job search process involves individual uncertainty. Immigrants have a reservation level for the expected present value of income (which should reflect the alternative income flows abroad and the once-and-for-all migration costs). Hence, assuming identical individuals, the immigrant "supply curve" is perfectly elastic at the reservation income level. Given that the number of immigrants also affects the capital/labor ratio and hence – through unemployment and real wages – the expected present value of income, the "demand curve for immigrants," is downward-sloping. The equilibrium immigration flows are then determined by the combination of these two factors. The tightening of foreign borrowing implies a lower path for the capital/labor ratio and hence yields lower present values of future income. In other words, this change implies a leftward shift of the "demand curve," and consequently lower immigration flows.

The mechanism described previously differs from the two-country neoclassical analysis of migration and capital mobility, which suggests that the opening of factor mobility between two economies with initially different capital/labor ratios causes factor migration until these ratios are eventually equalized (assuming the same constant-returns technology). Labor migrates to the capital-intensive country and/or capital flows to the labor-intensive country. Then, the lower the degree of capital mobility (for some exogenous reason), the larger should be the migration of labor. In other words, there should be a negative relationship between capital mobility and migration. By contrast, the present framework of a small open economy facing a given supply of funds schedule displays the opposite characteristic: The lower the degree of capital mobility, the *smaller* the migration of labor. The difference stems from the assumption that the interest rate schedule faced by the small open economy is unaffected by the opening of new world migration possibilities.

The analysis is carried out by simulating the model, after calibrating it to Israeli data. A simulation consists of computing paths for the different variables starting in a base period, taken here as

1992. Then the main analysis consists of changing the degree of capital mobility by shifting the schedule of the supply of funds and computing the resulting change in immigration and the other macroeconomic variables. Additionally, the present framework was used to address the quantitative implications of changes in the immigrants' income reservation level.

The remainder of the paper is organized as follows. Section 2 presents the model. Its empirical calibration to Israeli data is discussed in Section 3, and Section 4 addresses the simulation of the model and the results. Section 5 presents concluding remarks.

2. THE MODEL

The structure of the domestic economy is described in Section 2.1, where the number of immigrants is treated as exogenous. Section 2.2 incorporates the endogenous determination of immigration.

2.1. Exogenous Immigration

The population of a competitive open economy at time zero is N_0. All original residents at time zero are employed. Starting from period one an exogenous immigration wave of $\{A_t\}_{t=1}^{\tau}$ arrives for τ periods. The population N_t includes the employed E_t (N_0 plus the number of immigrants who found employment), and the unemployed, U_t, who are immigrants.

Production in the economy takes place according to the technology

$$Y_t = F(K_t, L_t) = [\alpha K_t^\sigma + (1 - \alpha]L_t^\sigma)^{1/\sigma}, \quad 0 < \alpha < 1, \quad \sigma < 1 \quad (6.1)$$

where K_t is the net capital stock and $L_t = N_0 \ell_t^o + (E_t - N_0)\ell_t^e$ is the total input of work hours, with ℓ_t^o and ℓ_t^e as the hours worked per member of the original population and employed immigrant, respectively. The capital stock is thought of as combining private (including housing) and public capital. In Hercowitz and Meridor (1993) the private nonresidential, the private residential, and the public capital stocks are determined separately in a simpler growth model with exogenous immigration and a constant interest rate.

The capital stock evolves according to

$$K_{t+1} = K_t(1 - \delta) + I_t, \qquad 0 < \delta < 1 \tag{6.2}$$

with I_t as gross investment. Changing the capital stock entails the adjustment costs

$$J_t = \frac{\phi}{2}(K_{t+1} - K_t)^2 \tag{6.3}$$

Social welfare in this economy is given by

$$\sum_{t=1}^{\infty} \beta^{t-1}\{(1 - \theta_t^e - \theta_t^u)u(c_t^o, \ell_t^o) + \theta_t^e u(c_t^e, \ell_t^e) + \theta_t^u u(c_t^u, 0)\}, \tag{6.4}$$

where $u(\cdot)$ is the momentary utility function, θ_t^e and θ_t^u are weights, and c_t^o, c_t^e, and c_t^u are the per-capita consumption levels of the original residents, employed immigrants, and unemployed immigrants respectively. The function $u(\cdot)$ is parametrized as

$$u(c, \ell) = \ln\left(c_t - \frac{\mu}{1 + \psi}\ell_t^{1+\psi}\right), \qquad \mu, \psi > 0 \tag{6.4'}$$

At time t the economy faces the real interest rate r_t. Defining $R_0 = 1$ and $R_t = 1/(1 + r_t)$ for $t > 0$, the intertemporal resource constraint is

$$\sum_{t=1}^{\infty} \prod_{i=1}^{t} R_{i-1}[C_t + K_{t+1} - (1 - \delta)K_t + J_t + G_t - Y_t - V_t] + (1 + r_0)D_0 \tag{6.5}$$

where $C_t = N_0 c_t^o + (E_t - N_0)c_t^e + U_t c_t^u$, G_t is government expenditures, V_t is unilateral transfers from abroad, and D_0 is the net foreign debt at the beginning of period one. The flows G_t and V_t are exogenous and are included for empirical purposes only.

The number of immigrants is $A_t > 0$ for $t = 1, 2, \ldots, \tau$ and zero for $t > \tau$. Hence, $N_t = N_{t-1} + A_t$ for $t \leq \tau$, and $N_t = N_\tau$ for $t > \tau$. The evolution of employment is determined by

$$E_t = E_{t-1} + \gamma_t(N_t - E_{t-1}), \qquad 0 < \gamma_t < 1 \tag{6.6}$$

where $\gamma_t = \gamma(\cdot)$ is the probability that a job seeker (the unemployed in $t - 1$ plus current immigrants) finds a job during period t. The probability γ_t depends on the degree of tightness in the labor market, but the individual takes γ_t as given. The form and arguments of the function $\gamma(\cdot)$ are specified in Section 3.

Finally, the economy is assumed to start with a positive foreign debt. Hence, the interest rate in the economy is determined along the supply function of foreign funds.

$$r_t = \left(\frac{D_{t-1}}{Y_{t-1}}\right) \quad \text{with} \quad r' \geq 0 \tag{6.7}$$

This function captures the imperfect nature of capital mobility, with $r' = 0$ for D/Y up to a critical value $(D/Y)_0$ and $r' > 0$ for higher values, up to a borrowing ceiling $\overline{(D/Y)}$. The case of perfect capital mobility would correspond to $(D/Y)_0 \to \infty$. This foreign borrowing cost function is of the type derived by Eaton and Gersovitz (1981) in a framework with default risk. In the present context the specification of $r(\cdot)$ is admittedly ad hoc because default risk is not analyzed.[1]

The Planning Problem. The artificial planning problem solved here is constructed so that its solution matches the outcome of a competitive environment. The problem is to find $[c_t^o, c_t^e, c_t^u, l_t^o, l_t^e, K_{t+1}]_{t=1}^\infty$ so as to maximize the social welfare function in (6.4), subject to the technological constraints (6.1), (6.2), and (6.3) and the resource constraint (6.5), taking as given $[r_t]_{t=0}^\infty$, D_0, K_0, $[G_t, V_t]_{t=1}^\infty$ and the probabilities $[\gamma_t]_{t=1}^\infty$ in the employment evolution equation (6.6). Hence, externalities through the functions $r(\cdot)$ and $\gamma(\cdot)$ are not taken into account. At each point in time, the state of the economy is given by the capital stock, K_t; the previous population and employment, N_{t-1} and E_{t-1}; and the foreign debt, D_{t-1}.

The first-order conditions for the planner's problem are

$$\beta^{t-1}(1 - \theta_t^e - \theta_t^u)u_c(c_t^o, \ell_t^o) - \lambda \prod_{i=1}^{t} R_{i-1}N_0 = 0 \qquad (c_t^o) \tag{6.8}$$

$$\beta^{t-1}(1 - \theta_t^e - \theta_t^u)u_\ell(c_t^o, \ell_t^o) - \lambda \prod_{i=1}^{t} R_{i-1}F_\ell(K_t, L_t)N_0 = 0 \qquad (\ell_t^o) \tag{6.9}$$

$$\beta^{t-1}\theta_t^e u_c(c_t^e, \ell_t^e) - \lambda \prod_{i=1}^{t} R_{i-1}(E_t - N_0) = 0 \qquad (c_t^e) \tag{6.10}$$

$$\beta^{t-1}\theta_t^e u_\ell(c_t^e, \ell_t^e) - \lambda \prod_{i=1}^{t} R_{i-1}F_\ell(K_t, L_t)(E_t - N_0) = 0 \qquad (\ell_t^e) \tag{6.11}$$

---

[1] In the present framework, D_t is the net debt and hence there is no separate demand for reserves. Ben-Bassat and Gottlieb (1992) estimate a model in which the country risk diminishes with the amount of reserves held.

$$\beta^{t-1}\theta_t^u u_c(c_t^u, 0) - \lambda \prod_{i=1}^{t} R_{i-1} U_t = 0 \qquad\qquad (c_t^u) \qquad (6.12)$$

$$\prod_{i=1}^{t} R_{i-1}[1 + \phi(K_{t+1} - K_t)] - \prod_{i=1}^{t+1} R_{i-1}[F_k(K_{t+1}, L_{t+1}) + 1 - \delta$$

$$+ \phi(K_{t+2} - K_{t+1})] = 0 \qquad\qquad (K_{t+1}) \qquad (6.13)$$

where λ is the Lagrangian multiplier associated with the constraint in (6.5).

Given the utility function in (6.4′) the hours of work of both original residents and employed immigrants are determined by[2]

$$\mu(\ell_t^o)^\psi = \mu(\ell_t^e)^\psi = \mu\ell_t^\psi = F_\ell(K_t, L_t) \qquad (6.14)$$

Labor effort depends only on its marginal productivity, and, hence, there is no wealth effect on this decision.

The individual consumption levels are

$$c_t^o = \left(\frac{1 - \theta_t^e - \theta_t^u}{N_0} \right) \frac{\beta^{t-1}}{\lambda\Pi_{i=1}^t R_{i-1}} + \frac{\mu}{1 + \psi}\ell_t^{1+\psi} \qquad (6.15a)$$

$$c_t^e = \left(\frac{\theta_t^e}{E_t - N_0} \right) \frac{\beta^{t-1}}{\lambda\Pi_{i=1}^t R_{i-1}} + \frac{\mu}{1 + \psi}\ell_t^{1+\psi} \qquad (6.15b)$$

$$c_t^u = \left(\frac{\theta_t^u}{U_t} \right) \frac{\beta^{t-1}}{\lambda\Pi_{i=1}^t R_{i-1}} \qquad (6.15c)$$

Total consumption is therefore

$$C_t = N_0 c_t^o + (E_t - N_0)c_t^e + U_t c_t^u = \frac{\beta^{t-1}}{\lambda\Pi_{i=1}^t R_{i-1}} + \frac{\mu}{1 + \psi}\ell_t^{1+\psi}E_t \qquad (6.16)$$

The solution to the preceding planning problem has the following decentralized interpretation. Competition in the labor market implies that $F_\ell(K_t, L_t)$ equals the real wage, w_t, while the government grants unemployment benefits, b, to each of the unemployed. The government finances the unemployment benefits and expenditures, G_t, partly with its share in the transfers from abroad, V_t, and the rest with lump-sum taxes. The weights θ_t^e and θ_t^u, determining the consumption levels in (6.15), are assumed to be such that the solutions for c_t^e and c_t^u match the decentralized consumption decisions of immigrants when they receive labor income when employed and unemployment benefits when unemployed. Note that

---

[2] This can be verified by substituting the marginal utilities from (6.4′) into (6.8)–(6.11) and dividing (6.9) by (6.8) and (6.11) by (6.10).

under the present utility function, labor supply of both individual types (equation [6.14]) and total consumption (equation [6.16]) are independent of the weights in the social welfare function.

Regarding foreign borrowing, it is assumed that the government does not intervene in a monopsonistic manner.

2.2. Endogenous Immigration

The previous planning problem can be easily extended to a situation where the immigration flows, $\{A_t\}_{t=1}^{\tau}$, are endogenous. The competitive interpretation implies that the immigration flows are taken as given by all individual agents, and hence the form of the solution does not change when immigration is endogenous. The model is now closed by incorporating the immigration decision.

From the point of view of the potential identical immigrants, the main economic magnitude is the expected present value of total income – defined as $w_t \bar{\ell}$, where $\bar{\ell}$ is the endowment of time. The expected present value of income depends on w_t, b, and the probability of being employed for each period after immigration. For an immigrant arriving in period t, the probabilities of being employed in $t, t + 1, \ldots$, and so on, are

$$_t P_t = \gamma_t$$

$$_t P_{t+1} = \gamma_t + (1 - \gamma_t)\gamma_{t+1}$$

$$_t P_{t+2} = \gamma_t + (1 - \gamma_t)\gamma_{t+1} + (1 - \gamma_t)(1 - \gamma_{t+1})\gamma_{t+2}$$

etc.

Then, the expected present value of income to a period t immigrant is

$$W_t = {}_t P_t w_t \bar{\ell} + (1 - {}_t P_t)b \sum_{j=1}^{\infty} \prod_{i=0}^{j-1} R_{t+i}[{}_t P_{t+j}w_{t+j}\bar{\ell} + (1 - {}_t P_{t+j})b] \quad (6.17)$$

The potential immigrant in period t has a reservation level, $\bar{W}_t$, for the expected present value of income, and thus immigrates only if $W_t \geq \bar{W}_t$. Given that all prospective immigrants are identical, the "supply curve" of immigrants at time $1 \leq t \leq \tau$ is infinitely elastic at $\bar{W}_t$. After τ, immigration is zero.

The model also generates a "demand curve" for immigrants, which reflects the diminishing marginal productivity of labor and the crowding of the labor market that reduces the probability of finding a job. Both effects imply that W_t falls with A_t, although each immigrant takes W_t as given. Hence, immigration in period t is such that it equates W_t to $\bar{W}_t$. Note that W_t depends not only on A_t, but also on the immigration flows in the other immigration years. Hence, all $\{A_t\}_{t=1}^{\tau}$ should be determined simultaneously.

It is assumed that the original residents do not emigrate. This is consistent with a situation in which the present value of income at home is higher than the alternative present value abroad less emigration costs. In any event, in the Israeli case emigration since 1989 is negligible relative to immigration.

3. CALIBRATION OF THE MODEL

Quantitatively, the dynamic behavior of the model depends crucially on the values of the base-period state variables, and on the parametrization of two functions: the probability of finding a job $\gamma(\cdot)$ and the supply of foreign funds $r(\cdot)$.

The base period of the simulation is taken as 1992, to capture the implications of the massive immigration during the 1989–92 period. The initial state variables are the population or labor force, N_{92}; the employment level, E_{92}; the foreign debt, D_{92}; and the capital stock, K_{93} (corresponding to the end of 1992). First, the normalization $N_{92} = 1$ is adopted, and D_{92} is determined so as to match the foreign debt/GDP ratio of 0.24 in 1992. The remaining state variables are E_{92} and K_{93}. Assuming that in 1989, prior to the influx of immigrants, the economy was at a steady state, initial 1992 employment and 1993 capital stock are specified as follows.

The unemployment rate in 1992 is 11.2 percent, whereas in the preimmigration year, 1989, it was 8.9 percent. Given that in the model only immigrants may be unemployed, the model's unemployment rate for the base year 1992 – $(N_{92} - E_{92})/N_{92}$ – is set equal to $0.112 - 0.089 = 0.023$. Given that $N_{92} = 1$, that equality implies that $E_{92} = 0.977$. According to this procedure the unemployment rate among 1989–92 immigrants in 1992 should be 27.8 percent. The actual figure is fairly close: 28.9 percent.

The initial capital stock is determined through similar considerations. Starting from a steady-state capital stock in 1989, K_{93} is computed according to the change in the net stock per participant in the labor force. Specifically, the total net stock increased from 1989 to 1992 by 10.3 percent, while the labor force increased by 17.2 percent. Hence, the initial 1992 capital stock is assumed to be $(1 + 0.172)/(1 + 0.103) - 1 = 0.059$ lower than the steady-state level corresponding to $N = N_{92}$.

The probability of finding a job is adopted from Flug, Hercowitz, and Levi (1993), who estimated the specification

$$\gamma_t = \gamma(\hat{u}_t, z_t) = \gamma_0 - \gamma_1 \hat{u}_t + \gamma_2 z_t, \qquad \gamma_0, \gamma_1, \gamma_2 > 0 \qquad (6.18)$$

where z_t represents the current innovation in labor demand and $\hat{u}_t$ is the unemployment rate net of the effects of current labor demand innovations. Equation (6.18) reflects externalities of immigration (which increase $\hat{u}_t$) and investment (affecting z_t) on the crowding of the labor market. They estimated $\hat{u}_t$ as a linear projection of the unemployment rate on various lagged variables. We implement (6.18) here by using

$$\hat{u}_t = u_{t-1} = \frac{(N_{t-1} - E_{t-1})}{N_{t-1}} + 0.089 \quad \text{and}$$

$$z_t = \log Y_t - \eta_{\ell t} \log L_t - (\log Y_{t-1} - \eta_{\ell t+1} \log L_{t-1})$$

where $\eta_{\ell t} = (1 - \alpha)(L_t/Y_t)^\sigma$ is the elasticity of output with respect to hours of work. The variable z_t, therefore, approximates the shift in labor productivity. The measure of $\hat{u}_t$ includes 0.089, which was the unemployment rate in 1989 prior to the immigration influx, because $(N_t - E_t)/N_t$ measures the unemployment of immigrants only. The estimates of the parameters in (6.18) from Flug, Hercowitz, and Levi (1993) are $\gamma_0 = 0.88$, $\gamma_1 = 4.7$, and $\gamma_2 = 1.58$. These values imply, for example, that if $\hat{u}_t = 0.1$ and $z_t = 0$ the probability that a job seeker finds a job within one year is $0.88 - 0.47 = 0.41$. If, at the same time, the productivity of labor increases by 2 percent, the probability increases by $1.58 \times 0.02 = 0.0216$ to 0.4316.

The supply curve of foreign debt was parametrized using data on the external debt and interest rates in the last decade, during which the debt/output ratio varied from 0.24 to 0.8. It also takes into account the $10 billion loan guarantees from the United States granted in 1993, by shifting the $r(\cdot)$ schedule to the right. The simulations reported in Section 4 address the effects of these loan

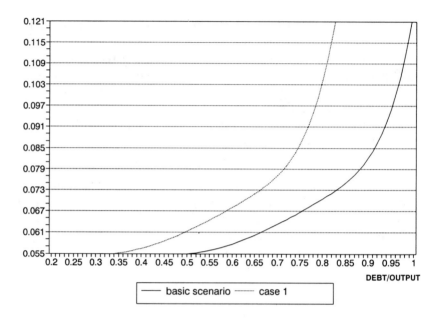

Figure 6.1. Borrowing cost function.

guarantees. The empirical $r(\cdot)$ function is accordingly set flat at 5.5 percent for $D/Y < 0.51$ and then the slope increases gradually as shown in Figure 6.1.

A key set of exogenous variables is $\{\bar{W}_t\}_{t=1}^{\tau}$ – the reservation levels for the expected values of future income. The discussion of how these values are computed is left for the next section.

To complete the calibration of the model, values have to be assigned to the technology parameters, α, σ, δ, and ϕ, and to the preference parameters, μ and ψ. Also, the exogenous sequences $[G_t, V_t]_{t=1}^{\infty}$ should be specified, along with the unemployment benefits, b. The considerations adopted and the resulting values for all parameters and exogenous variables appear in Appendix A.

4. SIMULATION OF THE MODEL

The focus of the simulation analysis is on the implications of the degree of capital mobility for immigration and macroeconomic performance. The degree of capital mobility, or the availability of foreign funds, is represented by the horizontal location of the $r(\cdot)$ curve. Increasing capital mobility implies that the $r(\cdot)$ curve shifts to the right, and hence the interest rate begins to rise at a higher debt/output ratio. The extreme case of perfect capital mobility corresponds to a flat interest rate curve at 5.5 percent. The technical aspects of the solution are described in Appendix B.

The simulation consists of two stages. The first is the computation of a basic scenario, resulting in benchmark paths for the endogenous variables from 1993 onward. In the second step, the supply of foreign funds is reduced by shifting the $r(\cdot)$ curve to the left by an amount corresponding to the $10 billion of U.S. loan guarantees. The purpose is to assess the implications of these guarantees for immigration and macroeconomic performance.

The basic scenario is characterized by three elements: (i) a base period that captures the main features of 1992, as described in Section 3; (ii) a supply function of foreign funds, as parametrized in Section 3; and (iii) a flow of 80,000 immigrants per annum for five years, starting in 1993. It is assumed, therefore, that the five-year flow of 80,000 immigrants is consistent with the conditions in (i) and (ii). This assumption is important because then the expected present values of future income W_t computed from the basic simulation (for each of the five immigration years) can be taken as the reservation levels, $\bar{W}_t$, of immigrants in the corresponding years.

The paths for the main macroeconomic variables in the basic scenario are presented in Figures 6.2 to 6.7. As shown in Figure 6.2, investment in the first years is high, given the initially low capital/labor ratio and the new immigration. Investment is financed by additional foreign borrowing of about $16 billion, or 117 percent of the initial debt, over the first nine years (Figure 6.3). The maximal debt/output ratio is 0.48, below the 0.51 level at which the interest rate begins to rise. Hence, in the basic scenario the imperfections of capital mobility are not at work.

Given the initial conditions, the starting (1992) real wage is lower than the steady-state level by 1.3 percent. This figure is between the actual decline from 1989 to 1992 of 0.43 percent, when the real wage is computed with the output price deflator, and the 5 percent decline when the cost-of-living index is used. The real wage in the simulation (Figure 6.5) declines further in 1993, and then it has a general upward trend that becomes clear after immigration stops in 1997.

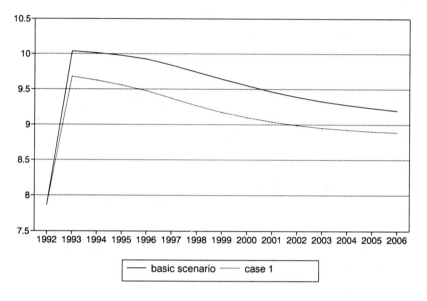

Figure 6.2. Investment (billions of 1992$).

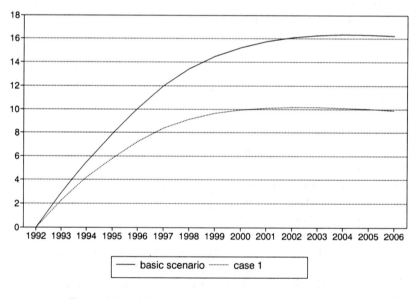

Figure 6.3. Additional external debt (billions of 1992$).

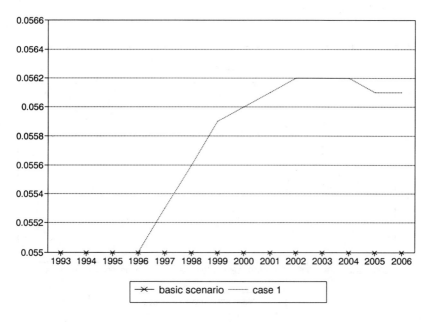

Figure 6.4. The interest rate.

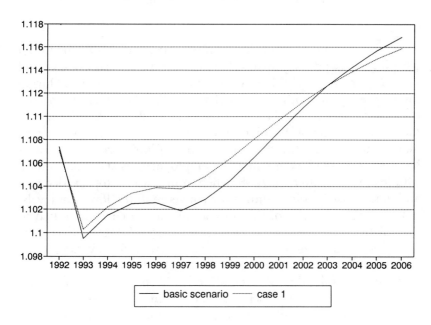

Figure 6.5. Real wage.

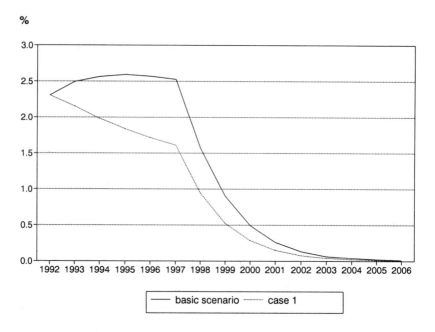

Figure 6.6. Unemployment rate over the 1989 level.

Figures 6.6 and 6.7 plot the unemployment rate above the initial 1992 level, u_t, and the probability of finding a job during one year of search, γ_t, respectively. The two variables interact strongly. During the first few years both γ_t and u_t increase. This behavior of γ_t occurs because capital accumulation increases labor demand, outweighing the negative effect of the unemployment rate. Similarly, the upward movement in u_t implies that the number of job searchers increases by more than the increase in γ_t. Unemployment is stabilized after a couple of years. After 1997–98, when immigration stops, u_t declines and γ_t increases rapidly, until they converge to the long-run levels.

In the second stage of the simulation the $r(\cdot)$ curve is shifted to the left by $10 billion, or 17 percent of the 1992 GDP. Given that $r(\cdot)$ depends on the current D/Y ratio, that shift may exaggerate somewhat the effects of the U.S. loan guarantees.

Reduced availability of foreign funds affects immigration by depressing the expected present value of immigrant income through three channels: (i) higher interest rates slow down capital accumulation and hence labor demand and real wages are reduced; (ii)

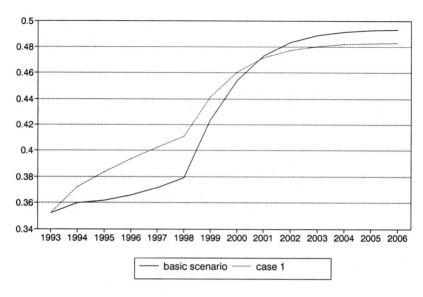

Figure 6.7. Probability of finding employment.

lower labor demand, and thus z_t values, also implies smaller probabilities, γ_t and $_tP_{t+i}$, $i = 0, 1, \ldots ,$ of finding a job and being
employed after immigration, respectively; and (iii) higher interest
rates directly depress the present values W_t. This can be visualized
as a leftward shift of the economy's demand curve for immigrants.
Given the reservation levels $\bar{W}_{93}, \ldots , \bar{W}_{97}$ computed in the basic
scenario, which represent flat supply curves of immigrants, the
immigration flows $A_{93}, \ldots , A_{97}$ decline. To simplify the calculations, a uniform flow during the five-year period is computed by
minimizing the absolute deviations of the five resulting W_t values
from the corresponding $\bar{W}_t$ values. Given that each of the resulting
present values is very close to the corresponding reservation levels,
this procedure seems to give a reasonable approximation.

As a result of tightening the supply of funds by \$10 billion immi-
gration is reduced from 400,000 over the 1993–97 period to 262,500
(or by 34 percent). Relative to the 1992 population, the impact is of
3 percent. It should be noted, however, that this is an average
calculation. Not all of the entire \$10 billion of loan guarantees is
effective, whereas the first dollars have a strong effect.

The resulting paths appear in Figures 6.2–6.7 under "Case 1."

As expected, the tighter supply of funds reduces investment and foreign borrowing (Figures 6.2 and 6.3) and increases interest rates (Figure 6.4). Note that tightening the supply of funds results in a *lower* unemployment path (Figure 6.6), and, for a number of years, both *higher* real wages and probabilities of employment (Figure 6.5 and 6.7). How are these developments consistent with a lower motivation to immigrate? Given that the expected present values $\bar{W}_t$ remain the same, higher γ_t and w_t values in the short run should imply lower values in the longer run. Hence, slower capital accumulation generated by credit tightening lowers the future prospects of immigrants. Thus, the diminished current immigration reduces the supply in the labor market, leading to the short-run results indicated.

5. CONCLUDING REMARKS

This chapter undertakes a small open economy analysis of immigration under increasing foreign borrowing costs. The model constructed here is an extension of a small-open economy growth framework in two directions. One is the endogenous immigration aspect, which is coupled for empirical purposes with a job-search process that is relevant to the immigration decision. The other direction is an upward-sloping supply function of foreign funds, which in the present context is taken as exogenous.

The main purpose of the discussion is to analyze the quantitative effects of an exogenous change in the availability of foreign funds for immigration and macroeconomic behavior. The channel is the effect on capital accumulation, which affects the paths of real wages and probability of employment. Tightening the supply of funds generates lower real wages and probabilities of employment in the long run. Hence, it reduces immigration during the immigration years; that reduction in turn causes the opposite behavior of real wages and probabilities of employment in the shorter run: Both increase.

The assumption of a given supply schedule of foreign borrowing makes it easier to concentrate on immigration and the macroeconomic variables. Given that the shape of this function should reflect default risk, that specification is a reasonable approximation if the current immigration shock does not systematically alter future borrowing needs – and hence the temptation to default.

APPENDIX A

PARAMETER VALUES

$\sigma = -1$ Parameter of the CES production function determining the elasticity of substitution between labor and capital. It is chosen from the range 0 (consistent with the Cobb–Douglas form) to the -1.5 derived from the estimates in Elkayam (1990).

$\alpha = 0.5$ Production function parameter determining the shares of labor and capital. See next.

$\delta = 0.07$ Depreciation rate of capital. The parameters α and δ are jointly determined using the steady state of the model so that the capital/output ratio is 2.0 and the labor share is 0.75.

$\phi = 1.4$ Capital adjustment cost parameter. Set so as to get a maximum ratio of adjustment costs to output of 0.1 percent. This criterion is adopted from Mendoza (1989).

$\beta = 1/1.055$ Rate of time preference.

$\psi = 2$ Set so that the elasticity of labor supply, $\psi - 1$, equals 1.

$\mu = 2.4$ Constant in utility function that normalizes leisure.

$\left.\begin{array}{l} \gamma_0 = 0.88 \\ \gamma_1 = 4.7 \\ \gamma_2 = 1.6 \end{array}\right\}$ Parameters in the job search function. See Section 3.

VALUES OF EXOGENOUS VARIABLES AND INITIAL STATE VARIABLES

V_t Unilateral transfers from abroad: constant at 11.2 percent of base year output (1989–92 average).

G_t Government expenditures: constant at 29.8 percent of base year output (1989–92 average).

D_{92} Initial foreign debt: 24.5 percent of base year output (1992).

b Unemployment benefits: 34 percent of the average salary. This calculation is based on unemployment benefit of NIS700 and the average salary in 1989.

K_{93} Initial capital stock: 5.9 percent lower than the model's
          steady-state value. See Section 4.
E_{92} Initial employment: 2.3 percent lower than steady-state
          value. See Section 4.

APPENDIX B

TECHNICAL ASPECTS OF THE SOLUTION

The infinite horizon problem is approximated by setting a finite horizon of
$T = 36$ years. The final capital stock K_{T+1} is set at the per-capita steady-
state level times N_{T+1}, and $D_T = 0.24\ Y_T$ – where 0.24 is the initial D/Y
ratio.

A "big" iteration starts with a given $\{A_t\}_{t=1}^{\tau}$ and a corresponding $\{N_t\}_{t=1}^{T}$.

A "small" iteration of the solution starts with a given $\{r_t,\ \gamma_t\}_{t=1}^{T}$, which,
along with $\{N_t\}_{t=1}^{T}$, generates $\{E_t,\ U_t\}_{t=1}^{T}$. Then the variables solved for are

$$\{\ell_t,\ C_t\}_{t=1}^{T},\ \{K_{t+1}\}_{t=1}^{T-1},\quad \text{and}\quad \lambda$$

a total of $3T - 1$ variables. The system of nonlinear equations in these
variables consists of the labor supply condition (6.14), the total consumption equation (6.16), both for $t = 1 \ldots T$; the optimal investment condition (6.13) for $t = 1 \ldots T - 1$; and the intertemporal resource constraint
(6.5): a total of $3T - 1$ equations.

The solution of the previous iteration implies a new $\{D_t,\ Y_t,\ u_t,\ z_t\}_{t=1}^{T}$,
from which a new $\{r_t,\ \gamma_t\}_{t=1}^{T}$ is computed, and so on, until convergence.
Each "small" iteration produces a $\{W_t\}_{t=1}^{T}$.

Then, a new "big" iteration is computed by adjusting $\{A_t\}_{t=1}^{\tau}$ (downward if the W_t values are lower than the reservation levels $\bar{W}_t$), and so on,
until convergence.

REFERENCES

Ben-Bassat, Avraham, and Daniel Gottlieb (1992), Optimal International
    Reserves and Sovereign Risk, *Journal of International Economics* 33: 345–
    62.
Eaton, Jonathan, and Mark Gersovitz (1981), Debt with Potential Repu-
    diation: Theoretical and Empirical Analysis, *Review of Economic Studies*
    48 (April): 289–311.
Elkayam, David (1990), Labor Supply and Demand in the Business Sec-
    tor, *Bank of Israel Economic Review* 64 (January): 37–49.
Flug, Karnit, Zvi Hercowitz, and Anat Levi (1993), A Macroeconomic
    Analysis of Migration, manuscript, The Bank of Israel.
Hercowitz, Zvi, and Leora Rubin Meridor (1993), On the Macroeco-

nomic Effects of Immigration: The Israeli Case, manuscript, The Bank of Israel.

Mendoza, Enrique G. (1989), "Dynamic Stochastic Analysis of a Small Open Economy," Ph.D. Dissertation, University of Western Ontario.

Razin, Assaf, and Efraim Sadka (1993), Interactions Between International Migration and International Trade: Positive and Normative Aspects, manuscript, Tel Aviv University.

PART III

Financial Innovation and Growth

CHAPTER 7

Interpreting Monetary Stabilization in a Growth Model with Credit Goods Production

S. Rao Aiyagari and Zvi Eckstein

1. INTRODUCTION

Recent episodes of high inflations and successful stabilizations in Latin America and Israel have provided substantial evidence on the behavior of the main monetary economic aggregates during the high-inflation period and in the poststabilization era (see, e.g., Bruno et al. 1993).[1] This recent evidence is roughly consistent with evidence on the monetary aggregates during the high-inflation episodes in Europe during the 1920s that are described by Sargent (1982).[2] There is less agreement on the evidence concerning the real consequences of the accelerating inflation and the abrupt stabilization programs on employment, unemployment, and output. A particular debate followed Sargent's (1982) claim that the evidence rejects the hypothesis of a "Phillips curve" trade-off between inflation and real output.[3]

We thank Kerstin Johnsson for outstanding research assistance and Neil Wallace for helpful comments on a previous version of this chapter. The views expressed herein are those of the authors and not necessarily those of the Federal Reserve Bank of Minneapolis or the Federal Reserve System.

[1] The main evidence includes the following: (i) average inflation accelerated toward the stabilization date and then abruptly fell to a small positive rate; (ii) velocity (real balances) increases (decreases) toward the stabilization date and then decreases (increases). After stabilization the level of velocity (real balances) is higher (lower) than the level before the high-inflation period; (iii) seigniorage and government deficit seem to follow almost no trend during the high-inflation period and both are reduced to zero during the poststabilization period; (iv) during the period after stabilization ex post real interest rates are extremely high (see Bental and Eckstein 1989; Vegh 1992; Bruno 1993, among many others).

[2] Bruno (1993) and Vegh (1992) provide a comprehensive discussion of the facts concerning the recent episodes, and the 1920s experiences of high inflations and stabilizations. They distinguish between short inflation episodes, such as those of the 1920s and in Bolivia, vis-à-vis chronic episodes, such as in Israel and Argentina. Vegh agrees (Bruno does not agree) with Sargent's claims concerning the facts about the real consequences of high-inflation stabilizations.

[3] Garber (1982) and Wicker (1986) provided evidence on sectoral shifts of employment and some delayed unemployment in Germany, Austria, and Hungary in the 1920s. They claim

The evidence on Germany in the 1920s (Garber 1982; Graham 1930) indicates that the growth rate of industrial output was higher on average in the poststabilization period, although a substantial sectoral shift in employment was associated with higher than average unemployment rates. Part of this sectoral shift was due to the increase in the banking sector during the period of accelerating inflation and the contraction of that sector after stabilization (Bresciani–Turroni 1937).

Wicker (1986) provided substantial evidence on the unemployment in Austria, Hungary, and Poland during the poststabilization period in the 1920s. In reference to the Hungarian case, he stated (1986, p. 358):

The most striking thing about these figures (incidence of trade union unemployment) is the extraordinary increase in the number of unemployed in the financial sector – 31.5 percent of the total net increase of 13,000. All of this increase can be attributed to the ending of hyperinflation which had increased substantially the money market as well as other operations of commercial banking.

Employment in the Hungarian industrial sector started to decrease prior to the stabilization of June 1924, whereas in December 1924 it was increasing. For Austria Wicker (1986) described a similar pattern, whereby ten thousand workers in the banking sector lost their jobs immediately after stabilization. Real gross national product (GNP) decreased by 1 percent during the first year following the stabilization but increased by 7 and 10 percent in the following two years.

Bruno (1993, table 1.2) claimed that the cross-country evidence shows that countries with high inflation rates have significantly lower per capita GDP growth rates. Furthermore, in recent episodes of high inflation the per capita growth rate was lower during the high-inflation period relative to the period with lower inflation.

Israel experienced an accelerating inflation from 1980 until July 1985. At that date the Israeli government implemented a stabiliza-

that their evidence contradicts the main claim of Sargent (1982) that there is no evidence of a stable trade-off between inflation and unemployment ("Phillips curve"). However, Sargent (1982), following Graham (1930), cites the evidence on short-run sectoral shifts of employment and capital but emphasizes Graham's (1930) conclusion that aggregate industrial output in Germany increased in the poststabilization period and was decreasing during the period of accelerating inflation.

tion program that resulted in an abrupt drop of the annual inflation rate from a high of close to 500 percent to a low of 16–20 percent. During the high-inflation period (1980–85) the business-sector output in Israel rose at an annual rate of about one half that during the poststabilization period (1986–90) (Bruno 1993, table 2.1). Moreover, total factor productivity growth rate was zero before the stabilization and 2.6 percent per annum after the stabilization (Bruno 1993, table 2.1).[4]

Melnik (1993) provided evidence on the Israeli banking sector that we present in Table 7.1. It is clear that during the period of accelerating inflation from 1968 to 1985 the three input indicators – labor, automated machines, and area of bank branches in Israel – has a significant upward trend. Although the aggregate business-sector growth rate was higher in the poststabilization period, as mentioned, the banking sector experienced a clear reduction in inputs during the period that followed the end of high inflation (see Figure 7.1).[5]

In this chapter we investigate a monetary growth model in which credit services are produced by labor and capital in order to facilitate trade in an alternative way to using fiat money. The motivations for analyzing such a model are the observations concerning the size of the credit producing sector and the private sector output growth rate before and after monetary stabilizations described previously. The observations may be summarized as follows. Moving from a regime of high monetary growth rate to one of low monetary growth rate we observe the following real changes in the economy:

i. The size of the credit (banking) sector decreases.
ii. The real GDP growth rate increases.

In view of these facts it seems that there should be an interest in providing an analytical model that combines the three variables that have a clear low-frequency comovement: the size of the banking sector, the growth rate of output, and the inflation rate. In this

---

[4] Leiderman (1993, p. 7) concludes that the data "does not conform well with the notion of a short-run tradeoff between inflation and unemployment."

[5] Melnik and Yashiv (this volume) make a similar point about the relationship between the banking sector in Israel and the inflation process. We do not have direct evidence on the banking sectors in Argentina and Bolivia during the high-inflation period and the poststabilization era. However, casual evidence supports the pattern we have reported for the other countries.

Table 7.1. *Indicators on the Israeli banking sector, 1968–1989*

Year	Employment in banks as % of total	Teller machines per 100 people	Area of banks per 1,000 people	Inflation (annual %)
1968	1.4	0.00	75.8	1.9
1969	1.5	0.00	74.4	3.9
1970	1.5	0.00	74.5	10.1
1971	1.6	0.00	74.4	13.4
1972	1.7	0.00	73.3	12.4
1973	1.8	0.00	73.5	26.4
1974	1.9	0.00	73.4	56.2
1975	2.0	0.00	76.4	23.5
1976	2.1	0.00	76.6	38.0
1977	2.2	0.02	77.1	42.5
1978	2.3	0.03	77.3	48.1
1979	2.5	0.04	77.4	111.4
1980	2.7	0.06	84.2	133.0
1981	2.7	0.08	92.1	101.5
1982	2.8	0.10	98.7	131.5
1983	2.8	0.12	103.2	190.7
1984	2.7	0.12	103.6	444.9
1985	2.5	0.12	105.6	185.2
1986	2.4	0.13	103.1	19.6
1987	2.2	0.13	101.5	16.1
1988	2.1	0.13	99.1	16.4
1989	2.1	0.13	100.8	20.7

Source: Melnick (1993). Annual Statistics of Israel's Banking System; Supervisor of Banks, Bank of Israel; Central Bureau of Statistics.

chapter we develop a general equilibrium monetary growth model that incorporates a banking and credit sector and that can be calibrated using data from the National Income and Production (NIP) accounts. Potentially, one can use the model to analyze low-frequency movements in inflation and the size of the banking and credit sectors.[6]

[6] Wicker (1986) claimed that the fact that we observe substantial sectoral shifts in employment and movements in and out of unemployment in the poststabilization period is inconsistent with the rational expectations hypothesis. The model developed here makes it clear that this claim is incorrect. In fact, Sargent (1982), at the end of the introduction, points out that sectoral shift of inputs as a result of the stabilization should be expected in a general equilibrium rational expectations model.

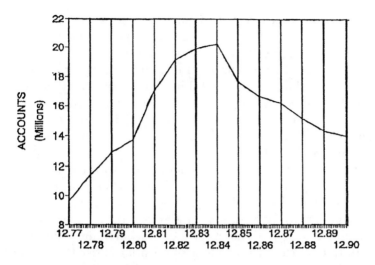

Figure 7.1. Total number of bank accounts (Israel, all types).

The model is a variant of the Lucas and Stokey (1987) model of cash goods and credit goods. The main innovation in the present model relative to Lucas and Stokey's is that unlike in their model we posit that cash goods and credit goods are perfect substitutes in consumption and investment but differ in their production technologies.[7] We think that this is sensible because gasoline is gasoline regardless of whether one pays for it with cash or check or credit card. The distinction ought to be traced to the additional resources in the form of the services of the banking sector or credit card companies that are required for the purchase of "credit gasoline" as opposed to "cash gasoline." That is, the production of a unit of credit gasoline requires a unit of cash gasoline plus some credit services. In turn, the differences in the technology of producing cash versus credit gasoline ought to be reflected in different prices for credit gasoline and cash gasoline. This is indeed the case for gasoline at many gas stations around the United States at which different prices are listed, depending on whether one pays with cash or with credit.

Aside from descriptive realism the major advantage of adopting

[7] Gillman (1993) followed the same approach to analyze the welfare cost of inflation. Ireland (1994) developed a growth model with transaction costs to analyze the trend in M_1 and M_2 velocities and the welfare cost of inflation. (See also Lacker and Shreft 1993; Marquis and Raffett 1993.)

the preceding alternative modeling strategy is that data can be brought to bear in calibrating the model and developing its quantitative implications. We can use data on the value added, capital input, labor input, and shares of capital and labor income in the credit and banking sectors to calibrate the technology for producing credit services that are needed for producing credit goods. This approach would not be possible if credit goods were treated simply as an additional argument of the utility function as in the model of Lucas and Stokey (1987).

As we will see the preceding modeling innovation not only enables us to capture the stylized facts mentioned earlier but also has new and interesting implications for the real effects of monetary policy and for the interrelationships among the money growth rate, the nominal and real interest rates, the inflation rate, and the growth rate of real output. These implications arise because in this model the nominal interest rate has a role in allocating resources between the goods-producing and credit-services-producing sectors. This role arises because the nominal interest rate determines the wedge between the prices of cash goods and credit goods. Equivalently, the nominal interest rate determines the relative price of credit services and production goods. As a consequence, the nominal interest rate also influences factor rewards in the two sectors. Because one of these factors is capital, the nominal interest rate influences the real rate through its allocative role. This is a channel for the real effects of monetary policy that leads to interesting interrelationships among the money growth rate, the nominal and real interest rates, the inflation rate, and the growth rate of real output. It is also the channel through which technological improvement in the provision of financial services, by making credit services, and, hence, credit goods relatively cheaper, affect the nominal interest rate and, thereby, currency velocity and inflation.[8]

Comparing steady states of an economy with high and low rates of monetary expansion shows that the model can interpret the main evidence on the banking sector and growth during and after the high-inflation period. That is, a reduction in the monetary growth rate implies a decrease in the size of the banking sector and an increase in the GDP growth rate.

The impact of a surprise stabilization is analyzed using a log-

---

[8] Thus, the technology of providing credit services is one of the determinants of the nominal interest rate. This feature of our model is similar to that of Bryant and Wallace (1979).

linear approximation to the stochastic model around a deterministic steady state. We simulate the model in response to a negative shock to the money growth rate assuming that this shock has high persistence (is almost a random walk). We show that the model's predictions are consistent with observations on the result of stabilization. That is, the inflation rate, the nominal interest rate, the wage rate, and the velocity all decrease immediately. The size of the credit sector is reduced, but the growth rate of the sector increases. The same is the case for real GNP and wages, while, as observed, consumption and growth rate also increase. The real interest rate increases as a result of the negative monetary shock.

The rest of this chapter is organized as follows. In Section 2 we describe the monetary growth model. Section 3 describes steady-state determination. In Section 4 we analyze the impact of a stabilization policy both by comparing steady states with high and low rates of monetary expansion as well as by analyzing the impact of a surprise stabilization. Section 5 concludes with a discussion that summarizes the results of the model in relation to the facts of stabilization policies that were adopted in high-inflation countries.

2. A MONETARY GROWTH MODEL WITH CREDIT GOODS PRODUCTION

The model we develop is a competitive equilibrium model and is described in terms of the behavior of its three decision units, namely, the households, the producers and the government, and equilibrium conditions. We start by describing the behavior of the representative household.

2.1. The Representative Household

There is a representative infinite-lived household that has one unit of labor endowment available each period. The household consumes the amount c_t of goods and supplies the exogenous amount n ($n = 1$) of labor input in each period t. The household's preferences are given by the following expected discounted sum of utility of consumption:

$$E_0 \left\{ \sum_{t=0}^{\infty} \beta^t U(c_t) \right\}, \qquad 0 < \beta < 1 \qquad (7.1)$$

The household purchases goods using cash ("cash goods") in the amount c_{1t} and purchases goods using credit ("credit goods") in the amount c_{2t} at the prices p_{1t} and p_{2t}, respectively. As mentioned, cash goods and credit goods are perfect substitutes in consumption and investment. Therefore, the household divides total goods purchases $c_{1t} + c_{2t}$ into consumption in the amount c_t and gross capital formation in the amount $k_{t+1} - (1 - \delta)k_t$, where k_t is the household's beginning of period t capital holding and $\delta \in (0, 1]$ is the depreciation rate of capital.[9] This leads to the following constraint on the household's optimization:

$$c_{1t} + c_{2t} \geq c_t + k_{t+1} - (1 - \delta)k_t \qquad (7.2)$$

In addition to capital, the household begins period t with m_t units of money and b_t units (in terms of face value) of nominal bonds. The household also receives nominal lump sum transfer payments from the government in the amount X_t. As is usual in cash-in-advance (CIA) models of money there is a financial market in which the household can rearrange its portfolio of money and bonds. Once this is done, the financial market closes and the goods markets (for purchasing cash goods and credit goods) open. In the cash goods market the household can purchase cash goods subject to the following CIA constraint:

$$\frac{(m_t + X_t)}{p_{1t}} + \frac{b_t}{p_{1t}} - \frac{b_{t+1}}{[(1 + R_t)p_{1t}]} \geq c_{1t} \qquad (7.3)$$

In (6.3) R_t is the nominal interest rate from t to $t + 1$. Note that the left side of (6.3) is the amount of cash the household has available after the close of the financial market.

The household can use any excess cash left over after the purchase of cash goods plus labor and capital income to purchase credit goods or accumulate cash for the next period. This leads to the following budget constraint:

$$\frac{(m_t + X_t)}{p_{1t}} + \frac{b_t}{p_{1t}} - \frac{b_{t+1}}{[(1 + R_t)p_{1t}]} - c_{1t} + w_t + r_t k_t \geq \frac{c_{2t} p_{2t}}{p_{1t}} + \frac{m_{t+1}}{p_{1t}} \qquad (7.4)$$

---

[9] Another advantage of our modeling strategy is that we do not arbitrarily designate consumption goods as cash goods and investment goods as credit goods as in, for example, Cooley and Hansen (1989). Both cash goods and credit goods may be used for consumption and/or investment.

In (7.4), w_t and r_t denote the wage and the rental on capital in units of the cash good.

The household's optimization problem now consists of maximizing (7.1) subject to the constraints (7.2)–(7.4) by choosing $\{c_t, c_{1t}, c_{2t}, m_{t+1}, b_{t+1}, k_{t+1}\}_{t=0}^{\infty}$ for given laws of motion for $\{p_{1t}, p_{2t}, X_t, R_t, w_t, r_t\}$.

2.2. The Producer

There are two primary production sectors that use only the primary factors of production (capital and labor) and a third sector that uses only intermediate inputs. Each of these satisfies constant returns to scale in the inputs used in that sector. Individual producers in each sector maximize profits taking prices of outputs and inputs as given.[10]

The first sector uses capital input in the amount K_{1t} and labor input in the amount n_{1t} to produce goods in the amount Y_t subject to the following constant returns to scale (in K_{1t}, n_{1t}, and Y_t) production function:

$$Y_t = F(K_{1t}, \theta_{1t}K_tn_{1t}) \tag{7.5}$$

The second sector uses capital input in the amount K_{2t} and labor input in the amount n_{2t} to produce "credit services" in the amount S_t subject to the following constant returns to scale (in K_{2t}, n_{2t}, and S_t) production function:

$$S_t = G(K_{2t}, \theta_{2t}K_tn_{2t}) \tag{7.6}$$

The output of goods Y_t of the first sector can be used in two ways. Some part can be sold directly for cash. This part is denoted c_{1t} and is referred to as "cash goods." The remaining part $(Y_t - c_{1t})$ is used as an intermediate input in the third sector along with the credit services produced by the second sector to produce "credit goods." This production relation in the third sector is of the following Leontief fixed coefficients type:

$$c_{2t} = \min[Y_t - c_{1t}, S_t] \tag{7.7}$$

The following special feature of this technology should be noted. In the production of goods and credit services (7.5) and (7.6), there

---

[10] The following specification is related to that in Fischer (1983).

is an external effect on labor productivity arising from the aggregate capital stock in the economy. This turns the model into an
endogenous growth model so that policies have growth as well as
level effects. Thus, we can analyze the effects of a monetary stabilization on the real growth rate. Because of this endogenous growth
feature, the labor augmenting technology shocks θ_{1t} and θ_{2t} in (7.5)
and (7.6), respectively, are assumed to follow stationary stochastic
processes.

We will refer to the production side of this economy as a two-
sector economy where the two sectors are the goods-producing
sector (7.5) and the credit-services-producing sector (7.6).

2.3. Government

In order to simplify the model we assume that the government sets
the supply of bonds and money as follows:

$$B_t = 0, t \geq 0 \qquad (7.8a)$$

$$M_{t+1} = M_t + X_t = (1 + x_t)M_t, \ t \geq 0 \qquad (7.8b)$$

In (7.8b), x_t is the money growth rate, which is assumed to follow
a stationary stochastic process that is independent of $\{\theta_{1t}, \theta_{2t}\}$.

2.4. Equilibrium

The following conditions (which are pretty self-explanatory) need
to hold in equilibrium:

$$K_{1t} + K_{2t} = K_t \qquad (7.9a)$$

$$n_{1t} + n_{2t} = 1 \qquad (7.9b)$$

$$c_t + K_{t+1} - (1 - \delta)K_t = c_{1t} + c_{2\,t} = Y_t = F(K_{1t}, \theta_{1t}K_t n_{1t}) \qquad (7.9c)$$

$$c_{2t} = S_t = G(K_{2t}, \theta_{2t}K_t n_{2t}) \qquad (7.9d)$$

$$k_t = K_t, K_0 \quad \text{given} \qquad (7.9e)$$

$$b_t = B_t = 0 \qquad (7.9f)$$

$$m_t = M_t, M_0 \quad \text{given} \qquad (7.9g)$$

In the next section we characterize the equilibrium for the preceding model and describe steady-state determination.

3. EQUILIBRIUM AND STEADY-STATE DETERMINATION

3.1. Consumer Optimization

The solution to the consumer's optimization problem is characterized by the following first-order necessary conditions (FONCs):

$$\frac{U_{c,t}}{(1 + R_t)} = \beta E_t \left[\frac{p_{1t} U_{c,t+1}}{p_{1,t+1}} \right] \tag{7.10a}$$

$$U_{c,t} = \beta E_t \left[\left(\frac{1 - \delta + r_{t+1}}{(1 + R_{t+1})} \right) U_{c,t+1} \right] \tag{7.10b}$$

$$1 + R_t = \frac{p_{2t}}{p_{1t}} \tag{7.10c}$$

In the preceding equations $U_{c,t}$ denotes the marginal utility of consumption at date t. Condition (7.10a) is standard. Condition (7.10b) is slightly different from the traditional model (e.g., Cooley and Hansen 1989), in that it exhibits an inflation tax effect on the return to capital. In the steady state, changes in the money growth rate and, hence, in the inflation rate and the nominal interest rate affect the real return to capital. This effect is absent in the traditional model because investment is treated as a credit good. In our model cash goods may also be used for investment, and this feature leads to an inflation tax effect on the return to capital and, hence, on the rate of investment. We think this feature of the model is sensible because there is no reason to suppose that candy must be paid for by cash whereas hammers can only be bought on credit.

What is entirely new is condition (7.10c), which is an arbitrage relation between the nominal interest rate and the price of the credit good relative to the cash good. It arises from the following consideration. A household can either purchase an extra unit of the cash good at price p_{1t} by borrowing in the financial market at the interest rate R_t, thereby reducing its cash holding at $t + 1$, or purchase an extra unit of the credit good at the price p_{2t} and reduce its cash holding at date $t + 1$. Because cash goods and credit goods are perfect substitutes in consumption and investment, the arbitrage relation (7.10c) must hold.

Thus, a key relation arising from consumer optimization is that the nominal interest rate equals the price of credit goods relative to cash goods. This is the channel through which money growth affects the allocation of resources between the cash goods and credit services sectors (by affecting the price of credit goods relative to cash goods). It is also the channel through which technological improvements in the provision of credit services, by making credit goods relatively cheaper, affect the nominal interest rate and, thereby, currency velocity and inflation.

3.2. Producer Optimization

Let p_{st} denote the price of credit services. Note that the price of goods Y_t will equal the price of cash goods (p_{1t}) so long as cash goods are being produced. The following obvious conditions reflecting the equality of factor prices and marginal products characterize producer profit maximization:

$$w_t = \theta_{1t} K_t F_{2t} = \left(\frac{p_{st}}{p_{1t}}\right)\theta_{2t} K_t G_{2t} \tag{7.11a}$$

$$r_t = F_{1t} = \left(\frac{p_{st}}{p_{1t}}\right)G_{1t} \tag{7.11b}$$

$$p_{2t} = p_{1t} + p_{st} \tag{7.11c}$$

Equations (3.1c) and (7.11c) imply the following relation between the nominal interest rate and the price of credit services relative to cash goods:

$$R_t = \frac{p_{st}}{p_{1t}} \tag{7.12}$$

3.3. Steady-State Analysis

Using the preceding optimality conditions for the representative household and producer we now study the model's nonstochastic steady-state properties. To do this we assume that the money growth rate x_t and the technology shocks θ_{1t} and θ_{2t} are all constant over time. Further, the utility function is assumed to have the following form:

$$U(c) = \frac{(c^{1-\mu} - 1)}{(1 - \mu)}, \qquad \mu > 0, \qquad \mu \neq 1, \qquad = \ln(c) \quad \text{if} \quad \mu = 1 \quad (7.13)$$

The parameter μ is the risk aversion coefficient and utility is logarithmic in consumption when μ equals unity.

Let g be the (endogenous) steady-state growth rate of the economy, that is, the common growth rate of K_t, K_{1t}, K_{2t}, c_t, c_{1t}, c_{2t}, Y_t, S_t, w_t. Using the CIA constraint (7.3) along with the supply of bonds and money given by (7.8) we can write the steady-state inflation rate for cash goods as follows:

$$\pi_{1,t+1} \equiv \left(\frac{p_{1,t+1}}{p_{1,t}}\right) - 1 = \frac{(1 + x)}{(1 + g)} - 1 \qquad (7.14)$$

Using the preceding relationship together with the household's optimality conditions (7.10a) and (7.10b) we can derive the following equations for the nominal and real interest rates:

$$1 + R = (1 + \varrho)(1 + x)(1 + g)^{(\mu - 1)} \qquad (7.15a)$$

$$\frac{r}{(1 + R)} + (1 - \delta) = (1 + \varrho)(1 + g)^{\mu} \qquad (7.15b)$$

where $\varrho = (1 - \beta)/\beta$ is the utility time preference rate.

Note that once the growth rate is determined, equations (7.14) and (7.15) determine the inflation rate, the real interest rate, and the nominal interest rate. The growth rate g is determined as follows. Equations (7.15) yield a relationship between R and r that is determined by the money growth rate and the preference parameters. The production side of the economy determines a second relation between R and r, because R equals the relative price of the output of the two sectors and r is the return to capital, which is one of the inputs. The growth rate g adjusts so that the relation between the nominal interest rate and the real interest rate implied by (7.15) is consistent with the relationship determined from the production side of the economy. A consequence of this feature of the model is that changes in the money growth rate (as well as changes in the technology parameters θ_1 and θ_2) have interesting level as well as growth effects. The relationships among the money growth rate, inflation rate, nominal interest rate, output growth rate, and real interest rate are different and more interesting than the usual Fisherian relationship.

As is clear from the preceding discussion a key relationship on which the properties of the model hinge is the relationship between the nominal interest rate (representing the relative price of the goods-producing and the credit-services-producing sectors) and the real interest rate (representing the price of capital services) arising from the production side of the economy. This relationship, in turn, depends on the relative capital intensities of the two sectors. For instance, if the goods-producing sector is more capital-intensive, then an increase in the nominal interest rate will (assuming diversification) raise the wage rate and lower the rental to capital independently of factor supplies.

For the rest of this chapter we consider the case in which the goods-producing sector is more capital-intensive.[11] We characterize the steady state of the economy using Figures 7.2a–c, which show the production side of the economy: the production possibility frontier (PPF) between production goods and credit services (Figure 7.2a), the PPF between cash goods and credit goods (7.2b), the relation between the factor returns r and w and the nominal interest rate $R = p_s/p_1$ (Figure 7.2c).

From Figure 7.2a it is clear that a higher nominal interest rate implies a higher output of credit services relative to goods. When the goods-producing sector is more capital-intensive a decrease in the nominal interest rate will (assuming that both goods are produced) increase the real interest rate and decrease the wage rate independently of factor supplies (see Figure 7.2c).

Figure 7.3 shows the determination of the nominal and real interest rates in steady state. The downward-sloping line is from the production side of the economy given in Figure 7.2c. The upward-real and nominal interest rates obtained by eliminating the growth sloping line in these figures represents the relationship between the rate g from equations (7.15). This relationship is characterized by the following equation:

$$r = (1 + R) \left\{ (1 + \varrho) \left[\frac{(1 + R)}{(1 + x)(1 + \varrho)} \right]^{\mu/(\mu-1)} - (1 - \delta) \right\} \qquad (7.16)$$

Assuming that the risk aversion coefficient μ exceeds unity, we get the upward-sloping line in Figure 7.3. The intersection of the two

---

[11] Empirically, the production function of financial services is more labor-intensive than the aggregate production function.

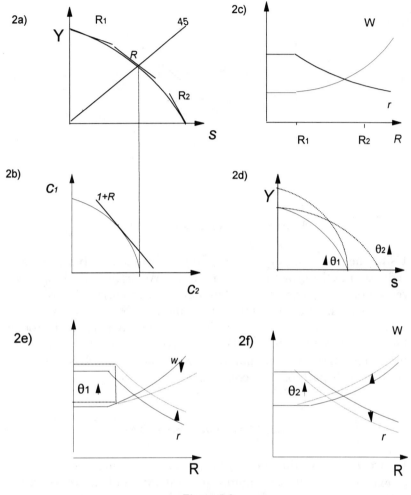

Figure 7.2.

lines determines the real and nominal interest rates.[12] Equations (7.14) and (7.15) then determine the real growth rate and the inflation rate. This completes the description of the steady-state determination of the economy.

---

[12] In the case that the capital intensities in production are identical for the two sectors, the PPF is flat and the price of financial services and the nominal interest rate are determined

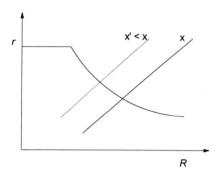

Figure 7.3.

4. PERMANENT STABILIZATION

Using the preceding model we define a permanent stabilization as a reduction in the growth rate of money, x. We discuss the impact of a reduction in the growth rate of money as a comparison between two steady states, where we start with a higher x. Next we consider the case when the change in x is a shock to a highly persistent process for the money growth rate. For the second part of the analysis we use a log-linear approximation around the nonstochastic steady-state growth path of the economy.

4.1. Steady-State Stabilization

Figure 7.3 shows the effects of a permanent change in the money growth rate, x, on the nominal interest rate and the real interest rate. As can be seen from Figure 7.3 a decrease in the money growth rate lowers the nominal interest rate and raises the real interest rate. Equation (7.15b) then shows that the real growth rate, g, increases. Figure 7.2c shows that the real wage decreases. From equation (7.14) it is clear that the inflation rate is reduced by

---

by technology. The downward-sloping line in Figure 7.3 is vertical, and, hence, changes in the money growth rate affect the real interest rate and the growth rate, but not the nominal interest rate. In this case the model becomes similar to that of Bryant and Wallace (1979).

more than the decrease in the money growth rate (because the real growth rate rises). Further, from (7.15a), the nominal interest rate decreases by less than the decrease in the money growth rate for the same reason.

The decrease in the nominal interest rate leads to a decrease in the output of credit services and credit goods and to an increase in the output of goods as well as cash goods (see Figures 7.2a and b). This is accomplished by a movement of labor out of the credit services sector (which is labor-intensive).

These features of the model are quite consistent with the observations on the growth of the credit services sector during periods of accelerating inflation and the decrease in the size of the sector following stabilization. In addition, the results are consistent with the observations on the growth rate of output and the real interest rate before and after the stabilization date.

The impact on currency velocity (denoted v) can be seen from the following expression:

$$v_t = \frac{(p_{1t}c_{1t} + p_{2t}c_{2t})}{M_{t+1}} = 1 + \frac{p_{2t}c_{2t}}{p_{1t}c_{1t}} = 1 + \frac{(1 + R_t)c_{2t}}{c_{1t}} \tag{7.17}$$

where $(p_{1t}C_{1t} + p_{2t}c_{2t})$ is nominal GNP. The second equality in (7.17) is derived by using the CIA constraint (7.3) together with (7.8), (7.9g), and (7.10d). It is now easy to see that currency velocity must decrease with a reduction in the money growth rate, because the nominal interest rate as well as the relative output of credit goods go down.

Another aspect of this model is the effect of improvements in the technology of producing credit services and, thereby, credit goods. As can be seen in Figure 7.2f an increase in θ_2 lowers the relationship between the real rate and the nominal rate. By combining this with the upward-sloping line in Figure 7.3, we see that an increase in θ_2 lowers the nominal interest rate, the real interest rate, and the real growth rate and raises the inflation rate. The relative output of credit services and credit goods goes up (see Figure 7.2d), but the impact on currency velocity is ambiguous. These effects are consistent with the observation that technological improvements in credit arrangements have led to an increase in the quantity of credit services and credit goods and, by reducing the demand for currency, have resulted in an increase in inflation.

4.2. Stabilization Shock

The analysis of a stabilization shock requires a stochastic specification of the money growth rate rule together with a closed form
solution for the equilibrium. For the solution we use a log-linear
approximation around the steady state. In order to analyze the
response of a high-inflation economy to a shock in the money
growth rate we assume that the money growth rate is a first-order
Markov process that is close to a random walk. That is

$$x_{t+1} = \varrho_x x_t + (1 - \varrho_x)\bar{x} + e_t \qquad (7.18)$$

where e_t is a white noise, $\bar{x}$ is the mean money growth rate, and ϱ_x is
close to unity ($\varrho_x = 0.99$). The high-inflation country has on average a monthly money growth rate of 10 percent. That is, we set the
period to be one month and set $\bar{x} = 0.10$.

We assume that the production functions $F(.)$ and $G(.)$ are both
Cobb–Douglas with capital share parameters denoted by α_1 and
α_2, respectively. Using data from the United States we found
(Aiyagari and Eckstein 1993) that $\alpha_1 = 0.41$ and $\alpha_2 = 0.35$, and we
use these values here.

The specification of the utility function has already been described in the previous section. We assume that the risk aversion
coefficient $\mu = 3$. The monthly depreciation rate of capital δ is
assumed to be 0.006 (annual 8 percent depreciation) and the
monthly growth rate g is set to 0.0016 (annual growth rate of 2
percent). We use data on y/k_1 to set r ($r = \alpha_1 [y/k_1]$) and this yields
a value of $r = 0.015$. We then set R using equations (7.15). Eliminating $(1 + \varrho)$ between (7.15a) and (7.15b) we obtain

$$\frac{r}{(1 + R)} + (1 - \delta) = \frac{(1 + R)(1 + g)}{(1 + x)} \qquad (7.19)$$

and we solve this equation for R and get a value of $R = 0.11$.

The amount of time that consumers spend working is normalized
to unity. We assume that for a high-inflation country the value
added share of credit services in GNP (denoted by ϕ) is 4 percent.
Note that $\phi = p_s S/(p_1 Y + p_s S) = RS/(Y + RS) = Rc_2/[c_1 + (1 +
R)c_2]$. The steady-state values of some key variables in the model
have been calculated using the steady-state characterization of the
economy in the following way. The efficiency conditions (7.11a)

and (7.11b) are used to calculate factor allocations and yield the following values.[13]

$$\frac{k_1}{k} = 0.985, \quad \text{and} \quad \frac{k_2}{k} = 0.015 \tag{7.20}$$

$$n_1 = 0.975, \quad \text{and} \quad n_2 = 0.025 \tag{7.21}$$

The shares of credit and cash goods in total goods are calculated using the preceding values of ϕ and R and yield the following values:

$$\frac{c_2}{c_1 + c_2} = 0.815, \quad \frac{c_1}{c_1 + c_2} = 0.125 \tag{7.22}$$

The preceding values imply a value for the ratio of credit goods to cash goods. This is used in (7.17) to calculate velocity and yields the following value:[14]

$$v = 1.25 \tag{7.23}$$

Lastly, the steady-state form of the resource constraint (7.9) is used to calculate the share of consumption in total goods as follows:

$$\frac{c}{y} = 1 - (g + \delta)\left(\frac{k}{k_1}\right)\left(\frac{k_1}{Y}\right) = 0.77 \tag{7.24}$$

In computing the impulse response dynamics of our endogenous growth model it is important to distinguish between level effects and growth effects of a transitory shock to the money growth rate. The variables we look at are divided into those that grow and those that are stationary. These are listed in the following discussion as "growth variables" in set A_t and "level variables" in set B_t.

$$A_t = \{K_t, K_{1t}, K_{2t}, c_t, c_{1t}, c_{2t}, Y_t, w_t, p_{1t}, p_{2t}\}, \text{ growth variables} \tag{7.25a}$$

$$B_t = \{\ln(n_{1t}), \ln(n_{2t}), R_t, r_t, v_t\}, \text{ level variables} \tag{7.25b}$$

Define the growth rate of a growth variable $a_t \in A_t$ by $g_{at} \equiv \ln a_t - \ln a_{t-1}$. Suppose that the shock hits the model economy at date 1 and let g_a^* be the steady-state growth rate of this variable before the shock hits. Then, for each growth variable, we report the level effect

---

[13] Equation (7.11a) can be written as $(1 - \alpha_1)Y/n_1 = R(1 - \alpha_2)S/n_2$. Using the definition of ϕ, this implies $n_1 = 1/[1 + (1 - \alpha_2)\phi/\{(1 - \alpha_1)(1 - \phi)\}]$. Further, $n_2 = 1 - n_1$. Equation (7.11b) can be written as $\alpha_1 Y/k_1 = R\alpha_2 S/k_2$. Using the definition of ϕ, this implies $k_1/k = 1/[1 + \alpha_2\phi/\{\alpha_1(1 - \phi)\}]$. Further, $k_2/k = 1 - k_1/k$.

[14] Note that velocity $v = (p_{1t}c_{1t} + p_{2t}c_{2t})/M_{t+1} = (p_{1t}c_{2t} + p_{2t}c_{2t})/p_{1t}c_{1t} = 1 + (1 + R)c_2/c_1$.

at date 1, which is given by $(g_{a,1} - g^*)$, and the growth rate effects for $t > 1$, which are given by $(g_{a,t} - g^*)$. Note that the aggregate capital stock K_t is predetermined at t, so that it is not subject to a level effect but only to a growth rate effect. Further, note that the level effect at date 1 should be interpreted as the percentage deviation from what the level of the variable would have been in the absence of the shock. This follows because $g_{a,1} - g_a^* \cong [\ln a_1 - \ln a_0] - [\ln((1 + g_a^*)a_0) - \ln a_0] = \ln a_1 - \ln((1 + g_a^*)a_0)$. Moreover, the growth rate effect for $t > 1$ is given as a deviation from the steady-state growth rate. Because we use a value of ϱ_x that is close to one, we can interpret the sign of the growth rate deviation as the direction of the impact of a permanent unexpected change in the growth rate of the money supply.

The level effect on a level variable $b_t \in B_t$ is defined as $(b_t - b^*)$, where b^* is the steady-state level of this variable. Therefore, the effects on labor input in the goods-producing sector (n_{1t}) and labor input in the credit services sector (n_{2t}) should be interpreted as percentage deviations from their steady-state values. As explained, the signs of these changes should be interpreted as the signs of the impacts of a permanent change in the money growth rate.

Table 7.2 presents the impact of a negative shock to the money growth rate with a serial correlation of 0.99: That is, the shock is very close to being permanent. The dynamics of the response of all variables is exactly that of the shock so that the persistence of the monetary shock implies persistence of each variable in the direction of the initial response. The first column in Table 7.2 presents the signs of the level effects on variables in group A and the effects on all variables in group B. The second column presents the signs of the growth rate effects on variables in group A.

The immediate effect of a surprise reduction in the growth rate of money is as we expect from the model. That is, the nominal interest rate decreases, leading to a reduction in credit goods production and the velocity of money. The inflation rate obviously goes down but by more than the nominal interest rate so that the real interest rate is going up. These responses are consistent with the wide observations on these variables during the poststabilization period. In addition, the growth rate of all real variables goes up, so that consumption level and growth rate are higher, as we usually observe in response to stabilization. Hence, the reduction in inflation has a real impact on the long-run path of the economy.

Table 7.2. *Response to a negative shock in the money growth rate (deviations from steady state)*

Variable	Level effect	Growth rate effect
K_t	na	+
K_{1t}	+	+
K_{2t}	−	+
c_t	+	+
c_{1t}	+	+
c_{2t}	−	+
Y_t	+	+
w_t	−	+
p_{1t}	−	−
p_{2t}	−	−
$\ln(n_{1t})$	+	na
$\ln(n_{2t})$	−	na
R_t	−	na
r_t	+	na
v_t	−	na

Note: na = not applicable.

5. CONCLUDING REMARKS

In this chapter we have developed a monetary growth model designed to address observations concerning changes over time in the relative size of the credit and banking sector, growth rate of the economy, and comovements among inflation, currency velocity, and relative size of the credit and banking sector. The model contains a new and hitherto unexplored channel for the long-run and short-run effects of changes in the money growth rate that can be interpreted as part of stabilization programs. This channel arises because although cash goods and credit goods are perfect substitutes in consumption and investment we posit different technologies for their production.

As a result of this feature the nominal interest rate has an allocative role in our model because it determines the price of credit goods relative to cash goods. Because of this same feature the nominal interest rate also determines factor returns, that is, the real wage and the real interest rate. As a consequence, the interrelationships among the money growth rate, inflation rate, nominal interest rate, real interest rate, and real growth rate are different from those that arise in the usual monetary growth models. In particular, we can provide an economic interpretation for the observations on the size of the banking sector and the economic growth rate in economies that experienced a transition from high inflation to low inflation due to a monetary stabilization program. In particular, we show that a permanent decrease in the growth rate of money increases the growth rate of output, decreases the share of the credit and banking sector in GNP, increases the real interest rate, and decreases inflation and the nominal interest rate.

So far we have provided a qualitative explanation for the observations. In future work we plan to extend the model quantitatively to analyze the business cycle implications during the period of stabilization. Furthermore, we are interested in exploring the extent to which technological innovations in the production of credit services and credit goods contribute to movements in inflation, interest rates, currency velocity, and output.

REFERENCES

Aiyagari, S. A., and Z. Eckstein (1993), Credit Goods Production in a Monetary Two Sector Growth Model, mimeo, Tel Aviv University.

Bresciani-Turroni, C. (1937), *The Economics of Inflation*, London: George Allen & Unwin.

Bruno, M., S. Fischer, N. Liviatan, and L. Meridor (1992), *Lessons of Economic Stabilization and Its Aftermath*, Cambridge, MA: The MIT Press.

Bruno, Michael (1993), *Crisis, Stabilisation, and Economic Reform: Therapy by Consensus*, Oxford: Claremont Press.

Bryant, John, and Neil Wallace (1979), The Inefficiency of Interest Bearing National Debt, *Journal of Political Economy* 87(2): 365–81.

Cooley, T., and G. Hansen (1989), The Inflation Tax in a Real Business Cycle Model, *American Economic Review* 79: 733–48.

Fischer, S. (1983), A Framework for Monetary and Banking Analysis, *Economic Journal* 1–16.

Garber, Peter M. (1982), Transition from Inflation to Price Stability, in K. Brunner and A. H. Meltzer, eds., *Monetary Regimes and Protectionism*, Carnegie–Rochester Conference Series on Public Policy, Amsterdam: North-Holland Publishing Co.

Gillman, Max (1993), The Welfare Cost of Inflation in a Cash-in-Advance Economy with Costly Credit, *Journal of Monetary Economics* (31): 97–115.

Graham, F. D. (1930), *Exchange, Prices and Production in Hyperinflation: Germany, 1920–1923.* New York: Russell & Russelle.

Ireland, Peter N. (1994), Money and Growth: An Alternative Approach, *American Economic Review* 84: 47–65.

Lacker, Jeffery M., and Stacy L. Schreft (1993), Money and Credit as Means of Payments, mimeo, Federal Reserve Bank of Richmond.

Leiderman, Leonardo (1993), *Inflation and Disinflation: The Israeli Experiment,* Chicago: The University of Chicago Press.

Lucas, Robert E., Jr., and Nancy Stokey (1987), Money and Interest in a Cash-in-Advance Economy, *Econometrica* 55: 491–513.

Marquis, Milton H., and Kevin L. Reffett (1993), Equilibrium Growth in a Monetary Economy with Transaction Costs, mimeo, Florida State University.

Melnick, Rafi (1995), Financial Services, Cointegration and the Demand for Money in Israel, *Journal of Money, Credit and Banking* 27: 140–153.

Sargent, Thomas J. (1982), The ends of four big inflations. In Robert E. Hall, ed., *Inflation: Causes and Effects,* Chicago: Chicago University Press.

Vegh, Carlos A. (1992), Stopping High Inflation: An Analytical Overview, *IMF Staff Papers* 39(3): 626–705.

Wicker, E. (1986), Terminating Hyperinflation in the Dismembered Habsburgh Monarchy, *American Economic Review* 76(5): 350–64.

CHAPTER 8

The Macroeconomic Effects of Financial Innovation: The Case of Israel

Rafi Melnick and Eran Yashiv

1. INTRODUCTION

This chapter examines the macroeconomic effects of financial innovation in the Israeli economy. Israel, like other economies in the
West, experienced significant innovation in financial services in the
1980s. Concurrently it experienced a high-inflation process followed by stabilization. This rich variation in the data allows hypothesis testing that is not possible in a stable environment. We
document the elements of financial innovation, propose a theoretical model of their macroeconomic implications, and empirically
test these implications.

By the term "financial innovation" we refer to the introduction of
new, liquid assets that partially replace traditional money in agents'
portfolios; technological progress in banking services that reduces
the costs of transactions; and changes in the regulatory environment that facilitate transactions. In Israel these innovations were
expressed in the increased use of foreign-exchange-linked (PA-
TAM) deposits in the period 1978–85 (a reversal of this process
occurred after the 1985 inflation stabilization program); the increased use of interest-bearing short-term deposits since 1982; and
a decline in traditional $M1$ use. All of this was accompanied by
significant technological progress in banking services.

We propose a theoretical model whereby financial innovation has
effects on production and consumption in an infinitely lived, utility-
maximizing representative agent model. Innovation affects the transactions costs of the consumer, generating a portfolio shift. This

We would like to thank Benjamin Eden, Zvi Hercowitz, Ben-Zion Zilberfarb, and seminar
participants at the Bank of Israel and at the World Bank–Horowitz Institute conference.
Research assistance by Jeremy Berkowitz and financial support from the World Bank are
gratefully acknowledged. Any errors are our own.

in turn affects financial intermediaries' resources and hence their lending rate. The change in the interest rate induces changes in the long-run level of capital and therefore in production and consumption.

We test the implications of the model empirically by estimating a series of VAR models, looking at the cumulative impulse responses of various real activity variables to shocks in the relative holdings of different financial assets. The model's predictions are borne out by the data.

The chapter bears upon two strands of recent literature in monetary economics: first, a growing literature on the effects of financial innovation on money demand, second, a body of literature on channels of transmission of monetary policy that go beyond the traditional textbook "money channel." The first strand studies the effects of the introduction of new instruments and new money management techniques on the demand for $M1$. Thus Gauger (1992) studies the portfolio redistribution impact of financial innovation for U.S. data. In the late 1970s and early 1980s new instruments were introduced (NOW and SuperNOW accounts) and there was wider use of money market accounts. Gauger finds substitution from traditional $M1$ (currency plus checking deposits) to the new interest-bearing checkable deposits. Arrau and de Gregorio (1992) show that the "missing money" phenomena in Chile and Mexico may be accounted for by financial innovation. Melnick (1995) uses a financial innovation variable as an explanatory variable of the demand for money in Israel, explicitly demonstrating the role of innovation in $M1$ demand reductions. A related article is Guidotti (1993), which studies the effects of financial innovation in the context of monetary integration among several economies. Innovation abroad may lead to substitution out of the domestic currency into the foreign currency. This type of discussion is naturally related to the question of seigniorage, an issue examined by de Gregorio (1991) and Melnick (1995).

The second strand of literature alluded to, the "credit" view of monetary transmission, proposes that the asset side of bank balance sheets plays an important role in monetary transmission: Following a tightening by the central bank (for example, an open market sale), banks reduce lending. This reduces firms' borrowing, particularly for firms heavily dependent on bank loans (such as small firms). The key assumption here is that alternative, nonbank borrowing is more costly or unavailable. Firms therefore reduce investment spending and subsequently cut employment and production.[1]

The model presented in this chapter embodies both a money channel and a credit channel, focusing on financial innovation rather than on monetary policy: As in the "money" view there is an effect on banks' liabilities through the change induced by innovation on the portfolio composition of consumers; this in turn affects banks' assets as the portfolio change interacts with differential reserve requirements to generate changes in loan supply, hence a credit supply effect.

We proceed as follows: Section 2 documents financial innovation in the Israeli economy, beginning in the late 1970s, and relates it to relevant macroeconomic events. Section 3 presents the theoretical model and Section 4 studies the effects of financial innovation. Section 5 reports the empirical tests of the model's implications. Section 6 discusses these results and draws conclusions.

2. FINANCIAL INNOVATION IN THE ISRAELI ECONOMY

In this section we look at some key developments pertaining to financial innovation in the Israeli economy. The process of innovation in Israel was closely linked to the dynamics of the inflationary process. We therefore begin by briefly surveying the development of inflation (2.1); we then look at major events of financial innovation (2.2), focusing on two major and distinct innovations: the introduction of liquid, foreign-currency-linked deposits, and the improvement and introduction of interest-bearing, unlinked deposits, similar to the new financial instruments offered in major Western economies. We then look (2.3) at the workings of the banking system and the credit market that have a bearing on the general equilibrium analysis, which is presented in the next section.

---

[1] See Bernanke and Blinder (1988, 1992), Gertler (1988), King (1986), and Romer and Romer (1990) for an extensive discussion.

2.1. The Inflationary Process

The inflationary process can be broken down into several sub-periods:

(i) The buildup of triple-digit annual inflation: 1978–83
(ii) An inflationary "explosion:": late 1983–June 1985
(iii) A major inflation stabilization program (July 1985) and its immediate aftermath
(iv) The post-stabilization period: 1986–92

Figure 8.1 shows quarterly CPI inflation in the period 1977 to 1990 in annual terms.

For detailed accounts of this process see Bruno (1993, chapters 3, 4 and 5), Bruno and Fischer (1986), Bruno and Meridor (1991), Helpman and Leiderman (1988), and Liviatan and Piterman (1986). Here we briefly delineate the major events that accompanied changes in inflation.

From the beginning of 1978 until early 1980 the inflation rate climbed rapidly from around 40 percent annually to 120 percent. The rise in inflation was associated with the liberalization of the foreign exchange market in November 1977, a large initial devaluation of the domestic currency, the introduction of the aforementioned PATAM deposits, and a decline in demand for money. The annual inflation rate stabilized at 120 percent annual rate in the period 1980–83. In October 1983 an acceleration occurred, initiated by a strong price shock due to a sharp nominal devaluation and a drastic rise in the prices controlled by the government. This was against the background of a profound balance of payments crisis. There followed a period in which the government had a commitment to maintain the level of the real exchange rate that was attained after the initial devaluation. This policy required an increasing rate of nominal devaluation, bringing the inflationary process to the verge of hyperinflation. Until mid-1985 there was a continuous and sharp rise in the public internal and external debts due to unsustainable deficits. A serious concern for a major collapse of the financial system developed and its main result was a shift from domestic assets to direct holding of foreign exchange. The

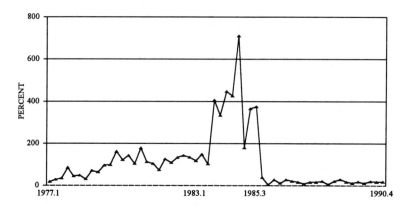

Figure 8.1. Inflation (quarterly data in annual terms).

high-inflation period led to the implementation of a radical stabilization program in July 1985. The program was successful and annual inflation rate was rapidly reduced to below 20 percent. In January 1986 a decline in the monthly CPI was recorded and though this was due to measurement problems, it was symbolic in representing the beginning of a new era. Since then the inflation rate has been remarkably stable, further declining in 1992. The fundamental change, implemented in 1985, was the balancing of the fiscal budget. The borrowing needs of the government were drastically curtailed and as a result the share of public debt to gross domestic product (GDP) steadily declined. This stable period is characterized by a process of reforms in the capital market, a process of liberalization in the foreign exchange market, and the introduction of new instruments of monetary policy and important changes in its conduct.

2.2. Financial Innovation

In this section we examine the process of innovation and related events by looking at the four subperiods identified previously.

The major changes occurred in the *first subperiod*, as inflation accelerated and settled at 120 percent a year:

(i) In November 1977 a capital-account liberalization plan, coupled with new foreign exchange management, introduced a

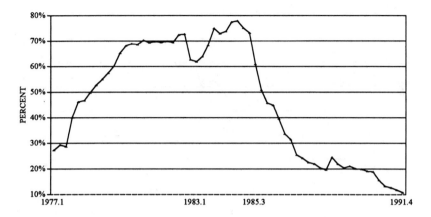

Figure 8.2. Share of PATAM in *M*3.

new asset, the PATAM deposits. Several types of foreign-currency-linked deposits, demand and time deposits, paying interest close to the Euro rate, were offered. The deposits could be easily liquidated and it was possible to transfer money from one account to another. Figure 8.2 shows the share of PATAM accounts in *M*3 (which also includes currency, demand deposits, and short-term deposits). As seen in the figure, soon after the 1977 liberalization, the PATAM became a dominant asset.

(ii) In the early 1980s the Bank of Israel announced its intention to abandon a longstanding policy of targeting the rate of return on government bonds (mostly CPI-indexed). This resulted in further substitution from government bonds into PATAM accounts.

(iii) Beginning in 1982 the Bank of Israel implemented a policy of facilitating the use of short-term, unlinked time deposits (STDs) and short-term certificates of deposit (CDs). This was a regulatory change that enabled the banks to create new types of such deposits and improve the conditions related to the use of existing ones. The result of this policy was a sharp increase in STD and a sharp decline in demand deposits as shown in Figure 8.3. The figure is drawn in terms of shares in *M*2, an aggregate composed of *M*1, STD, and CD.

(iv) There was marked technological change in banking facilities: a sharp increase in the number of automatic teller machines

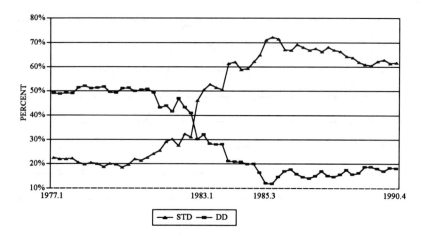

Figure 8.3. *M*2 components.

and an expansion of credit card uses, telephone banking, and automatic payment mechanisms (see the details in Melnick 1995).

(v) These developments and the rapid rise in inflation led to a continuous decline in the narrowly defined money aggregate, *M*1. This is shown in Figure 8.4 in terms of velocity.

(vi) A change in the composition of *M*1 took place: the share of currency (CU) increased while the share of demand deposits (DD) declined as seen in Figure 8.5.

This change was probably due to the fact that it became very easy to get cash or transfer money from interest-bearing deposits, so the attractiveness of demand deposits that bear no interest declined.

(vii) There was a trend decline in liquidity requirements.

In the *second subperiod*, when inflation accelerated into hyperinflation levels, the following events were observed:

(i) The PATAM accounts continued to be the dominant asset (see Figure 8.2). In addition there was widespread dollarization of the Israeli economy. Most financial contracts were linked to the U.S. dollar and many prices were denominated in U.S. dollars. This served to strengthen the importance of the PATAM accounts.

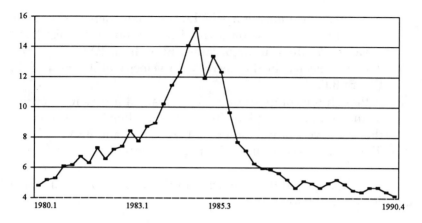

Figure 8.4. Velocity of $M1$.

(ii) There was continued substitution of unlinked DD into CD and STD. The traditional, narrow money almost disappeared from the system (see Figures 8.3 and 8.4).

(iii) There was an increase in liquidity requirements.

The *third subperiod*, following the July 1985 stabilization plan, saw the occurrence of the following developments:

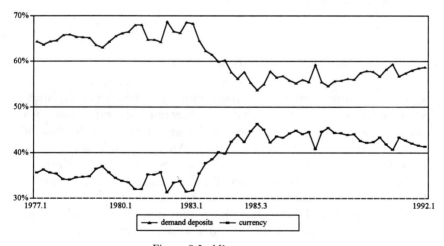

Figure 8.5. $M1$ components.

(i) A financial disinnovation – PATAM demand deposits could be drawn upon but new ones could not be opened. This disinnovation resulted in major substitution from PATAM to $M2$. This is reflected in the decrease in velocity of $M2$ as seen in Figure 8.6.
(ii) Although the composition of $M1$ remained just as it was prior to the stabilization plan, its velocity declined in response to the new levels of inflation (see Figures 8.3 and 8.4).
(iii) There was a rise in liquidity requirements.

The main financial developments in the *fourth subperiod* of stable inflation were the following:

(i) Substitution from PATAM into $M2$, mainly into CD and STD, continued.
(ii) Relative stability of the velocity of different monetary aggregates after a two year period of adjustment prevailed.
(iii) Reserve requirements were sharply reduced.
(iv) There began a period of reforms in the capital market that consisted of the gradual elimination of subsidized government credit; facilitation of direct access by private firms to the capital market; reduction in the formal requirements imposed on provident funds, pension funds, and banks' savings schemes to hold government bonds; and a drastic reduction of the segmentation of the capital market.

2.3. Innovations, the Banking System, and Credit

In order to appreciate the macroeconomic significance of the innovations discussed in the preceding subsection, several issues concerning the banking system, reserve requirements, and the flow of credit in Israel should be examined. An excellent discussion of these issues is provided by Cukierman and Sokoler (1989). Here we will limit ourselves to discussion of the particular issues relevant to the question of innovation.

First, one should note that short-term deposits are subject to lower reserve requirements than demand deposits, whereas PA-

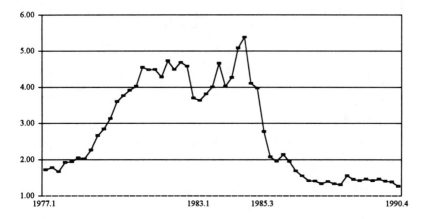

Figure 8.6. *M2* velocity.

TAM deposits are subject to very high reserve ratios. Table 8.1 delineates the various reserve ratios. Second, it should be noted that in creating PATAM deposits, banks basically acted as agents for the government. In fact, the main difference between a PATAM deposit and a government bond linked to the dollar issued on the Tel Aviv Stock Exchange is that the PATAM is not traded. Third, savings schemes operate in a similar way: The banks were subject to very high reserve requirements. Thus the resources for lending to the private sector come mainly from the nonindexed deposits.

Combining the details about the various innovations outlined and these characteristics, the following scenario may be depicted:

(i) From 1982 onward there was increased use of nonindexed, interest-bearing short-term deposits; the use of these did not diminish after stabilization. This acted to enlarge banks' resources for private lending.

(ii) The use of indexed PATAM deposits was prevalent in the high-inflation period and was facilitated by regulatory changes; following stabilization in 1985, demand for such deposits fell and further regulatory changes placed limits on the creation of new deposits. The expansion (contraction) of the PATAM accounts relative to the nonindexed assets served to reduce (expand) the resources used for private lending by banks.

Table 8.1. *Reserve requirements (percent)*

Type of deposit	1980	1987	1990
Demand deposits	60	48	10
CD	26	48	10
One-week STD	na	38	7.5
Two-week STD	na	30	7.5
One-month STD	na	20	7.5
PATAM	90	100	100

Note: na = asset not available.

Source: Bank of Israel, The Comptroller of the Banks Annual Survey, various issues.

(iii) There was significant technological progress in banking services throughout the 1980s. This acted to reduce the demand for conventional $M1$. The fact that $M1$ did not return to its former levels following stabilization is a result of this technological change.

It is instructive to look at the evolution of interest rates for the period analyzed. Figure 8.7 depicts the basic short-term lending rate and the CD rate for the period surveyed in real (ex post) terms. Figure 8.8 shows the real return on the five-year government bond.

It is clear from Figure 8.8, and to some extent from Figure 8.7, that the real rate of interest climbed from the early 1980s till 1985 and declined since then. Note that the first half of the 1980s was dominated by the portfolio shift into PATAM deposits, which contracted banks' resources for lending; moreover in the subperiod 1983–85 reserve requirements were raised. In the second half of the decade short-term deposits with sharply lower reserve requirements became dominant while the share of PATAM declined. These developments will be important for the empirical examination of the theoretical model to which we turn now.

3. THE MODEL

We consider a small open economy made up of a representative agent (to simplify the exposition we abstract from population growth), a representative firm, the government, and financial inter-

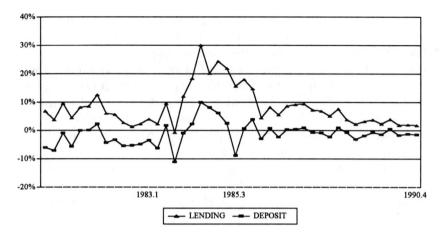

Figure 8.7. Real interest rates.

mediaries (banks). There are three financial assets: money, which is entirely held as demand deposits; interest-bearing short-term deposits; and bonds or savings deposits, which are indexed to the price level and bear a rate of interest closely related to the foreign rate. In terms of the Israeli financial system we thus lump together PATAM accounts, savings schemes, and government bonds into this last category. The consumer devotes real resources to making transactions. The transactions technology is modeled as a function of demand and short-term deposits and the regulatory environ-

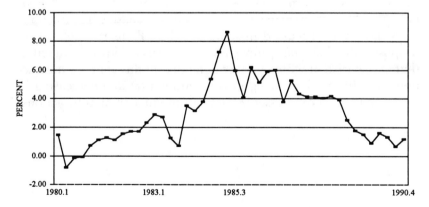

Figure 8.8. Yield on 5-year bond (real terms, ex post).

ment. The consumer decides on the allocation of income into consumption and holdings of demand and short-term deposits (which then implies a certain amount of savings deposits). Banks use demand and short-term deposits to lend to firms that buy capital used in production. Bonds or savings deposits are used to finance government expenditure, which is also financed by taxes and seigniorage revenues from the two types of deposits held as reserves (differential reserve ratios being imposed by the government). The structure of lending and borrowing is summarized in Figure 8.9, where m denotes demand deposits, d denotes short-term deposits, b denotes bonds, and τ_1 and τ_2 denote the reserve ratios on m and d, respectively. In what follows we spell out formally the behavior of these different sectors.

3.1. Transactions Technology

Numerous models in monetary theory use the notion of a costly transactions technology whereby consumers forgo real resources when making transactions. Several underlying mechanisms have been proposed to support this notion. One is that the consumer incurs costs when converting bonds into cash, as in the Baumol (1952)–Tobin (1956) money demand model; another is that there is a penalty associated with a cash shortfall when making a transaction as in the Whalen (1966) money demand model. A related notion (see, for example, McCallum 1983) is that the consumer sacrifices leisure in making transactions: That is, there are "shopping time" costs incurred when making purchases. Transactions costs have been discussed in some detail by Feenstra (1986), who proposed the following properties for a transactions cost function that are consistent with a variety of models in this context: transaction costs (θ) are increasing in consumption (c) and decreasing in the amount of a liquid asset (h) held for use in making transactions. Thus

$$\begin{gathered} \forall\, c \geq 0, \quad h \geq 0 \\ \theta \geq 0, \quad \theta(c = 0) = 0 \\ \theta_c \geq 0, \quad \theta_{cc} \geq 0 \\ \theta_h \leq 0 \quad \theta_{hh} \geq 0 \\ \theta_{hc} \leq 0 \end{gathered} \tag{8.1}$$

In the following analysis we shall assume that two assets provide liquidity services (i.e., fulfill the role of h): demand deposits (m in

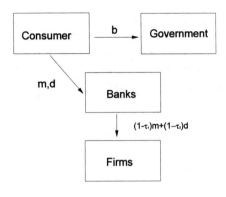

Figure 8.9.

real terms) and short-term deposits (d). Financial innovation may affect this cost function in two ways: First, it may increase the relative contribution of short-term deposits to liquidity; second, it may reduce transaction costs altogether. In the Israeli context, the former innovation relates to the introduction of STD and CD and the changes in regulation facilitating their use. The latter innovation refers to the technological progress and regulatory changes that made the PATAM accounts fairly easy to convert into liquidity. In the terminology of the Baumol–Tobin model the first type of innovation enhances the role of a near money as the liquidity aggregate, where the second type reduces the costs of converting bonds into cash.

In the analysis that follows we shall sometimes assume separability between the various arguments in the transactions costs function. Although this is not necessary to the analysis, it makes it more tractable. We consider then the following general specification:

$$
\begin{aligned}
&\theta(c, m, d; \gamma, \delta) \geq 0 \\
&\theta_c \geq 0, \qquad \theta_{cc} \geq 0 \\
&\theta_m \leq 0, \qquad \theta_{mm} \geq 0 \\
&\theta_d \leq 0, \qquad \theta_{dd} \geq 0 \\
&\theta_{cm} = 0, \qquad \theta_{cd} = 0, \qquad \theta_{md} = 0 \\
&\theta_\gamma > 0, \qquad \theta_\delta?
\end{aligned}
\tag{8.2}
$$

The transaction costs function exhibits the properties described in (8.1), adding separability between the arguments, and considers two parameters: The first is γ, which stands for the costs associated with transactions between liquid assets and bonds. Increases in this parameter represent increases in transaction costs. The second parameter, δ, stands for the value of liquidity services provided by short-term deposits relative to those provided by money (demand deposits). It represents the marginal reduction in transaction costs by the liquid aggregate for a given mix of money and short-term deposits.

Additional clarity will be obtained by considering the following special case of the function described in (8.2):

$$\theta(c, m, d) = \gamma[\phi(c) - (\ln m + \delta(\ln d - \ln m)] \qquad (8.2')$$

where

$$\phi_c \geq 0, \quad \phi_{cc} \geq 0, \quad [\phi\phi_{cc} - \phi_c^2] \geq 0$$
$$0 \leq \delta < 1$$

The innovation relating to the introduction of STD and CD is expressed as increasing δ, that is, enhancing the role of d relative to m. The innovation that generates a reduction in transaction costs is expressed as a reduction in γ.

3.2. Consumers' Optimization

The representative agent holds the three assets delineated: demand deposits (m), short-term deposits (d), and bonds (b). Demand deposits pay no interest and are nonindexed; this is "traditional" money; short-term deposits pay the nominal interest rate i^d; bonds are indexed and pay the real rate of interest r.[2] The consumer receives income from labor (w) and pays taxes (t). He or she devotes resources to making transactions as discussed previously. The consumer chooses a stream of consumption (c), money balances (demand deposits), and short-term deposits so as to maximize

$$\max \int_0^\infty U(c_t)e^{-rt}\, dt \qquad (8.3)$$

subject to the constraint

$$\dot{a} = ra + w - c - \theta(c, m, d) - t - (\pi + r)m + (i^d - \pi - r)d \qquad (8.4)$$

---

[2] The open economy assumption implies that $r = r^* + \zeta$, where r^* is the foreign real interest rate and ζ is a term reflecting risk premia and constraints on capital flows.

where

$$a = m + d + b \tag{8.5}$$

π is the rate of inflation.

The opportunity cost of real money balances is $r + \pi$; the real rate of return on short-term deposits is $i^d - \pi$.

The first-order conditions are

$$\begin{aligned}
U'(c) &= \lambda(1 + \theta_c) \\
-\theta_m &= \pi + r \\
\theta_d &= i^d - \pi - r \\
\lim \lambda_t a_t e^{-rt} &= 0
\end{aligned} \tag{8.6}$$

and the budget constraint. λ denotes the costate variable.

We have thus defined implicit demand functions for the two liquid assets: Demand for money (demand deposits) is decreasing in the rate of inflation and the real rate; short-term deposits are decreasing in these variables too and increasing in the rate of interest paid on them, or alternatively they are increasing in the difference between the real rate on deposits and the real rate on bonds.

3.3. The Government

The consolidated government finances its consumption (g) and debt service (rb) by lump-sum taxes (t), by the inflation tax on reserves held at the central bank, and by bond issuance. Reserves at the central bank relate to two types of assets: demand deposits and short-term deposits.

The government flow constraint is

$$g + rb = t + \dot{b} + \mu[\tau_1 m + \tau_2 d] \tag{8.7}$$

where τ_1 and τ_2 are the reserve ratios on m and on d, respectively, and μ is the rate of growth of the monetary base.

We take the reserve ratios and the rate of growth of the monetary base as exogenous; the primary deficit ($g - t$) is adjusted so as to satisfy the stability conditions of the dynamic system.[3]

In the steady state, equation (8.7) becomes

$$g + rb = t + \pi[\tau_1 m + \tau_2 d] \tag{8.8}$$

---

[3] See the discussion in Liviatan (1983) on the dynamic stability of deficit finance under a similar setup and in particular the discussion on adjusting government transfers to satisfy stability requirements.

3.4. The Banks

The banks receive consumers' demand and short-term deposits; they hold the required reserves at the central bank; they lend the remainder to firms charging them $i^l = \pi + r^l$;[4] and they pay the consumers i^d for short-term deposits. If banks are competitive and there is free entry, then the zero profit condition is

$$i^l \left[(1 - \tau_1)m + (1 - \tau_2)d \right] = i^d d \tag{8.9}$$

or

$$(r^l + \pi)(1 - \tau_1)m + (r^l - r^d)(1 - \tau_2)d - (r^d + \pi)\tau_2 d = 0 \tag{8.10}$$

3.5. The Firms

Firms borrow each period from banks in order to finance capital used together with a fixed amount of labor (normalized to be one) in a constant returns to scale production function f. If we consider a constant depreciation rate v, then the firms borrow

$$k = vk = (1 - \tau_1)m + (1 - \tau_2)d \tag{8.11}$$

Thus the first-order condition for profits maximization is

$$f'\left(\frac{[(1 - \tau_1)m + (1 - \tau_2)d]}{v} \right) = r^l \tag{8.12}$$

Firms pay wages, which are given by

$$w = f - r^l \left[\frac{(1 - \tau_1)m + (1 - \tau_2)d}{v} \right] \tag{8.13}$$

3.6. General Equilibrium

We can consolidate the private and public budget constraints using the wage equation and the zero profits condition for banks to obtain the overall budget constraint for the economy

$$f\left[\frac{(1 - \tau_1)m + (1 - \tau_2)d}{v} \right] = c + g + \theta(c, m, d) + k \tag{8.14}$$

---

[4] Perfect foresight is assumed throughout the analysis.

This equation together with the three first-order conditions of the consumer (the equations in [8.6]), the government budget constraint (equation [8.8]), the zero profit condition for the banks (equation [8.10]), and the first-order-condition for firms (equation [8.12]) constitute the seven equations that determine the seven endogenous variables of the economy in the *steady state:* the amount of deposits (m and d), the value of government debt (b), the level of consumption (c), the shadow price of the consumer problem (λ), and the two interest rates r^l and r^d. The rate of inflation (π) and the reserve ratios (τ_1 and τ_2) are set exogenously. The primary deficit is adjusted so as to satisfy the budget constraint. The interest rate (r), which is the rate paid on bonds, is taken as given to the economy. Knowing the value of the seven endogenous variables we can derive the level of output, the deficit, and transaction costs.

In the general case we have to solve the seven-equation system simultaneously to derive the steady-state values. However, to keep the analysis tractable, we assume separability of the three arguments of the transaction costs function (consumption, demand deposits, and short-term deposits). We can thus solve for the level of the two types of deposits as a function of r^d using the consumer optimization conditions and then solve for the two interest rates using the profit conditions for banks and firms. Subsequently we can derive the level of production and consumption.

Thus separability allows the formulation of following two implied demand functions for financial assets.

$$m = m\,(r, \pi; \gamma, \delta) \tag{8.15}$$

$$d = d\,(r^d, r; \gamma, \delta) \tag{8.16}$$

Note that (8.15) and (8.16) include the parameters of the transaction function.

For the special case of the transaction cost function specified in (8.2′) these demand equations are given as follows:

$$m = \frac{\gamma(1 - \delta)}{r + \pi} \tag{8.15′}$$

$$d = \frac{\gamma\delta}{r - r^d} \tag{8.16′}$$

Equations (8.10) and (8.12) can therefore be rewritten with r^l and r^d as the only endogenous variables:

$$(r^l + \pi)(1 - \tau_1) \frac{m[r, \pi; \gamma, \delta]}{d[r^d, r; \gamma, \delta]} + (r^l - r^d)(1 - \tau_2) - (r^d + \pi)\tau_2 = 0 \quad (8.17)$$

$$f'\left[\frac{(1 - \tau_1)m[r, \pi; \gamma, \delta] + (1 - \tau_2)d[r, r^d; \gamma, \delta]}{v} \right] = r^l \quad (8.18)$$

These equations can be portrayed in r^l and r^d space as shown in Figure 8.10.

The slopes of the two curves are given as follows:

Banks: $\dfrac{\partial r^l}{\partial r^d} = \dfrac{d[r^d, r; \gamma, \delta] + (\partial d/\partial r^d)[r^d(1 - \tau_2) + (r^d + \pi)\tau_2]}{(1 - \tau_1)m[r, \pi; \gamma, \delta] + (1 - \tau_2)d[r^d, r; \gamma, \delta]} > 0 \quad (8.19)$

Firms: $\dfrac{\partial r^l}{\partial r^d} = f''(1 - \tau_2)\dfrac{\partial d}{\partial r^d} < 0 \quad (8.20)$

The banks' zero profit condition yields an upward-sloping schedule (equation [8.19]) as an increase in interest paid on deposits has to be matched by an increase in the interest charged on loans. The firms' optimality condition (equation [8.18]) yields a downward-sloping curve as demand for capital declines with increases in the borrowing rate facing firms. Note that the level of capital is a positive function of the interest rate paid on deposits.

4. FINANCIAL INNOVATION

We turn now to look at the effects of financial innovation.

4.1. Short-Term Deposits

The first type of innovation is the introduction of new short-term deposits coupled with a change in regulations so that the liquidity services provided by them are enhanced relative to regular demand deposits. In terms of the separable function (equation [8.2]) discussed in Section 3.1 this is expressed as increasing δ. There will thus occur a substitution away from m and into d in the consumer portfolio. This is derived from the first-order conditions (equation [8.6]) and will be reflected in the implied asset demand functions (equations [8.15'] and [8.16']). If the reserve ratio on short-term deposits is lower than that on demand deposits, as has been the

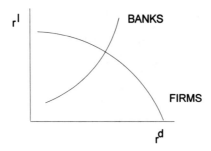

Figure 8.10.

case for Israel and most Western countries, then the resources available for bank loans unambiguously increase.[5] For any given level of the deposit rate (r^d) firms now face a higher supply of loans and thus the rate on loans (r^l) declines. Examination of the bank profit equation (8.10) indicates the following changes:

$$\frac{\partial r^l}{\partial \delta} = [(1 - \tau_1)m + (1 - \tau_2)d]^{-1}\left[\frac{\partial d}{\partial \delta}(r^d + \pi\tau_2) \right.$$

$$\left. - \frac{\partial m}{\partial \delta}\pi(1 - \tau_1) - r^l(1 - \tau_2)\left(\frac{\partial d}{\partial \delta} + \frac{\partial m}{\partial \delta} \right) \right] > 0 \qquad (8.21)$$

Banks face several changes: On the one hand, their revenue from the inflation tax on demand deposits declines, and they have to pay interest on more short-term deposits and the inflation tax on bigger reserves of short-term deposits; on the other hand, their resources for lending to firms have increased. However, the former effects dominate and so the expression in (8.21) is positive and the banks would like to raise the lending rate for any given deposit rate. In terms of Figure 8.10 both schedules will shift leftward. These changes are shown in Figure 8.11.

The fall in the deposit rate is unambiguous. However, the lending rate may either fall or increase (B may be below or above A).

---

[5] Note that m is not replaced for d one to one. If, for example, θ is given by the function in (8.2′), then the change in banks resources for lending when δ increases is given by $(\partial[(1 - \tau_1)m + (1 - \tau_2)d]/\partial\delta) = (\gamma[(\tau_1 - \tau_2)r + (1 - \tau_1)r^d + (1 - \tau_2)\pi]/(\pi + r)(r - r^d)) > 0$, and banks' resources may go up even if the reserve ratio on short-term deposits exceeds the reserve ratio on demand deposits.

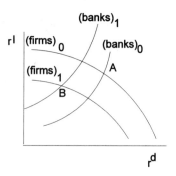

Figure 8.11.

This is so because as the banks lower the rate paid on deposits, the latter contract after their initial expansion. If the initial effect is dominant, then the introduction of short-term deposits will be expansionary: Firms will use more capital and production will increase.

4.2. Reduction in Transaction Costs

The second type of innovation is the introduction of new indexed assets, which, combined with technological progress and regulatory changes, generates a portfolio shift out of the two types of deposits. In terms of the discussion in Section 3.1 this would be a lowering of γ. In this case resources for bank lending decrease; the firms' schedule in Figure 8.10 shifts up. The effect on the banks' profit condition is ambiguous and depends on the ratio of demand to short-term deposits. If this ratio remains constant, as in the case of the logarithmic and separable specification discussed, then the banks' schedule does not shift.[6] Both rates increase and thus production and consumption decrease.[7] This is shown in Figure 8.12.

---

[6] Algebraically this is given by $(\partial r^l / \partial \gamma) = \{d[r^d + \pi\tau_2 - r^l(1 - \tau_2)] - m[(1 - \tau_1)(r^l + \pi)]/(1 - \tau_1)m + (1 - \tau_2)d\} = 0$.

[7] Unless the reduction in transaction costs is of such significant magnitude that consumption can remain constant or even increase.

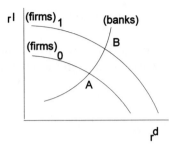

Figure 8.12.

4.3. Implications for Estimation

To recapitulate the basic economic mechanism that operates here (comparing steady-state situations): When financial innovation occurs, consumers change their portfolio allocation. This affects banks' resources for lending and hence interest rates. The change in the lending rate affects the level of capital and therefore production and consumption. Thus what begins as an effect on money demand translates into real macroeconomic effects via the banks' asset side of the balance sheet.

The model, in conjunction with the preceding discussion on the Israeli financial system, therefore implies two major macroeconomic effects:

(i) The introduction of short-term deposits with lower reserve requirements expanded banks' resources for lending and therefore led to a decrease in the short-term deposit rate and to a probable decrease in the lending rate, and thus to an increase in the capital stock, in production, and in consumption in the steady state.

(ii) The use of PATAM accounts, facilitated by regulation and technological progress, reduced the amount of nonindexed deposits in 1978–85. Hence there were a contraction in banks' resources, a rise in the lending rate, and a reduction in capital stock, production, and consumption in the long run. The opposite occurred after the 1985 stabilization plan.

5. ESTIMATION

We test the model's implications by estimating a series of VAR models. In each model we include the following four endogenous variables:

(i) A real activity variable, which corresponds to f in the model
(ii) The deposit and lending real interest rates, corresponding to r^d and r^l
(iii) A financial ratio, corresponding to the ratios among m, d, and b

We also control for monetary policy responses and for the inflationary developments that are considered exogenous in the analysis. In particular we include the following:

(i) The loan from the Bank of Israel to the banks, which is a key monetary policy variable. One possible interpretation in terms of the model is that it reflects changes in μ.
(ii) The rate of inflation (π).

We use three different real activity variables: nondurables consumption; the "State of the Economy" index, which is a coincident indicator for the business cycle (see Melnick and Golan 1992); and nonresidential investment. Exact data definitions are given in the Appendix.

The VAR models were estimated in first differences of the levels (for the activity variable first differences of the logs). The differencing is needed because for all the levels we were not able to reject the presence of a unit root. The sample covers quarterly data from 80.1 until 90.4. Two lags were used for each variable.

In terms of the notation used in section 3 the VAR model is as follows:

$$Y_t = A(L)Y_t + B(L) X_t + \varepsilon_t \tag{8.22}$$

where

$$Y_t = [\Delta \ln f, \Delta r^l, \Delta r^d, \Delta ratio]$$
$$X_t = [\Delta \pi, \Delta l] \tag{8.23}$$

Y and X are the vectors of endogenous and exogenous variables, respectively; $A(L)$ and $B(L)$ are finite lag polynomial matrices;

f is the real activity variable used; ratio is either $m/(m + d)$ or $(m + d)/a$ and l indicates the Bank of Israel loan.

5.1. Testing the Effects of Short-Term Deposits

We test the first proposition by using the ratio $M1/M2$ as the relevant financial ratio. A decrease in the ratio is the first type of innovation discussed in Section 4. The three graphs in Figure 8.13 show the cumulative impulse response responses for the three real activity variables given a negative shock to the ratio. Responses are shown over an expanse of twelve quarters. The responses are for orthogonalized innovations imposing the ordering that contemporaneous innovations on interest rates impact all variables; whereas contemporaneous innovations on the activity variable impact no other variable. The financial ratio is in the middle; its contemporaneous innovations impact the activity variable but do not impact the interest rates.

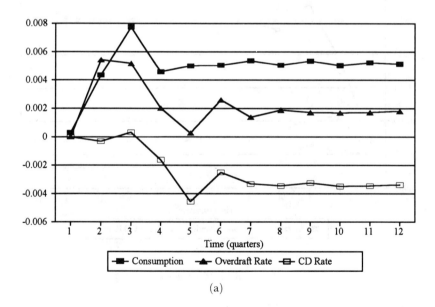

(a)

Figure 8.13. Cumulative impulse response: (a) Consumption – Shock to the $M1/M2$ ratio; (b) "S" index – Shock to the $M1/M2$ ratio; (c) Investment – Shock to the $M1/M2$ ratio.

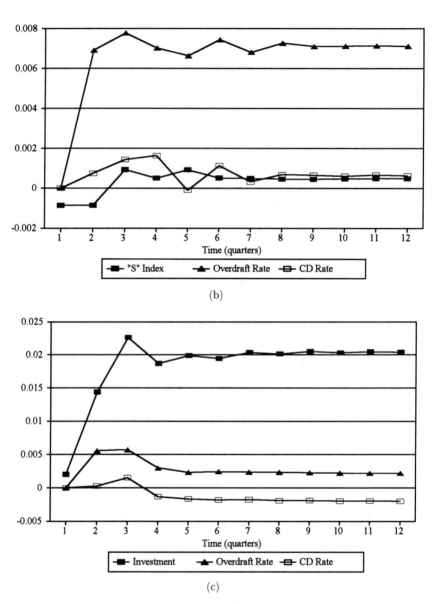

(b)

(c)

Figure 8.13. (*Continued*)

The cumulative responses are as expected; this is so, except for r^l: Although the model does not have a clear-cut prediction about this rate, the positive real activity response is consistent with a fall in r^l rather than the rise that was actually obtained.

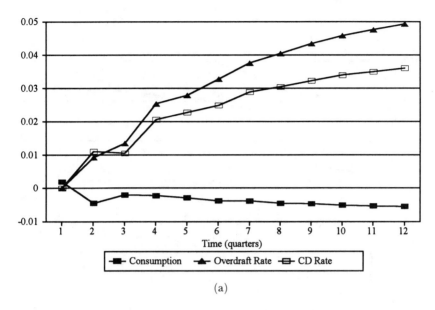

(a)

Figure 8.14. Cumulative impulse response: (a) Consumption – Shock to the
$M2/M3$ ratio; (b) "S" index – Shock to the $M2/M3$ ratio; (c) Investment –
Shock to the $M2/M3$ ratio.

5.2. Testing the Effects of PATAM Deposits

We test the second proposition by using the ratio $M2/M3$ as the
relevant financial ratio. A decrease in the ratio is the second type of
innovation discussed in Section 4. The three graphs in Figure 8.14
show the cumulative impulse response responses for the three real
activity variables given a negative shock to the ratio. Responses are
shown over an expanse of twelve quarters.

The results are fully consistent with the model's predictions: a
contraction in activity and a rise in both interest rates.

A summary of the cumulative impulse response is presented in
Table 8.2.

6. CONCLUSIONS

The effects of financial innovation in Israel in the 1980s may be
summarized as follows:

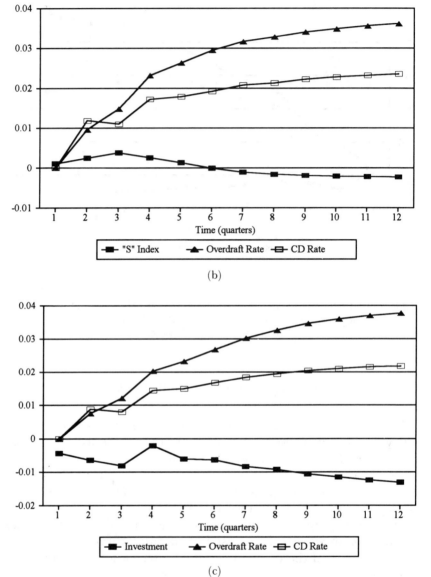

(b)

(c)

Figure 8.14. (*Continued*)

(i) The introduction of the PATAM indexed deposits, as part of the 1977 liberalization program, coupled with technological progress and regulatory change, had a contractionary effect on real activity as it reduced banks' resources for lending. This

Table 8.2. *Cumulative impulse responses*
after 12 quarters

	M1/M2	M2/M3
Consumption	−	+
r^l	−	−
r^d	+	−
"S" index	−	+
r^l	−	−
r^d	−	−
Investment	−	+
r^l	−	−
r^d	+	−

was the dominant development in the high-inflation years 1978–85. With inflation stabilization in July 1985, regulation changed and the share of PATAM in financial assets declined, generating an expansionary effect.

(ii) After 1982, the use of short-term deposits increased at the expense of regular demand deposits. The 1985 stabilization did not change the bigger role played by these deposits. This innovation has expansionary effects.

This chapter has demonstrated that there are real macroeconomic effects of financial innovation. A major question that remains open to further analysis is the endogenous derivation of the innovation process itself.

APPENDIX

The data series used and their sources are as follows (CBS indicates Central Bureau of Statistics; BOI indicates Bank of Israel):

Consumption: nondurables consumption, constant prices (National Accounts, CBS)

Investment: nonresidential investment, constant prices (National Accounts, CBS)

"S" index: index of coincident indicators for the business cycle, based

on industrial production, vacancies, retail sales, and imports net of
investment goods, fuel, and diamonds (BOI)

Monetary aggregates: BOI data

Inflation: CPI rates of change (CBS)

Lending rate: overdraft rate charged by banks; ex post real rate using
actual inflation (BOI) used in model

Borrowing rate: rate on bank CDs; we use the ex-post real rate using
actual inflation (BOI) used in model

Bank of Israel monetary loan: value in NIS of the loan made by the
Bank of Israel to commercial banks (BOI)

REFERENCES

Arrau, Patricio, and Jose de Gregorio (1992), Financial Innovation and
Money Demand: Application to Chile and Mexico, mimeo, International Monetary Fund.

Baumol, William J. (1952), The Transactions Demand for Cash: An
Inventory-Theoretic Approach, *Quarterly Journal of Economics* 66 (November): 545–56.

Bernanke, Ben S., and Alan S. Blinder (1988), Credit, Money and Aggregate Demand, *American Economic Review Papers and Proceedings* 78
(May): 435–39.

Bernanke, Ben S., and Alan S. Blinder (1992), The Federal Funds Rate
and the Channels of Monetary Transmission, *American Economic Review* 82 (September): 901–21.

Bruno, Michael (1993), *Crisis, Stabilization and Economic Reform*, Oxford:
Clarendon Press.

Bruno, Michael, and Stanley Fischer (1986), The Inflationary Process:
Shocks and Accommodation, in Y. Ben-Porath, ed., *The Israeli Econ-
omy: Maturing through Crises,* Cambridge, MA: Harvard University
Press.

Bruno, Michael, and Leora Meridor (1991), The Costly Transition from
Stabilization to Sustainable Growth: Israel's Case, in Bruno, Fischer,
Helpman, and Liviatan, eds., *Lessons of Economic Stabilization and Its
Aftermath*, Cambridge, MA: MIT Press.

Cukierman, Alex, and Meir Sokoler (1989), Monetary Policy and Institutions in Israel: Past, Present and Future, *Economics Quarterly* 139 (January): 371–426 (in Hebrew).

De Gregorio, Jose (1991), Welfare Costs of Inflation, Seigniorage, and
Financial Innovation, *IMF Staff Papers* 38: 675–704.

Feenstra, Robert C. (1986), Functional Equivalence between Liquidity
Costs and the Utility of Money, *Journal of Monetary Economics* 17
(March): 271–91.

Gauger, Jean (1992), Portfolio Redistribution Impacts within the Narrow

Monetary Aggregate, *Journal of Money, Credit, and Banking* 24 (May): 239–57.

Gertler, Mark (1988), Financial Structure and Aggregate Activity: An Overview, *Journal of Money, Credit, and Banking,* 20 (August): 559–88.

Guidotti, Pablo E. (1993), Currency Substitution and Financial Innovation, *Journal of Money, Credit, and Banking* 25: (February): 109–24.

Helpman, Elhanan, and Leonardo Leiderman (1988), Stabilization in High Inflation Countries: Analytical Foundations and Recent Experience, *Carnegie–Rochester Conference Series* 28: 9–84.

King, Steven (1986), Monetary Transmission: Through Bank Loans or Bank Liabilities, *Journal of Money, Credit, and Banking* 18 (August): 290–303.

Liviatan, Nissan (1983), Inflation and the Composition of Deficit Finance, in F. G. Adams and B. G. Hickman, eds., *Global Econometrics,* Cambridge, MA: MIT Press, 84–100.

Liviatan, Nissan, and Sylvia Piterman (1986), Accelerating Inflation and Balance of Payments Crises: Israel 1973–84. In Y. Ben-Porath, ed., *The Israeli Economy: Maturing through Crises,* Cambridge, MA: Harvard University Press.

McCallum, Bennet T. (1983), The Role of Overlapping Generations Models in Monetary Economics, *Carnegie–Rochester Conference Series on Public Policy* 18: 9–44.

Melnick, Rafi (1995), Financial Services, Cointegration and the Demand for Money in Israel, *Journal of Money, Credit, and Banking* 24 (February): 140–53.

Melnick, Rafi, and Yehudit Golan (1992), Measurement of Business Fluctuations in Israel, *Bank of Israel Economic Review* 67 (July): 3–20 (in Hebrew).

Romer, Christina D., and David H. Romer (1990), New Evidence on the Monetary Transmission Mechanism, *Brookings Papers on Economic Activity* 1 (August): 149–213.

Tobin, James (1956), The Interest Elasticity of the Transactions Demand for Cash, *Review of Economics and Statistics* 38 (August): 241–47.

Whalen, Edward L. (1966), A Rationalization of the Precautionary Demand for Cash, *Quarterly Journal of Economics* 80 (May): 314–24.

Index

251